Ethical Considerations
FOR
Research Involving Prisoners

Committee on Ethical Considerations for
Revisions to DHHS Regulations for
Protection of Prisoners Involved in Research

Board on Health Sciences Policy

Lawrence O. Gostin, Cori Vanchieri, and Andrew Pope, *Editors*

INSTITUTE OF MEDICINE
OF THE NATIONAL ACADEMIES

THE NATIONAL ACADEMIES PRESS
Washington, D.C.
www.nap.edu

THE NATIONAL ACADEMIES PRESS • 500 FIFTH STREET, N.W. • Washington, DC 20001

NOTICE: The project that is the subject of this report was approved by the Governing Board of the National Research Council, whose members are drawn from the councils of the National Academy of Sciences, the National Academy of Engineering, and the Institute of Medicine. The members of the committee responsible for the report were chosen for their special competences and with regard for appropriate balance.

This study was supported by Award No. N01-OD-4-2139, TO #149 (DHHS-5294-249) between the National Academy of Sciences and the DHHS (Office for Human Research Protections)/National Institutes of Health and by a grant from The Greenwall Foundation. Any opinions, findings, or conclusions expressed in this publication are those of the author(s) and do not necessarily reflect the view of the organizations or agencies that provided support for this project.

International Standard Book Number-10: 0-309-10119-0
International Standard Book Number-13: 978-0-309-10119-6

Library of Congress Control Number: 2006937620

Additional copies of this report are available from the National Academies Press, 500 Fifth Street, N.W., Lockbox 285, Washington, DC 20055; (800) 624-6242 or (202) 334-3313 (in the Washington metropolitan area); Internet, http://www.nap.edu.

For more information about the Institute of Medicine, visit the IOM home page at: **www.iom.edu.**

Copyright 2007 by the National Academy of Sciences. All rights reserved.

Printed in the United States of America.

The serpent has been a symbol of long life, healing, and knowledge among almost all cultures and religions since the beginning of recorded history. The serpent adopted as a logotype by the Institute of Medicine is a relief carving from ancient Greece, now held by the Staatliche Museen in Berlin.

"Knowing is not enough; we must apply.
Willing is not enough; we must do."
—Goethe

INSTITUTE OF MEDICINE
OF THE NATIONAL ACADEMIES

Advising the Nation. Improving Health.

THE NATIONAL ACADEMIES
Advisers to the Nation on Science, Engineering, and Medicine

The **National Academy of Sciences** is a private, nonprofit, self-perpetuating society of distinguished scholars engaged in scientific and engineering research, dedicated to the furtherance of science and technology and to their use for the general welfare. Upon the authority of the charter granted to it by the Congress in 1863, the Academy has a mandate that requires it to advise the federal government on scientific and technical matters. Dr. Ralph J. Cicerone is president of the National Academy of Sciences.

The **National Academy of Engineering** was established in 1964, under the charter of the National Academy of Sciences, as a parallel organization of outstanding engineers. It is autonomous in its administration and in the selection of its members, sharing with the National Academy of Sciences the responsibility for advising the federal government. The National Academy of Engineering also sponsors engineering programs aimed at meeting national needs, encourages education and research, and recognizes the superior achievements of engineers. Dr. Wm. A. Wulf is president of the National Academy of Engineering.

The **Institute of Medicine** was established in 1970 by the National Academy of Sciences to secure the services of eminent members of appropriate professions in the examination of policy matters pertaining to the health of the public. The Institute acts under the responsibility given to the National Academy of Sciences by its congressional charter to be an adviser to the federal government and, upon its own initiative, to identify issues of medical care, research, and education. Dr. Harvey V. Fineberg is president of the Institute of Medicine.

The **National Research Council** was organized by the National Academy of Sciences in 1916 to associate the broad community of science and technology with the Academy's purposes of furthering knowledge and advising the federal government. Functioning in accordance with general policies determined by the Academy, the Council has become the principal operating agency of both the National Academy of Sciences and the National Academy of Engineering in providing services to the government, the public, and the scientific and engineering communities. The Council is administered jointly by both Academies and the Institute of Medicine. Dr. Ralph J. Cicerone and Dr. Wm. A. Wulf are chair and vice chair, respectively, of the National Research Council.

www.national-academies.org

COMMITTEE ON ETHICAL CONSIDERATIONS FOR REVISIONS TO DHHS REGULATIONS FOR PROTECTION OF PRISONERS INVOLVED IN RESEARCH

Lawrence O. Gostin (*Chair*), Georgetown University Law Center, Washington, DC
Hortensia Amaro, Northeastern University, Boston, MA
Patricia Blair, University of Texas Health Center at Tyler, Tyler, TX
Steve J. Cambra, Jr., Cambra, Larson & Associates, Elk Grove, CA
G. David Curry, University of Missouri, St. Louis
Cynthia A. Gómez, University of California, San Francisco
Bradford H. Gray, The Urban Institute, Washington, DC
Michael S. Hamden, North Carolina Prisoner Legal Services, Inc., Raleigh, NC
Jeffrey L. Metzner, University of Colorado School of Medicine, Denver
Jonathan Moreno, University of Virginia, Charlottesville
Larry I. Palmer, University of Louisville, Louisville, KY
Norman G. Poythress, Jr., University of South Florida, Tampa
William J. Rold, New York
Janette Y. Taylor, University of Iowa, Iowa City
Wendy Visscher, RTI International, Research Triangle Park, NC
Barry Zack, Centerforce, San Quentin, CA

Expert Advisor and Liaison, Board on Health Sciences Policy

Nancy Dubler, Montefiore Medical Center, Bronx, NY

Consultants

Ben Berkman, Georgetown University Law Center, Washington, DC
Sarah Shalf, Bondurant, Mixson, & Elmore, LLP, Atlanta, GA
Cori Vanchieri, Silver Spring, MD

Intern

Jason E. Farley, The Johns Hopkins University, Baltimore, MD

IOM Staff

Andrew Pope, Study Director (from August 2005)
Adrienne Stith Butler, Senior Staff Officer (from August 2005)
Tracy G. Myers, Study Director (through August 2005)
Eileen Santa, Research Associate (from August 2005)
Susan McCutchen, Research Associate
Vilija Teel, Senior Project Assistant

BOARD ON HEALTH SCIENCES POLICY[*]

Fred H. Gage (*Chair*), The Salk Institute for Biological Studies, San Diego, CA
Gail H. Cassell, Eli Lilly and Company, Indianapolis, IN
James F. Childress, University of Virginia, Charlottesville
Ellen Wright Clayton, Vanderbilt University Medical School, Nashville, TN
David Cox, Perlegen Sciences, Mountain View, CA
Lynn R. Goldman, Johns Hopkins Bloomberg School of Public Health, Baltimore, MD
Bernard Goldstein, University of Pittsburgh, PA
Martha N. Hill, Johns Hopkins University School of Nursing, Baltimore, MD
Alan Leshner, American Association for the Advancement of Science, Washington, DC
Daniel Masys, Vanderbilt University Medical Center, Nashville, TN
Jonathan Moreno, University of Virginia, Charlottesville
E. Albert Reece, University of Maryland, Baltimore
Myrl Weinberg, National Health Council, Washington, DC
Michael J. Welch, Washington University School of Medicine, St. Louis, MO
Owen N. Witte, University of California, Los Angeles
Mary Woolley, Research!America, Alexandria, VA

IOM Staff

Andrew Pope, Director
David Codrea, Financial Associate
Amy Haas, Board Assistant

---

[*]IOM boards do not review or approve individual reports and are not asked to endorse conclusions and recommendations. The responsibility for the content of the report rests with the authoring committee and the institution.

Independent Report Reviewers

This report has been reviewed in draft form by individuals chosen for their diverse perspectives and technical expertise, in accordance with procedures approved by the NRC's Report Review Committee. The purpose of this independent review is to provide candid and critical comments that will assist the institution in making its published report as sound as possible and to ensure that the report meets institutional standards for objectivity, evidence, and responsiveness to the study charge. The review comments and draft manuscript remain confidential to protect the integrity of the deliberative process. We wish to thank the following individuals for their review of this report:

George J. Annas, Department of Health Law, Bioethics and Human Rights, Boston University School of Public Health
B. Jaye Anno, Consultants in Correctional Care, Santa Fe, New Mexico
Kenneth Appelbaum, Correctional Mental Health Program, University of Massachusetts Medical School
Ronald Braithwaite, Rollins School of Public Health, Emory University
Vivian Brown, PROTOTYPES: Centers for Innovation in Health, Mental Health and Social Services, Culver City, California
Jeff Cohen, HRP Associates, Inc., New York, New York
Amy Craddock, Department of Criminology, General Education Program, Indiana State University
Madeline Delone, The Innocence Project, Benjamin N. Cardozo School of Law, Yeshiva University

Nicholas Freudenberg, Department of Urban Public Health, Hunter College, City University of New York
George Gasparis, Institutional Review Board—Human Research Protection Program, Columbia University
John K. Irwin, Professor Emeritus, San Francisco State University
Leodus Jones, Community Assistance for Prisoners, Philadelphia, Pennsylvania
Nancy E. Kass, Berman Bioethics Institute, Johns Hopkins Bloomberg School of Public Health
Elaine L. Larson, School of Nursing, Columbia University
John T. Monahan, School of Law, University of Virginia
Jonathan Seltzer, Applied Clinical Intelligence, Bala Cynwyd, Pennsylvania
Anne C. Spaulding, Department of Epidemiology, Emory University Rollins School of Public Health

Although the reviewers listed above have provided many constructive comments and suggestions, they were not asked to endorse the conclusions or recommendations nor did they see the final draft of the report before its release. The review of this report was overseen by **Neil R. Powe,** Welch Center for Prevention, Epidemiology and Clinical Research, Johns Hopkins Medical Institutions, and **Elena O. Nightingale,** Scholar-in-Residence at the Institute of Medicine. Appointed by the National Research Council and the Institute of Medicine, they were responsible for making certain that an independent examination of this report was carried out in accordance with institutional procedures and that all review comments were carefully considered. Responsibility for the final content of this report rests entirely with the authoring committee and the institution.

Preface

The Committee's task—to review the ethics regarding research involving prisoners—was as challenging as it was important. Research is critically important in providing knowledge needed for informed and enlightened prison policy, as well as for affording health benefits to prisoners. At the same time, research could impose unacceptable risks on prisoners, complicated by serious concerns about the potential for coercion in the prison environment. The history of prisoner research is plagued with illustrations of unconscionable abuses. Getting the balance right between scientifically rigorous research and ethically appropriate treatment of prisoners is vital in a decent, humane society. It was a difficult task in which the Committee had to take account of history, demography, vulnerability, and the restrictions of prisoner life.

The charge of our Committee, the Institute of Medicine Committee on Ethical Considerations for Revisions to the DHHS Regulations for Protection of Prisoners Involved in Research, was to explore whether the conclusions reached in 1976 by the National Commission for the Protection of Human Subjects of Biomedical and Behavioral Research remain appropriate today. The Commission's path-breaking report on the ethical values of human subject research resulted in regulation of all human subject research funded by the U.S. Department of Health and Human Services (DHHS). The provisions regarding research on prisoners are contained in Subpart C of the regulations.

Specifically, the Committee was asked to: (1) consider whether the ethical bases for research with prisoners differ from those for research with nonprisoners, (2) develop an ethical framework for the conduct of research with prisoners, (3) based on the ethical framework developed, identify considerations or safeguards necessary to ensure that research with prisoners is conducted ethically, and (4) identify issues and needs for future consideration and study.

Past abuse in biomedical research in prisons has engendered deep distrust among prisoners and their advocates. It is impossible to ignore the historical exploitation of prisoners and their current misgivings about the biomedical research enterprise. The prison population, moreover, has markedly changed since 1976. It is vastly larger in number with disproportionate representation of African Americans, Latinos, persons with mental illness, and other historically disenfranchised populations. Many women and children are also incarcerated in American prisons today. Prisoners are particularly vulnerable to exploitation not only because of their low socioeconomic status, but also due to the realties of prison life. Although conditions are widely variable, overall prisoners are subjected to high levels of coercion (explicit and implicit). The prison environment makes it difficult to assure even minimal standards for ethical research such as voluntary informed consent and privacy.

Given these realities, the easiest thing would have been to recommend a virtual ban on human subject research involving prisoners. Yet, the Committee felt that this would be a mistake. Research affords the potential of great benefit as well as burden. It can help policy makers to make correctional settings more humane and effective in achieving legitimate social goals such as deterrence and rehabilitation. Research can also help policy makers better understand and respond to the myriad health problems faced by prisoners such as HIV/AIDS, tuberculosis, hepatitis C, mental illness, and substance abuse. Respect for prisoners also requires recognition of their autonomy. If a prisoner wants to participate in research, his or her views should be taken into account. The overall goal, then, is to permit scientifically rigorous research to the extent that it confers significant benefit without undue risk and in accordance with the prisoner's wishes.

The critical question facing the Committee was whether, given all these factors, current federal regulation is ethically sound and has achieved an appropriate balance between scientific knowledge and prisoner vulnerability. Our answer, after an exhaustive study, was an emphatic "no." Although the ethical principles articulated by the National Commission are still largely apt, the Committee found that the federal system of human subject protection is deficient.

The Committee was surprised and disappointed to find that there were no systematic data sources on the quantity and quality of prisoner research in the United States. Committee members searched the literature and determined there is a great deal of research involving prisoners taking place that appears to be largely unregulated. The most glaring problem is that the federal rules cover only a small fraction of the research being undertaken in prisons. This is because the regulations (45 C.F.R. Part 46) do not cover human subject research unless it is funded by a few federal agencies, or the sponsoring institution has voluntarily adopted Subpart C. Much of the research supported through other sources (e.g., federal, state, or private) is outside the scope of regulatory protection. Subpart C also only applies to narrowly defined "prisoners," not including individuals who are under state-imposed limitations of liberty but not in traditional prison settings. There appears to be no morally defensible reason for excluding a large number of prisoners from human subject protection, as is currently the case.

The Committee boldly recommends five paradigmatic changes in the system of ethical protections for research involving prisoners. First, expand the definition of the term *prisoner* to include a much larger population of persons whose liberty is restricted by virtue of sentence, probation, parole, or community placement. Second, ensure universal, consistent standards of protection so that safeguards based on sound ethical values apply to prisoner research irrespective of the source of funding. Third, shift from a category-based to a risk-benefit approach to defining ethically acceptable research so that prisoners are never exposed to research risks unless there is a distinctly favorable benefit-to-risk ratio. Fourth, update the ethical framework established by the National Commission to include collaborative responsibility—the concept that research should be conducted in meaningful collaboration with the key stakeholders—notably prisoners and prison staff. Finally, enhance systematic oversight of research involving prisoners so that human subject protections are more rigorous and more reliable than those that exist under the existing institutional review board (IRB) mechanism.

The treatment of prisoners (both respect for their rights and concern for their health and well-being) is a principal measure of a decent and civilized society. Therefore, the committee strongly encourages the executive and legislative branches give due consideration to the proposals in this report.

Finally, and importantly, I express my sincere gratitude to the DHHS Office for Human Research Protections for commissioning this project, the Institute of Medicine (IOM) leadership for its support and insights, and to my fellow Committee members for their exceptional wisdom and service. Committee members worked hard and long in devising solutions to apparently intractable problems. The Committee is particularly grateful to the 10 members of the prisoner liaison committee who educated us about prison life. Without their involvement, we could not have fully understood the problems or solutions. Cori Vanchieri and her team (Ben Berkman and

Sarah M. Shalf) wrote extraordinarily incisive drafts for the Committee to review. Andrew Pope is not only the Director of the IOM Board on Health Sciences Policy, but also brilliantly assumed the position of Study Director of our Committee. His leadership is warmly appreciated.

> Lawrence O. Gostin, *Chair*
> *Committee on Ethical Considerations*
> *for Research Involving Prisoners*

Contents

ACRONYMS xvi

SUMMARY 1

1 INTRODUCTION 21
   Why Now?, 22
   Committee's Task and Approach, 24
      Methods and Approach, 26
   Organization of This Report, 27

2 TODAY'S PRISONERS: CHANGING DEMOGRAPHICS,
   HEALTH ISSUES, AND THE CURRENT RESEARCH
   ENVIRONMENT 29
   Changing Demographics and Health Issues, 30
      Descriptions of Prisons, Jails, and Other Correctional
         Settings, 30
      The Prisoner Population, 31
      Summary of Findings on Changing Demographics
         and Health Issues, 58
   Current Research Environment, 59
      Current Status of Prisoner Research, 59
      Results from the Surveys with Key DOC Personnel, 59
      Published Literature: A Review of Selected Prisoner Studies, 61
      Data Retrieval Needs Improving, 64
      Summary of Findings on Current Research Environment, 66

3 FEDERAL REGULATORY LANDSCAPE 73
Adoption of DHHS Human Subjects Protection Regulations, 74
    The Common Rule, 76
    Subpart C: Prisoners as Research Subjects, 79
    Report of the SACHRP Subcommittee, 81
Other Federal Human Subjects Protections, 84
    Subpart D, 85
    Other DHHS Agencies: FDA Regulations, 86
    DOJ Regulations, 89
Analysis, 94
    Existing Authority for Broader Regulation, 95
    Can the DHHS Be Guaranteed Broader Authority?, 96
    Alternatives to Comprehensive Regulation, 99

4 DEFINING PRISONERS AND CORRECTIONAL SETTINGS 101
Ethical Foundations of Current Research Regulations, 101
Current Regulations Pertinent to Places of Prisoner Research, 102
Correctional Settings Encompass More than Prisons and Jails, 103
Definition of Prisoner, 105
Delineation of Settings, 109
    When Proposed Regulations Should Apply, 109
    When Proposed Regulations Should Not Apply, 110
When Liberty Status Changes, 110

5 THE ETHICAL FRAMEWORK FOR RESEARCH INVOLVING PRISONERS 113
The 1976 Commission's Ethical Framework, 114
    Historical Context, 114
    Justice and Respect for Persons, 115
An Updated Ethical Framework, 116
    Respect for Persons, 117
    Justice, 127

6 SYSTEMS OF OVERSIGHT, SAFEGUARDS, AND PROTECTIONS 137
Overarching Principle, 137
Defining and Reviewing Prisoner Research, 138
    What Is Reviewed, 139
    Who Reviews, 141
    How Reviews Are Conducted, 143
    When Reviews Are Done, 150

Systematic Oversight of Research with Prisoners, 151
  Prison Research Subject Advocate, 153
  IRB Postapproval Monitoring, 156
  National Oversight, 157
Applying Safeguards for Particular Kinds of Research, 160
  Sample Situations, 162
Other Categories and Types of Research Involving
  Prisoners Prohibited, 170
Impact of Committee Recommendations on
  Stakeholder Responsibilities, 170

APPENDIXES

A	Data Sources and Methods	175
B	The National Commission's Deliberations and Findings	191
C	Report of the SACHRP Subcommittee and Human Subjects Protections	199
D	Code of Federal Regulations Title 45: Public Welfare, Part 46: Protection of Human Subjects	205
E	Committee, Expert Advisor, Liaison Panel, and Staff Biographies	239

INDEX 253

Acronyms

AE	adverse events
AIDS	acquired immunodeficiency syndrome
BJS	Bureau of Justice Statistics
BOP	Bureau of Prisons
BRRB	Bureau Research Review Board
CDC	Centers for Disease Control and Prevention
CDCR	California Department of Correction and Rehabilitation
CIA	Central Intelligence Agency
CMF	California Medical Facility
CQI	comprehensive quality improvement
CRA	clinical research associate
CRC	clinical research center
CYA	California Youth Authority
DHHS	Department of Health and Human Services
DOC	Department of Corrections
DOJ	Department of Justice
DHEW	Department of Health, Education, and Welfare
FBP	Federal Bureau of Prisons
FDA	Food and Drug Administration
FWA	federal-wide assurance

ACRONYMS

GAO	General Accounting Office
GED	General Equivalency Development (test)
HIV	human immunodeficiency virus
HIPAA	Health Insurance Portability and Accountability Act
HRPPP	Human Research Participant Protection Program
IRB	institutional review board
IOM	Institute of Medicine
JPI	Justice Policy Institute
LRRB	local research review board
National Commission	The National Commission for the Protection of Human Subjects of Biomedical and Behavioral Research
NCCHC	National Commission on Correctional Health Care
NIC	National Institute of Corrections
NIH	National Institutes of Health
NIJ	National Institute of Justice
NFCMH	New Freedom Commission on Mental Health
OHRP	Office for Human Research Protections
ORE	Office of Research and Evaluation
OSI	Open Society Institute
PHI	protected health information
PRSA	prison research subject advocate
QA	quality assurance
QI	quality improvement
RA	research assistant
SACHRP	Secretary's Advisory Committee on Human Research Protections
SAMHSA	Substance Abuse and Mental Health Services Administration
SSA	Social Security Administration
TB	tuberculosis
TQI	total quality improvement
U.S.	United States

Summary

ABSTRACT

In the past 30 years, the population of prisoners in the United States has expanded more than 4.5 fold, correctional facilities are increasingly overcrowded, and more of the country's disadvantaged populations—racial minorities, women, people with mental illness, and people with communicable diseases such as human immunodeficiency virus (HIV)/acquired immune deficiency syndrome (AIDS), hepatitis C, and tuberculosis—are under correctional supervision. Because prisoners face restrictions on liberty and autonomy, limited privacy, and often inadequate health care, they require specific protections when involved in research, particularly in today's correctional settings. Given these issues, the Department of Health and Human Services (DHHS) Office for Human Research Protections (OHRP) commissioned the Institute of Medicine (IOM) to review the ethical considerations regarding research involving prisoners. The resulting analysis emphasizes five broad actions to provide prisoners involved in research with critically important protections. (1) expand the definition of the term prisoner; (2) ensure universally and consistently applied standards of protection; (3) shift from a category-based to a risk-benefit approach to research review; (4) update the ethical framework to include collaborative responsibility; and (5) enhance systematic oversight of research involving prisoners.

In many important ways, the U.S. correctional system is different than it was in the 1970s, when current regulations regarding prisoners as research subjects were promulgated. The total correctional population (persons in prisons, jails, probation, and parole) increased to nearly 7 million individuals between 1978 and 2004 (Bureau of Justice Statistics [BJS], 2000a, 2005a,b,c; U.S. Census, 1994, 1998). Correctional facilities are increasingly overcrowded (BJS, 2005a), and access to programs, services, and health care has not kept pace with the rising tide of prisoners (Metzner, 2002; Sturm, 1993). More of our country's disadvantaged populations are under correctional supervision: racial minorities, women, persons with mental illness, and persons with communicable diseases such as HIV/AIDS, hepatitis C, and tuberculosis (BJS, 2005b; National Commission on Correctional Health Care [NCCHC], 2002).

Prisoners have been exploited in the past, carrying a heavier burden of the risks of research than the general population (Hornblum, 1998; Jones, 1993; Murphy, 2005). Although the level of severity varies depending on the correctional setting, prisoners face restrictions on liberty and autonomy, limited privacy, and potentially inadequate health-care services. These factors can be barriers to the prerequisites of ethical research, namely the acquisition of voluntary informed consent, protection of privacy, and access to adequate health care such that a choice between research participation and nonparticipation is not simply a desperate action to obtain treatment.

However, research can impart benefits. Responsible research has the potential of improving the health and well-being of prisoners as well as improving the conditions in which they live. Adherence to the highest ethical values, however, is critically important in designing and conducting human research involving prisoners.

Title 45 Part 46 of the Code of Federal Regulations (45 C.F.R. Part 46) contains Subpart A, the basic DHHS regulations for the protection of human research subjects, also known as the Common Rule. The Common Rule provides requirements and guidance on issues such as review by an institutional review board (IRB), informed consent by subjects, analysis of risks and benefits, protecting privacy, plus further requirements for approval of proposed research. Additional subparts of 45 C.F.R. Part 46 provide more specific protections for certain particularly vulnerable populations: pregnant women, fetuses, and neonates (Subpart B); prisoners (Subpart C); and children (Subpart D). Subpart C (Additional Protections Pertaining to Biomedical and Behavioral Research Involving Prisoners as Subjects), the principal focus of this report, was first finalized in 1978 and was developed in response to the *Report and Recommendations: Research Involving Prisoners* by the National Commission for the Protection of Human Subjects of Biomedical and Behavior Research (NCPHSBBR, 1976).

The general stance of Subpart C is that only research that fits within four or five categories is permitted in prisoner populations.

The committee's review of current research revealed that most research involving prisoners is taking place outside the purview of Subpart C, and many prisoner studies are being conducted without IRB review. There is no ethically defensible reason to exclude certain prisoners from most, if not all, human subject protections afforded by federal regulation. All of these factors point to a population that is more vulnerable and requires stronger protections than those inspired by the national commission in the 1970s.

With these concerns in mind, the OHRP of the DHHS commissioned the IOM to review the ethical considerations in research involving prisoners as a basis for updating DHHS regulations to protect prisoners as research subjects.

The committee was charged with the following tasks:[1]

- Consider whether the ethical bases for research with prisoners differ from those for research with nonprisoners.
- Develop an ethical framework for the conduct of research with prisoners.
- Identify considerations or safeguards necessary to ensure that research with prisoners is conducted ethically.
- Identify issues and needs for future consideration and study.

MAJOR RECOMMENDATIONS

The committee developed each recommendation in this report with the interests of prisoners in mind. Throughout its deliberations, the committee was well aware of the dark history of research involving prisoners (Hornblum, 1998; Jones, 1993; Murphy, 2005) and was determined not to permit the exposure of prisoners to the kind of research abuses that oc-

---

[1] The committee decided to exclude children (unless treated as adults), military personnel, persons under restricted liberty due to mental illness, and persons outside the criminal justice system, such as those detained under the U.S. Patriot Act. By excluding these groups, the committee emphasizes that these groups face very similar circumstances and that very strong ethical safeguards are required. However, the committee lacks the expertise to address the needs of these special populations and such an inquiry exceeds the committee's charge. Parallel studies, such as the one undertaken by this committee, may be needed to explore ethical issues of research involving these groups. If, however, juveniles are transferred from the original jurisdiction of the family court (or the equivalent, such as a juvenile court) to the jurisdiction of a state or federal criminal court, then they would fall under the provisions of this report.

curred before the national commission released its report (NCPHSBBR, 1976). In this report, in fact, the committee adds further protections both by expanding the population of prisoners covered by rigorous ethical rules and by recommending additional ethical safeguards. At the same time, access to research may be critical to improve the health of prisoners and the conditions in which they live, as the committee was told by prisoners during prison site visits. The task was to strike a balance between potential benefits and risks of specific research protocols. The goal is to ensure rigorous responsible research that improves the well-being of prisoners while taking great care to protect their health, well-being, and human rights.

The recommendations discussed later (and presented in Box S-1) will allow research, in limited circumstances, that might benefit prisoners. These limited circumstances cannot be captured by a rigid categorical approach but need to be rooted in an ethically relevant risk-benefit analysis that grapples with the balance between a need for protection and access to potentially beneficial research protocols. During the course of the committee's deliberations, five themes emerged as organizing categories for the committee's recommendations: (1) expand the definition of the term *prisoner*; (2) ensure universal, consistent ethical protection; (3) shift from a category-based to a risk-benefit approach to research review; (4) update the ethical framework to include collaborative responsibility; and (5) enhance systematic oversight of research with prisoners.

Expand the Definition of Prisoner

Subpart C defines a prisoner as any person who is "involuntarily confined or detained in a penal institution" as a result of violating a criminal or civil statute, detained in other facilities as an alternative to criminal prosecution or incarceration, or detained pending arraignment, trial, or sentencing (45 C.F.R § 46.303[c]). The present regulation's emphasis on custodial detention is too narrow. Of the nearly 7 million persons under adult correctional supervision in 2004, only 2.1 million were in prisons and jails. The rest—4.9 million—were on parole and probation, groups that do not clearly fit under the definition in the current regulations (BJS, 2005c). The committee, therefore, recommends an expansion of the definition of prisoner to afford protections for a larger population of prisoners involved in human subjects research.

> **Recommendation:** *Redefine the term* prisoner *to expand the reach of human subjects protections.* The Department of Health and Human Services and other relevant agencies that write, implement, or enforce regulations pertaining to research with prisoners should expand the definition of the term *prisoner* to include all settings, whether a correc-

> **BOX S-1**
> **Ethical Considerations for Revisions to DHHS Regulations for Protection of Prisoners Involved in Research**
>
> **Recommendations**
> Redefine the term *prisoner* to expand the reach of human subjects protections. (4.1)
>
> **Ensure Universal, Consistent Ethical Protection**
> - Establish uniform guidelines for all human subjects research involving prisoners. (3.1)
> - Maintain a public database of all research involving prisoners. (2.1)
> - Ensure transparency and accountability in the research enterprise. (6.7)
>
> **Shift from a Category-Based to a Risk-Benefit Approach to Research Review**
> - Apply a risk-benefit framework to research review. (5.1)
>
> **Update the Ethical Framework to Include Collaborative Responsibility**
> - Use a collaborative research approach. (5.2)
> - Ensure adequate standards of care. (5.3)
> - Support critical areas of correctional research. (5.4)
>
> **Enhance Systematic Oversight of Research Involving Prisoners**
> - Strengthen monitoring of research involving prisoners. (6.3)
> - Modify institutional review board considerations for independent ethical review of research protocols. (6.4)
> - Enhance the Office for Human Research Protections's capacity to provide systematic oversight of research involving prisoners. (6.5)
> - Establish systematic oversight of all research with prisoners. (6.6)
> - Ensure voluntary informed consent. (6.1)
> - Protect the privacy of prisoners engaged in research. (6.2)

tional institution or a community setting, in which a person's liberty is restricted by the criminal justice system. *(Recommendation 4.1)*

The goal of this recommendation is to expand the reach of the regulatory procedures and oversight mechanisms recommended in this report to the fuller population of individuals whose liberty is restricted by the criminal justice system. These individuals face greater risks than those in the general population. The freedom of a prisoner to make a choice as well as the ability to protect his or her privacy can be hampered in any of the correctional settings that restrict liberty. Throughout this report, the term *prisoner* is used with this expanded meaning in mind. An exclusion, however, was provided by the committee so that prisoners living in a noncustodial community setting could enroll in research that is open to any citizen in the community when his or her status as a prisoner is not relevant or related to enrollment in the study.

Ensure Universal, Consistent Ethical Protection

The committee was asked to make recommendations regarding research under the oversight jurisdiction of OHRP, but currently OHRP jurisdiction is severely limited by the terms and conditions of Subpart C; its oversight extends only to research funded by 3 of 17 federal agencies. The Department of Justice's Bureau of Prisons (BOP) has its own set of rules (BOP, 1999, 2005), and other federal agencies and nonfederal entities (e.g., state and private) that support research with prisoners are not required by statute or regulation to offer special protections for prisoner subjects. The committee recommends more uniform application of regulations and oversight of all prisoner research regardless of the source of funding or supervising agency as well as a better accounting of research involving prisoners and greater openness throughout the universe of prisoner research.

Recommendation: *Establish uniform guidelines for all human subjects research involving prisoners.* **Congress should mandate a uniform set of guidelines for human research participant protection programs[2] for all research involving prisoners.** *(Recommendation 3.1)*

All human subjects research involving prisoners should be regulated by the same ethical standards irrespective of source of funding, supporting agency, or type of correctional facility (federal, state, local, or private) or program that houses the prisoner. This would mean that all 17 federal agencies that are signatories to the Common Rule, any additional federal agencies, and all nonfederal sponsors of research would be required to comply with a newly drafted Subpart C.[3] All research involving prisoners, therefore, would be under OHRP oversight (see Recommendations 6.5 and 6.6). There is no justification for variability across agencies, sponsors, and

---

[2]The term *human research participant protection program* (HRPPP) is used throughout this report to mean the network of entities with direct responsibility for the safety of those enrolled in the studies carried out under its purview. The HRPPP most often includes the research organization, the study sponsor, investigator, IRB, and, when relevant, the data safety monitoring board (IOM, 2003). In the contexts described in this report, prison research subject advocates would be an important part of this network as well.

[3]Federal regulation of state and private research would be constitutionally permissible by using, for example, the federal spending power. See, e.g., *South Dakota v. Dole*, 483 U.S. 203, 211 (1987) (upholding the constitutionality of a federal statute conditioning states' receipt of federal funds on adoption of a minimum drinking age of 21).

facilities regarding their approaches to protecting the rights, health, and dignity of prisoners participating in human subjects research, individuals who are among the most vulnerable human subjects of research.

Establishing uniformity within the research protections systems specific to prisoners would enable a second, important step to be realized. Currently, there is no central repository of information about the amount and type of research with prisoners as subjects. For the same reasons that registries of clinical research on drugs and biologics exist and have garnered strong support (DeAngelis et al., 2004; IOM, 2006), a national database would bring clarity to the currently murky landscape of research involving prisoners.

> **Recommendation:** *Maintain a public database of all research involving prisoners.* **The Department of Health and Human Services, in cooperation with the Department of Justice, should systematically and comprehensively document all human subjects research with prisoners.** *(Recommendation 2.1)*

The establishment of a publicly available, national registry of research involving prisoners should include data such as who is conducting research with what support, with what kind of research on what populations, and the nature and extent of ethical oversight provided. A national registry would shed light on the totality of research taking place on prisoners and the quality of ethical oversight provided for each protocol. To enable consideration of questions of justice, it could be used to examine the magnitude and volume of prisoners in different types of research to determine the allocation of benefits and burdens of research among prisoners. A registry would also enhance the application of research findings to prisoner populations.

> **Recommendation:** *Ensure transparency and accountability in the research enterprise.* **Human research participant protections programs and prison administrations conducting human subject research should be open, transparent, and accountable.** *(Recommendation 6.7)*

A sound, ethical protection program involves an open, transparent research process. It requires that the mechanisms used to protect participants from undue harm and to respect their rights and welfare must be apparent to everyone involved. This transparency requires open communication and interaction with the local community, research participants, investigators, and other stakeholders in the research enterprise. Accountability entails maintaining fidelity to the methodology stipulated in the protocol as well as accountability to ensure the quality and performance of the protection program itself.

Shift from a Category-Based to a Risk-Benefit Approach to Research Review

The current categorical approach used in Subpart C to review proposals for research involving prisoners is dependent on narrowly defined stipulated research categories that are subject to various interpretations. If a protocol does not fit a category, it is not allowed. This approach does not provide sufficient or reliable protections for the human subject because it does not consider the potential benefits and risks involved in the study and might disallow research that would be quite acceptable on risk-benefit grounds. In addition, the present structure does not address the actual conditions of confinement or the restrictions on liberty experienced by the prisoner subject (whether incarcerated or subject to restraints on liberty in connection with community-based alternatives to incarceration).

> Recommendation: *Apply a risk-benefit framework to research review.* The Department of Health and Human Services should revise regulations regarding research with prisoners from a model based on categories to a system based on weighing of risks and benefits for the individual human subject, similar to the approach currently used in Subpart D. *(Recommendation 5.1)*

A risk-based approach is preferable because it requires human research participant protection programs (HRPPPs) and OHRP to (1) focus on the potential benefits and harms of each suggested research protocol, and (2) identify the particular ethical issues that each protocol raises in the specific context of the correctional setting. As in Subpart D (45 C.F.R. § 46.407), protections should increase as the risk-benefit scale tilts more toward risk (IOM, 2004).

A risk-benefit approach should apply to all types of research: biomedical, social/behavioral, and epidemiological. Ethically permissible research must offer potential benefits to prisoners that outweigh the risks. Under this framework, it is clear that studies offering no potential benefit to subjects would be precluded (i.e., testing of cosmetic products). Biomedical research in correctional settings would be severely limited. Phase 1 and 2 studies, as defined by the Food and Drug Administration (FDA), for example, would not be allowable because safety and efficacy are not yet clear in these early phases of biomedical research; therefore, risk would overshadow potential benefit.

Biomedical research involving prisoners in two narrow circumstances may be ethically acceptable:

1. In normal circumstances, a biomedical research study may be ethically acceptable if:

- for research on new therapies or preventive measures, there is already some evidence of safety and efficacy, as in Phase 3 testing for new drugs, as defined by the FDA; and
- the ratio of prisoner to nonprisoner subjects does not exceed 50 percent.

2. In exceptional circumstances, a biomedical research study may be ethically acceptable even if the benefit of an intervention has not been completely established, or if the research population is disproportionately comprised of prisoners. These two criteria may be waived if the research addresses a condition or behavior that is solely or almost exclusively found in incarcerated populations (e.g., repetitive sexual assaults). Studies of this nature could only proceed, however, with a federal-level review. The protocol must be submitted to a national, specially convened panel of experts, who, in a public process, consider the ethical acceptability of a particular protocol and make recommendations to the responsible government authority (OHRP) regarding the special circumstances that do or do not provide a basis for research and the safeguards that must apply. This review would be very similar to the process outlined under Subpart D (45 C.F.R. § 46.407) that requires DHHS secretarial consultation for studies that are not otherwise approvable that present an opportunity to understand, prevent, or alleviate a serious problem affecting the health or welfare of prisoners (rather than children), except that the panel of experts could be convened by an entity outside DHHS if appropriate.

This approach comports with the committee's risk-benefit approach. Given the history of and continued potential for prisoner exploitation, biomedical research should be permitted only if there is a strongly favorable benefit-risk ratio for the prisoner. The distribution of burdens should also be considered, thus the requirement that at least half of the research subjects must come from nonprisoner populations. Research should only involve prisoners to provide a benefit to prisoners, not because they are a convenient source of subjects. This approach would enable fair distribution of potential benefits and burdens to prisoners.

To provide extra protections in the area of biomedical intervention research, which likely carries the greatest risks for subjects, the only benefits that should be considered are the benefits to the subjects themselves. Benefits to prisoners as a class are not a strong enough justification for a biomedical intervention study to proceed. These biomedical inquiries may include drug studies and surgical, radiological, or any interventional study in which the outcome of the biomedical intervention is the question of interest.

There may be research proposals, most likely within social/behavioral and epidemiological categories, that carry very low risks for the prisoner subjects but no personal benefit for the subjects. Instead, the potential benefits may be for prisoners as a class (e.g., studies to identify factors that predict recidivism or that seek to understand the effects of prior trauma on antisocial behavior). Applying a risk-benefit analysis may determine that, because the risks are very low and important knowledge or benefits may accrue for prisoners as a class, the research is ethically acceptable. The same may hold true for epidemiological studies that require analysis of biomedical samples, such as tissue, blood, or urine, but are not designed to assess outcomes of an intervention.

For all studies under consideration, the greater the risk and the more restrictive the correctional setting, the stronger the design and monitoring safeguards need to be.

Update the Ethical Framework to Include Collaborative Responsibility

In the Belmont Report (NCPHSBBR, 1979), the national commission identified respect for persons, justice, and beneficence as the fundamental ethical principles that should guide the conduct and regulation of research with prisoners. These three principles should continue to anchor discussions of research with prisoners. However, ideas about ethical research have evolved over the past three decades, leading the committee to suggest that collaborative responsibility be added as a derivative of the principle of justice to give attention to the needs and responsibilities of all parties who will be involved with or affected by a research endeavor.

> **Recommendation:** *Use a collaborative research approach.* Under an ethic of collaborative responsibility, investigators should find ways to obtain input from prisoners and other stakeholders on the design and conduct of any research protocol involving prisoners. *(Recommendation 5.2)*

Collaborative responsibility is intended to convey the idea that, to the extent feasible, all aspects of research (design, planning, and implementation) should include the active participation of relevant institutional stakeholders (prisoners, correctional officers, medical staff, administrators). A focus on collaboration would help cope with the reality that each institution has its own unique conditions and may facilitate openness of the research environment. The responsibility for collaboration lies with investigators, who need to make the effort to engage prison administration and prisoners themselves for their input, and with the other components of the HRPPP, which must determine that the effort was made.

This report contains two additional recommendations that are part of the updated ethical framework aimed at protecting prisoners:

Recommendation: *Ensure adequate standards of care.* Human research participant protection programs, together with the prison administration and prison health-care professionals, are responsible for ensuring that research with prisoners occurs in an environment that is appropriate to the health and well-being of prisoners, including access to existing medical and mental health care that is adequate, protection from inmate attempts to coerce or manipulate participation or non-participation in research, and prompt access to decent health-care services in case the research causes physical or mental harm. *(Recommendation 5.3)*

Justice requires more than the protection of prisoners from harm caused by the research itself. Ethical research carries with it a responsibility to grapple with the fact that potential harm is ubiquitous in everyday prison life, creating an environment for research in which the choice to participate in a study can be inherently coercive and potentially dangerous. Thus, in order for research to be ethical, justice requires that it must be done in a setting in which there is an adequate standard of health care in place.

Ethical research requires an environment that is humane and provides reasonable access to supportive care, particularly when human subjects are exposed to physical or psychological risks. Without adequate medical or psychological care, subjects may be vulnerable to undue inducements to participate in research in order to gain access to medical care or other benefits they would not normally have. Finally, researchers have an ethical obligation, if they expose subjects to risk, to rapidly and professionally remedy any harms caused by the research.

Recommendation: *Support critical areas of correctional research.* Government agencies should fund and researchers should conduct research to identify needed supports to facilitate prisoners' successful reentry into society, reduce recidivism, and inform policy makers about the most humane and effective strategies for the operation of correctional systems. *(Recommendation 5.4)*

Society creates a correctional system for clear purposes such as deterrence to future crime and rehabilitation of those who are convicted of committing offenses. It is of utmost social importance to better understand how best to achieve the purposes of incarceration, including reduction of recidivism and successful introduction back into the community. Perhaps unavoidably, the criminal justice system inflicts some harm on those it punishes. As ethical people, we strive to develop and use corrective measures that are effective and humane without causing unnecessary physical or mental harm to prisoners. However, prisoners are a vulnerable population subject to abuse and exploitation. Indeed, several subclasses of prisoners are some of society's most vulnerable populations, such as young people, persons with mental disabilities, racial minorities, women, and people with diseases (addiction, hepatitis, HIV, hypertension, diabetes) that may or may not be treated during imprisonment. It is, therefore, especially important to better understand how to protect and promote the welfare and well-being of this large and growing segment of our society. Scientific knowledge and information about best practices gained from high-quality research are critically important to understanding how best to achieve all of the legitimate purposes of the criminal justice system.

Enhance Systematic Oversight of Research Involving Prisoners

If limited opportunities for research are to be allowed, safeguards and oversight must be strengthened, made consistent, and applied in relation to the levels of study risk and liberty restrictions experienced by the prisoner population. Informed consent must be obtained and privacy protected in the context of the correctional setting.

Approval of research by the IRB is a critical step, but it is not sufficient. Research involving prisoners must be monitored throughout the course of the study to verify that procedures are being conducted as approved and to detect adverse events or unanticipated problems in a timely manner. The monitoring process may need to differ depending on the setting or study type. Studies that take place in closed institutions, where liberty restrictions are the greatest, require more proactive monitoring than studies within community settings, where subjects can more easily pick up the phone to express concerns or complaints. Similarly, higher risk or more intrusive studies (e.g., research that involves medical, pharmaceutical, or biological interventions) would likely require more intrusive monitoring than social/behavioral studies of nonsensitive issues (e.g., involving questionnaires). The committee suggests that monitoring be accomplished by a prison research subject advocate (PRSA), who is familiar with the local correctional setting but not an employee of the facility, to ensure credibility among the prisoner subjects and maintain independence. The IRB should have free access to the PRSA and be able to meet with the PRSA separate from the investigator and correctional staff.

Recommendation: *Strengthen monitoring of research involving prisoners.* **Institutional review boards that review and approve research involv-**

ing prisoners should establish an onsite, ongoing monitoring function through a prison research subject advocate. *(Recommendation 6.3)*

The activities of the PRSA go beyond the routine annual reviews that IRBs currently conduct. The PRSA's activities are study specific (although a single person could be a PRSA for more than one study) and are "on the ground" activities, involving varying degrees of direct observation of specific research activities (depending on the type and risk level of the research).

Recommendation: *Modify institutional review board considerations for independent ethical review of research protocols.* Institutional review boards should focus on the particular ethical issues that each protocol raises in the specific context of the correctional setting. Institutional review boards would no longer be required to forward research proposals to Office for Human Research Protections for certification, except for those rare proposals that require federal-level review. *(Recommendation 6.4)*

IRBs should accomplish the following:

- Review studies at the local level, make the initial assessments of risk and potential benefits, and approve or reject individual studies based on detailed information about the protocol and correctional setting.
- Determine if a study requires federal-level review.
- Evaluate investigator efforts to obtain input from prisoners and other stakeholders on the design and conduct of the protocol.
- Evaluate the proposed research environment in terms of adequacy of existing health services.
- Calibrate the extent of safeguards and monitoring to the level of restrictions imposed upon prisoners in the particular correctional setting and the degree of risk involved in study participation.
- Receive monitoring reports directly from PRSAs and researchers, at a scope and frequency determined during study review.

The committee recommends that, although IRBs should retain the bulk of the approval and monitoring functions to keep these at a local level, a national independent body is also needed as an additional safeguard.

Recommendation: *Enhance the Office for Human Research Protections's capacity to provide systematic oversight of research involving prisoners.* The Department of Health and Human Services should strengthen the capacity of the Office for Human Research Protections to provide systematic oversight of research involving prisoners that is within its purview. *(Recommendation 6.5)*

Four necessary functions are currently lacking in whole or in part in oversight of research involving prisoners:

1. Maintain a national registry of all prisoner research that is conducted.
2. Make determinations if a study requires federal-level review.
3. Enforce compliance with the regulations, investigate reports of possible problems, intervene to curtail abuses, and impose sanctions for noncompliance.
4. Serve as a national resource for HRPPPs to promote a uniform understanding and consistent application of the regulations.

OHRP is designed to perform three of the four functions above, but does not currently have the funding or personnel to adequately carry out the tasks. OHRP needs to be revitalized and refocused to carry out the three functions already within its purview. In addition, it should be charged with the task of creating and maintaining a national registry of research involving prisoners. This recommendation, however, covers only research supported by DHHS and two other federal agencies. The majority of research involving prisoners is being conducted in the absence of any obligation to provide safeguards or oversight. To remedy that inadequacy and ensure that these protections apply to all research involving prisoners, the enhanced OHRP model must be replicated for all agencies and privately funded research.

> **Recommendation:** *Establish systematic oversight of all research involving prisoners.* **Congress should establish a national system of oversight that is applied uniformly to all research involving prisoners.** *(Recommendation 6.6)*

To expand prisoner protections beyond the narrow jurisdiction of DHHS, Congress should establish a national system of oversight that is applied uniformly to all research involving prisoners, performing all of the functions listed in the recommendation before last. The vast majority of research involving prisoners does not fall within OHRP overview jurisdiction. Strengthening the safeguards provided for all prisoners involved in research, regardless of funding source, will facilitate safe and ethical research across the full range of research involving prisoners. These functions could be performed by the revitalized and properly funded OHRP if OHRP's jurisdiction were extended to the entire range of research involving prisoners regardless of funding source (i.e., federal or nonfederal, public or private). An alternative is to compose a national entity to perform the necessary oversight functions. Placing the functions within OHRP may be more feasible and less disruptive, but it must be done with serious attention to the extra support needed within OHRP to undertake those tasks fully and much more broadly than its current limits to Common Rule agencies. The committee is calling for substantial improvements to the existing system of oversight, and if a new entity is necessary to make it happen, then it should be created.

> **Recommendation:** *Ensure voluntary informed consent.* **Human research participant protection programs should ensure that voluntary informed consent is obtained from subjects in all research involving prisoners.** *(Recommendation 6.1)*

Informed consent is vital to autonomous decision making and respect for persons and is considered a bedrock of ethical research. Informed consent is an interactive and ongoing process to ensure that participants are voluntarily participating in research and that they understand the level and nature of the risks and the uncertainty of potential benefits. The written consent form—one part of the process—is the mechanism for documenting that communication with the participant regarding relevant considerations to enrollment in a protocol has taken place. The informed consent process must help the prisoner to exercise autonomous decision making. The process poses special challenges in the correctional setting, where autonomy is incompatible with institutional order and judicially imposed limitations on liberty. In a correctional setting, a prisoner's capacity to exercise independent judgment may have atrophied. The consent process and discussion must focus on the risks and potential benefits of the research in the context of confinement and the nature of restrictions imposed on the prisoner's liberty. This would include the impact of research data on a prisoner (e.g., how would testing positive for a communicable disease impact housing, work opportunities, medical treatment, family visiting). There is no question that, within correctional settings, it is more difficult to provide integrity to the process of informed consent, but this does not remove the obligation. If it is determined that voluntary informed consent is not obtainable, then a research proposal should not go forward.

> **Recommendation:** *Protect the privacy of prisoners engaged in research.* **Human research participant protections programs should collaborate with prison officials, probation officers, and other staff relevant to the correctional setting to protect the privacy of subjects in prisoner research.** *(Recommendation 6.2)*

Privacy is considered one of the necessary prerequisites for ethical research. In most circumstances, this means nondisclosure of the identity of the research subject and ensuring confidentiality of the specific data collected. Privacy is exceedingly difficult to attain in prison settings, however, because of the inherently coercive and institutionalized contexts and the controlled and public nature of physical movement. Maximizing privacy within a correctional setting will require collaborative planning efforts specific to the particular correctional setting that involve potential subjects and staff from the correctional setting to consider the impact of participation on privacy issues.

Given that it may not be possible to guarantee absolute privacy in some situations, researchers and IRBs should consider the extent to which core privacy issues can be protected from disclosure through realistic and practical approaches. For instance, it may be clear to prisoners and staff that medical research is being conducted, but the specific nature of the study or the characteristics common to human subjects need not be generally known or discernible. These measures, and their limits, should be discussed in detail with prospective participants in the context of the consent process.

CONCLUDING REMARKS

The recommendations offered within this report are intended to encourage the development of a uniform system that provides critically important protections for prisoners involved in research. Research has the potential to help society better understand how to protect and promote the welfare and well-being of this large and growing segment of our society. For any research to go forward, however, it must offer more benefits than risks to prisoners, and the setting in which the prisoners are consigned must allow for the ethical conduct of research, including autonomous decision making, voluntary informed consent, and privacy protection. Strengthening systems of oversight and requiring collaboration at every level of the research process will require substantial commitments from every stakeholder (Table S-1). The committee acknowledges that the collaboration model, for example, will be new within most correctional settings and among many researchers. However, if research is to be supported to improve the welfare of prisoner populations, which the committee recommends, it must be done with rigorous safeguards and under a comprehensive HRPPP. The hallmark of a decent society is to ensure humane, respectful treatment of all prisoners. Responsible, ethically appropriate research is one important aspect of the kind of society to which we aspire.

TABLE S-1 Impact of Committee Recommendations on Stakeholder Responsibilities

Stakeholders	Current Duties	Proposed Duties Based on Committee Recommendations
Congress		1. Mandate uniform guidelines 2. Adequately fund OHRP to strengthen its capacity to provide uniform oversight 3. Establish national oversight entity (OHRP or other) to provide same OHRP oversight functions for the larger universe of research involving prisoners that is not within DHHS jurisdiction.
DHHS/OHRP	1. DHHS agencies follow Subpart C, OHRP also has oversite for research involving prisoners for two other agencies (CIA, SSA) that signed on to Subpart C. 2. For above mentioned studies involving prisoners, OHRP must certify that IRB has followed Subpart C. 3. If a protocol does not fit within one of five categories, regardless of risk benefit, it is not approved.	1. Expand definition of the term *prisoner*. 2. Support critical areas of correctional research. 3. Revise Subpart C regulations to reflect a risk-benefit approach to research review similar to Subpart D. 4. Establish a system of safeguards to be applied uniformly. 5. Revitalize OHRP to enhance its capacity to provide uniform oversight. 6. Maintain a national registry of all prisoner research. 7. OHRP no longer certifies all studies, although it still oversees process of "exceptional" study review. 8. OHRP focus shifts to national oversight, data collection, compliance, enforcement, and technical assistance role.
Other federal agencies	Only CIA and SSA follow Subpart C.	1. All federal agencies follow Subpart C. 2. Support critical areas of correctional research.
Nonfederal and private sponsors	Not required to follow Subpart C.	Must follow revised Subpart C.

continued

TABLE S-1 Continued

Stakeholders	Current Duties	Proposed Duties Based on Committee Recommendations
Correctional settings	1. No clear, standard expectations for providing input in design or access for onsite monitoring. 2. May or may not require IRB review for research at their facility.	1. Be open to providing input to investigators regarding the design and conduct of research protocols involving prisoners. 2. Require that research be approved by an IRB before it is conducted at their facility. 3. Assist in protection of subject privacy. 4. Provide for timely and adequate medical response to adverse events experienced by the research subjects. 5. Ensure that PSRAs have open access to monitor research activities.
HRPPP/IRB	1. Protocol review is based on categories. 2. For DHHS-supported research involving prisoners, submit to OHRP for certification, and if necessary, federal-level review. 3. Wait for OHRP certification before study can be approved. 4. Ensure informed consent. 5. Protect subject privacy. 6. Include prisoner representative as voting member of IRB.	1. Review shifts from category-based to risk-benefit approach, with focus on the particular ethical issues that each protocol raises in the specific context of the correctional setting. 2. Only "exceptional" studies are submitted to OHRP for federal-level review. 3. Evaluate investigator efforts to obtain input from prisoners and other stakeholders on the design and conduct of research protocols involving prisoners. 4. Evaluate the proposed research environment in terms of adequacy of existing health services to ensure that prisoner participation is truly voluntary, and assess existing capacity to provide for timely and adequate medical response to adverse events experienced by the research subjects. 5. Ensure informed consent.

	6. Protect subject privacy.
7. Include prisoner representative as voting member of IRB.
8. Be open, transparent, and accountable.
Investigators	1. Present studies to IRB and await IRB approval and OHRP certification.
2. No standards for getting input or ensuring adequate medical response
3. Obtain informed consent.	1. Present study to IRB for approval. Only requires OHRP review for "exceptional" studies.
2. Demonstrate efforts to obtain input on study design and implementation from stakeholders, including prisoners.
3. Demonstrate to the IRB that the proposed research environment provides for timely and adequate medical response to adverse events experienced by the research subjects.
4. Obtain informed consent.
5. Be open, transparent, and accountable.
PRSAs	Do not exist.	1. Provide assurance, via ongoing, onsite monitoring, such that research subjects within a specific facility or program are protected.
2. Multisite studies would likely have more than one PRSA.
3. Duties expand as potential risks to participants increase.
Prisoners	1. Provide informed consent.	1. Provide informed consent.
2. Provide input, on request, on study design and implementation.

NOTE: OHRP, Office for Human Research Protections; DHHS, Department of Health and Human Services; CIA, Central Intelligence Agency; SSA, Social Security Administration; IRB, institutional review board; PRSA, prison research subject advocate.

REFERENCES

BOP (Bureau of Prisons). 1999. *Program Statement 1070.07.* [Online]. Available: http://www.bop.gov/DataSource/execute/dsPolicyLoc [accessed January 4, 2006].

BOP. 2005. *Program Statement 6031.01.* [Online]. Available: http://www.bop.gov/DataSource/execute/dsPolicyLoc [accessed January 4, 2006].

BJS (Bureau of Justice Statistics). 2000. *Prisoners in Custody 1977-1998.* [Online]. Available: http://www.ojp.usdoj.gov/bjs/prisons.htm [accessed January 3, 2006].

BJS. 2005a. *Prisoners in 2004.* [Online]. Available: http://www.ojp.usdoj.gov/bjs/abstract/p04.htm [accessed January 23, 2006].

BJS. 2005b. *Prison and Jail Inmates at Midyear 2004.* NCJ 208801. Washington DC: U.S. Department of Justice.

BJS. 2005c. *Probation and Parole in the United States, 2004.* NCJ 210676. [Online]. Available: http://www.ojp.usdoj.gov/bjs/pub/pdf/ppus04.pdf [accessed December 20, 2005].

DeAngelis CD, Drazen JM, Frizelle FA, Haug C, Hoey J, Horton R, Kotzin S, Laine C, Marusic A, Overbeke AJ, Schroeder TV, Sox HC, and Van Der Weyden MB. 2004. International Committee of Medical Journal Editors. Clinical trial registration: A statement from the International Committee of Medical Journal Editors. *Journal of the American Medical Association* 292(11):1363–1364.

Hornblum AM. 1998. *Acres of Skin.* New York: Routledge.

IOM (Institute of Medicine). 2003. *Responsible Research: A Systems Approach to Protecting Research Participants.* Washington, DC: The National Academies Press.

IOM. 2004. *The Ethical Conduct of Clinical Research Involving Children.* Washington, DC: The National Academies Press.

IOM. 2006. *Developing a National Registry of Pharmacologic and Biologic Clinical Trials Workshop Report.* Washington, DC: The National Academies Press.

Jones JH. 1993. *Bad Blood: The Tuskegee Syphilis Experiment.* New York: The Free Press.

Metzner JL. 2002. Class action litigation in correctional psychiatry. *Journal of the American Academy of Psychiatry and the Law* 30:19–29.

Murphy D. 2005. Health care in the federal bureau of prisons: Fact or fiction. *California Journal of Health Promotion* 3(2):23–37.

NCCHC (National Commission on Correctional Health Care). 2002. *The Health Status of Soon-to-Be-Released Inmates: Executive Summary.* [Online]. Available: http://www.ncchc.org/stbr/Volume2/ExecutiveSummary.pdf [accessed October 10, 2005].

NCPHSBBR (National Commission for the Protection of Human Subjects of Biomedical and Behavioral Research). 1976. *Report and Recommendations: Research Involving Prisoners.* Washington, DC: U.S. Department of Health, Education, and Welfare, Pub. No. (OS) 76–131.

NCPHSBBR. 1979. *The Belmont Report: Ethical Principles and Guidelines for the Protection of Human Subjects of Research.* [Online]. Available: http://ohsr.od.nih.gov/guidelines/belmont.html [accessed October 10, 2005].

Sturm SP. 1993. The legacy and future of corrections litigation. *University of Pennsylvania Law Review* 142:638–738.

U.S. Census. 1998. *Table No. 377: Federal and State Prisoners: 1970 to 1996.* In: Statistical Abstracts of the United States: 1998. [Online]. Available: http://www.census.gov/prod/3/98pubs/98statab/sasec5.pdf [accessed December 23, 2005].

U.S. Census. 2004. *Table: Number and Rate of Sentenced Prisoners Under Jurisdiction of State and Federal Correctional Authorities on December 31.* [Online]. Available: http://www.albany.edu/sourcebook/pdf/t6282004.pdf [accessed December 23, 2005].

1

Introduction

Prisoners are an especially vulnerable class of potential research participants who historically have been exploited by physicians and researchers seeking expedient solutions to complex research problems (Hornblum, 1997, 1998; Mitford, 1974). They are the classic "captive population."

The ethical issues surrounding research on any human population require serious consideration. Certain unique circumstances faced by prisoners,[1] however, require particular attention. Numerous ethical problems surrounding research with prisoners grow out of the complexity of the correctional settings and the disempowered status of the potential research participants. Although the limitations on personal choice and control are perhaps most evident and oppressive in locked detention facilities (e.g., jails, prisons), the power differential between criminal justice agents and prisoners exists in many other contexts as well (e.g., probation, parole); the differences are a matter of degree.

First among the problems are those related to informed consent, ensuring that the setting permits the processes of informed consent and refusal. Second, privacy is much more difficult to ensure within a correctional setting. In a prison or jail, everyone sees who moves where and can specu-

---

[1]The term *prisoner* is defined by the Committee in Chapter 4 and used throughout this report to mean all persons whose liberty has been restricted by decisions of the criminal justice system. The setting is not limited to prisons and jails but can include community settings, such as work release programs, probation, parole, and so on.

late on what that movement means. For example, an inmate's trip to a medical clinic that is investigating acquired immune deficiency syndrome (AIDS) or hepatitis C makes quite clear what the inmate's visit portends.

Third, ethical research involves ensuring, as a prerequisite for research, that the standard of medical health care available in the correctional setting permits the inmate to have a meaningful choice between the existing care that is available and the experimental intervention. In addition, other matters that generally are not complex issues in research outside of correctional settings appear as ethical dilemmas in the prison or jail. For example, in a correctional setting it may be difficult to distinguish between a refusal of care and a denial of care. Likewise, there can be difficulties in distinguishing between compliance and noncompliance in the research protocol. For example, if an inmate does not appear for a scheduled research meeting, which may also provide access to health care, it may not be clear whether the inmate has (1) decided not to come, (2) been barred or precluded from coming, (3) been taken to court for an unanticipated appearance, or (4) been presented with an unscheduled family visit.

These concerns are readily apparent in the context of research involving prisoners. However, what about questions of justice and fairness? How much of the burden of research should prisoners be asked to bear? How many of the potential benefits of research will be directed toward the prisoners? The acne medication Retin-A was basically developed in the Philadelphia prison system, with serious harms and few benefits afforded the prisoners who were involved in the research (Hornblum, 1998). Alternatively, many inmates would choose to live and work in a research unit if they could, regardless of the risks and benefits associated with research participation. Should that be encouraged, permitted, or, as it is now, barred from the prison setting? What if the burdens of research are actually experienced by inmates as benefits to be coveted in the deprived and stark setting of the prison? Should that overcome the current stance of the regulations in the U.S. Department of Health and Human Services (DHHS, 2005a) 45 C.F.R. Part 46 (see Appendix D)?

WHY NOW?

In response to a request from the Office for Human Research Protections (OHRP), the Institute of Medicine (IOM) formed the Committee on Ethical Considerations for Protection of Prisoners Involved in Research to address ethical considerations for protecting prisoners involved in research. The broad purpose was to examine whether the conclusions reached in 1976 by the National Commission for the Protection of Human Subjects of Biomedical and Behavioral Research (see Appendix B) remain appropriate today. The national commission's report (NCPHSBBR, 1976) was the basis for 45 C.F.R. Part 46, which contains four subparts. Subpart A, also known as the Common Rule, is "Basic U.S. DHHS Policy for Protection of Human Research Subjects" (DHHS, 2005a). Subparts B, C, and D of 45 C.F.R. Part 46 provide further and more specific protection for certain particularly vulnerable populations: pregnant women, fetuses, and neonates; prisoners; and children, respectively (DHHS, 2005a). Subpart C, "Additional Protections Pertaining to Biomedical and Behavioral Research Involving Prisoners as Subjects," the focus of this project, was first finalized in 1978 (DHHS, 2005a).

This examination will consider the impact of developments in correctional systems since that time (1976) as well as societal perceptions of the balance between burdens and potential benefits of research.

Many changes have occurred within the U.S. correctional system since the late 1970s, and these changes have important ramifications for research involving prisoners. They include the following:

- An escalating prisoner population. For example, persons under prison supervision grew from 216,000 in 1974 to 1.4 million in 2004, largely as a result of the war on drugs, harsher sentencing laws, and high recidivism rates (Bureau of Justice Statistics [BJS], 2003, 2005a; Human Rights Watch [HRW], 2003; Jacobson, 2005). The overall correctional population, including persons in prison, jail, and on parole and probation, has jumped from 1.5 million in 1978 to nearly 7 million in 2004 (BJS, 2005a,b,c,d).
- The overrepresentation of men and women of color in prisoner populations (BJS, 2003). One out of eight black men in their late 20s is under the jurisdiction of the criminal justice system, including, jail, prison, probation, and parole (Lotke, 1997; Mauer and King, 2004).
- Increased overcrowding in correctional facilities, resulting in diminished availability of and access to programs and services. Construction has not kept pace with the increasing number of inmates (Jacobson, 2005).
- Inadequate health-care services is a reality of some correctional settings, notwithstanding Eighth Amendment proscriptions against "deliberate indifference to the serious medical needs" of prisoners (Braithwaite et al., 2005; HRW, 2003; Metzner, 2002; Restum, 2005; Sturm, 1993).
- Increasing population of female inmates—growing at a faster rate than that of male inmates—who face unique challenges (BJS, 1999). As with male prisoners, female inmates are more likely to be a minority, poor, and undereducated, but as women they are more likely to be the primary caregiver for children, and they suffer disproportionate victimization from sexual and physical abuse (BJS, 1999).
- Increased number of prisoners serving their sentences in alternative programs, outside the traditional "bricks and mortar" prisons and jails

(BJS, 2004). The environments to which prisoners are consigned have expanded to include work-release programs, halfway houses, electronic monitoring programs, and other alternatives to incarceration (BJS, 2004).
- Overrepresentation of communicable diseases, such as HIV/AIDS, hepatitis B and C, and tuberculosis, in prisons (Hammett et al., 2002; Khan et al., 2005; MacNeil et al., 2005; National Commission on Correctional Health Care [NCCHC], 2002). In addition, among an aging prison population, chronic diseases such as diabetes and hypertension are critical management issues (NCCHC, 2002).
- Increasing admissions of mentally ill prisoners with the closing of the large state mental institutions (HRW, 2003). Mental illness and violence take a heavy toll on the prisoner population (BJS, 1999; New Freedom Commission on Mental Health [NFCMH], 2004).

At the same time that prison populations have been expanding, there has been a considerable amount of confusion and disagreement in the research community regarding the interpretation and application of Subpart C of 45 C.F.R. Part 46 ("Additional Protections Pertaining to Biomedical and Behavioral Research Involving Prisoners as Subjects" [DHHS, 2005a]) to current issues of research involving prisoners. The OHRP's responsibilities include implementation of the DHHS Regulations for the Protection of Human Subjects (DHHS, 2005a) and the provision of guidance on ethical issues in biomedical and behavioral research. OHRP has oversight and educational responsibilities wherever DHHS funds are used to conduct research involving human participants. The Secretary's Advisory Committee for Human Research Protections(SACHRP), the advisory committee to OHRP, has asked OHRP to rewrite Subpart C, taking into consideration the current prison environment (see Appendix C).

OHRP recommended that, before such an effort is undertaken, there should be a thorough review of the ethical considerations in research involving prisoners, which could serve as the basis for developing new regulations. Beyond its importance regarding revisions to Subpart C, such a review would be instructive for developing ethical bases for making future changes to the DHHS Regulations for the Protection of Human Subjects and the Common Rule.

COMMITTEE'S TASK AND APPROACH

This report addresses ethical considerations for the protection of prisoners involved in research. The overall purpose of the committee was to examine whether the conclusions reached by the national commission in 1976 remain appropriate today. This examination considered the impact of developments in correctional systems since that time and societal perceptions of the balance between research burdens and potential benefits of research. The committee was asked to

- consider whether the ethical bases for research with prisoners differ from those for research with nonprisoners;
- develop an ethical framework for the conduct of research with prisoners;
- based on the ethical framework developed, identify considerations or safeguards necessary to ensure that research with prisoners is conducted ethically; and
- identify issues and needs for future consideration and study.

The committee was asked to address the following three questions:

1. What are the unique features of the prison setting as an environment for research with respect to the general characteristics of the prison population, its specific and general health-care needs, the adequacy of existing health-care services, and the legal constraints placed on prisoners and the institutions that house them? Considerations include the following:

- How should the term *prisoner* be defined?
- What features of the current system of incarceration must be considered in conducting and reviewing research?
- What constitutes voluntariness in the prison setting? Are special measures needed to ensure informed consent in this setting?
- Must there be a finding that no alternative population is available in order for ethical research involving prisoners to occur?
- What safeguards are necessary to ensure that research proceeds ethically? For example, how can privacy and confidentiality be protected in a setting in which individuals are institutionalized?

2. What criteria or factors are relevant to determining whether research with prisoners can be conducted ethically? Specifically:

- Does the national commission's conclusion that research involving prisoners should only be conducted if it benefits prisoners individually or as a group merit continued support?
- What should constitute minimal risk in the context of research with prisoners?
- Should prisoner research be limited to "not greater than minimal risk?"
- What are the priorities for research involving prisoners?

3. What is an appropriate ethical framework for the conduct of such research? How should the concepts of minimal risk, voluntary informed consent, privacy and confidentiality, and distributive justice be incorporated into such a framework? Specifically:[1]

- Are the criteria for allowing prisoner research expressed by the national commission regarding voluntariness and openness (e.g., public scrutiny, grievance procedures) still appropriate?
- What measures beyond exclusion from research are appropriate for protecting the rights and welfare of prisoners?
- How should the standard of existing medical care be valued when reviewing research protocols involving control or placebo-control arms?
- Should there be a risk threshold for allowing research with prisoners? If so, how should the prospect of benefit affect that threshold?

Methods and Approach

In conducting its work, the committee cast a broad net for the collection of information. In addition to the traditional sources of information (e.g., literature, workshops, commissioned papers [see Box A-1 in Appendix A]), the committee also had a liaison group (see Box A-2) and visited two correctional facilities. Appendix A provides a detailed summary of the committee's methods and data sources.

ORGANIZATION OF THIS REPORT

This report is organized into six chapters. This introduction is followed by a thorough discussion of the demographics of today's correctional system in Chapter 2, which also details the committee's efforts to determine

---

[1]The committee decided to exclude children (unless treated as adults), military personnel, persons under restricted liberty due to mental illness, and persons outside the criminal justice system, such as those detained under the U.S. Patriot Act. By excluding these groups, the committee emphasizes that these groups face very similar circumstances and that very strong ethical safeguards are required. However, the committee lacks the expertise to address the needs of these special populations and such an inquiry exceeds the committee's charge. Parallel studies, such as the one undertaken by this committee, may be needed to explore ethical issues of research involving these groups. If, however, juveniles are transferred from the original jurisdiction of the family court (or the equivalent, such as a juvenile court) to the jurisdiction of a state or federal criminal court, then they would fall under the provisions of this report.

the type and scope of research involving prisoners within the past two years. Chapter 3 provides a description of the current federal regulatory landscape, with a discussion of its limitations. Chapter 4 introduces the committee's broadened definition of *prisoner* aimed at expanding protections to a wider group of people who have restricted liberties because of decisions of criminal courts. Chapter 5 describes a new framework for research involving prisoners, based on the ethical principles of respect for persons and justice, and introduces the derivative concept of collaborative responsibility as being particularly important for planning and implementing research involving this vulnerable population. Finally, Chapter 6 contains the committee's recommendations for a new, more comprehensive system of oversight, safeguards, and protections for research involving prisoners, with more intrusive monitoring for higher risk studies. Appendix A contains a thorough description of the committee's methods and data sources; Appendix B, the national commission's deliberations and findings; Appendix C, the report of the SACHRP Subcommittee and Human Subjects Protections; Appendix D, the Code of Federal Regulations 45 Part 46 (Protection of Human Subjects); and Appendix E, brief biographies of the committee members, liaison group, and IOM staff.

REFERENCES

BJS (Bureau of Justice Statistics). 1999. *Mental Health and Treatment of Inmates and Probationers.* [Online]. Available: http://www.ojp.usdoj.gov/bjs/pub/pdf/mhtip.pdf [accessed December 23, 2005].

BJS. 2003. *Prevalence of Imprisonment in the U.S. Population, 1974–2001.* [Online]. Available: http://www.ojp.usdoj.gov/bjs/pub/pdf/piusp01.pdf [accessed December 30, 2005].

BJS. 2004. *Probation and Parole in the United States, 2003.* [Online]. Available: http://www.ojp.usdoj.gov/bjs/pub/pdf/ppus03.pdf [accessed January 20, 2005].

BJS. 2005a. *Prison and Jail Inmates at Midyear 2004.* [Online]. Available: http://www.ojp.usdoj.gov/bjs/pub/pdf/pjim04.pdf [accessed January 20, 2006].

BJS. 2005b. *Prisoners in Custody, 1977-98.* [Online]. Available: http://www.ojp.usdoj.gov/bjs/prisons.htm#selected [accessed April 4, 2006].

BJS. 2005c. *Adults on Probation, Federal and State by State, 1977–2004.* [Online]. Available: http://www.ojp.usdoj.gov/bjs/pandp.htm#selected [accessed April 4, 2006].

BJS. 2005d. *Adults on Parole, Federal and State by State, 1977–2004.* [Online]. Available: http://www.ojp.usdoj.gov/bjs/pandp.htm#selected [accessed April 4, 2006].

Braithwaite RI, Treadwell HM, Arriola KRJ. 2005. Health disparities and incarcerated women: A population ignored. *American Journal of Public Health* 95(10):1679–1680.

DHHS (Department of Health and Human Services). 2005a. *Code of Federal Regulations: Title 45. Public Welfare. Part 46: Protection of Human Subjects.* Washington, DC: DHHS.

Hammett TM, Harmon MP, Rhodes W. 2002. The burden of infectious disease among inmates of and releasees from US correctional facilities, 1997. *American Journal of Public Health* 92:1789–1794.

Hornblum AM. 1997. They were cheap and available: Prisoners as research subjects in twentieth century America. *British Medical Journal* 315:1437–1441.

Hornblum AM. 1998. *Acres of Skin: Human Experiments at Holmesburg Prison.* New York: Routledge.
HRW (Human Rights Watch). 2003. *Ill-Equipped: U.S. Prisons and Offenders with Mental Illness.* [Online]. Available: http://www.hrw.org/reports/2003/usa1003/index.htm [accessed October 13, 2005].
Jacobson, M. 2005. *Downsizing Prisons: How to Reduce Crime and End Mass Incarceration.* New York: New York University Press.
Khan AJ, Simard EP, Bower WA, Wurtzel HL, Khristova M, Wagner KD, Arnold KE, Nainan OV, LaMarre M, Bell BP. 2005. Ongoing transmission of hepatitis B virus infection among inmates at a state correctional facility. *American Journal of Public Health* 95(10): 1793–1799.
Lotke E. 1997 *Hobbling a Generation: Young African American Men in D.C.'s Criminal Justice System Five Years Later.* National Center on Institutions and Alternatives. [Online]. Available: http://66.165.94.98/stories/hobblgen0897.html [accessed April 6, 2006].
MacNeil JR, Lobato MN, Moore M. 2005. An unanswered health disparity: Tuberculosis among correctional inmates, 1993 through 2003. *American Journal of Public Health* 95(10):1800–1805.
Mauer M, King RS. 2004. *Schools and Prisons: Fifty Years After Brown V. Board of Education.* [Online]. Available: http://sentencingproject.org/pdfs/brownvboard.pdf [accessed January 2, 2006].
Metzner JL. 2002. Class action litigation in correctional psychiatry. *Journal of the American Academy of Psychiatry and the Law* 30:19–29.
Mitford J. 1974. *Kind and Usual Punishment.* New York: Vintage.
NCCHC (National Commission on Correctional Health Care). 2002. *The Health Status of Soon-to-Be-Released Inmates: Executive Summary.* [Online]. Available: http://www.ncchc.org/stbr/Volume2/ExecutiveSummary.pdf [accessed October 10, 2005].
NCPHSBBR (National Commission for the Protection of Human Subjects of Biomedical and Behavioral Research). 1976. *Report and Recommendations: Research Involving Prisoners.* Washington, DC: NCPHSBBR.
NFCMH (New Freedom Commission on Mental Health). 2004. *Subcommittee on Criminal Justice Background Paper.* DHHS Pub. No. SMA-04-3880, Rockville, MD. Available: http://www.mentalhealthcommission.gov/papers/CJ_ADACompliant.pdf [accessed March 20, 2006].
Restum ZG. 2005. Public health implications of substandard correctional health care. *American Journal of Public Health* 95(10):1689–1691.
Sturm SP. 1993. The legacy and future of corrections litigation. *University of Pennsylvania Law Review* 142:638–738.

2

Today's Prisoners: Changing Demographics, Health Issues, and the Current Research Environment

The conditions of confinement in today's prisons and jails have many of the same characteristics that were of concern to the National Commission for the Protection of Human Subjects of Biomedical and Behavioral Research (NCPHSBBR) some 30 years ago (see Appendix B). Yet important new factors have emerged that require consideration. The correctional population has expanded more than 4.5 fold between 1978 and 2004—from 1.5 million to almost 7 million as a result of tougher sentencing laws and the war on drugs (Bureau of Justice Statistics [BJS], 1997, 2005a,f,g,h; Human Rights Watch [HRW], 2003; Jacobson, 2005). Just within prisons and jails, the population grew from 454,444 to 2.1 million (BJS, 2005a,f). The rest of the expansion occurred among probationers and parolees (BJS, 2005g,h).

In addition, with the closing of large state mental institutions, prisons have effectively become the new mental illness asylums. Prisoners suffer higher rates of communicable diseases, such as human immunodeficiency virus (HIV)/acquired immune deficiency syndrome (AIDS) and hepatitis, than the general population, and chronic diseases such as diabetes are on the rise, especially among the growing older population of prisoners (National Commission on Correctional Health Care [NCCHC], 2002). Health care within some prison systems is less than satisfactory. Through class actions over the inadequacies of state prison health-care systems, the most serious problems were largely addressed and health-care delivery systems were put in place (Metzner, 2002; Sturm, 1993). However, problems remain. Most recently, a federal district court judge placed California's entire prison medical health-care system into federal receivership, taking it out of control of the state and placing it under the control of a trustee appointed by the court.[1] In addition, the entire state prison mental health system is being monitored by another federal court after being found to be providing constitutionally inadequate mental health services to inmates with serious mental illnesses (*Coleman v. Wilson*, 912 F.Supp. 1282 [E.D.Cal 1995]). And New York regulators have faulted the private firm Prison Health Services in several deaths within the state's prison system (Von Zielbauer, 2005d). This follows by 30 years the case of *Estelle v. Gamble*, in which the U.S. Supreme Court articulated a constitutionally protected right to health care in prisons and jails (U.S. Supreme Court, 1976).

The committee's review of current research indicated that the majority of research involving prisoners is happening outside the purview of Subpart C, and many prisoner studies are being conducted without review or approval by an institutional review board (IRB). Prison research committees that may serve some type of proxy IRB role only infrequently include prisoners or prisoner representatives among their membership. All of these factors point to a population of prisoners who may be more vulnerable and require stronger protections than those inspired by the commission in the 1970s.

CHANGING DEMOGRAPHICS AND HEALTH ISSUES

Descriptions of Prisons, Jails, and Other Correctional Settings

Within the United States, correctional settings, which constrain liberty, entail more than prisons. Local jails, usually county or city facilities, house prisoners from arraignment through conviction and for sentences usually no longer than one year. State and federal prisons incarcerate those sentenced for longer periods. About 6 percent, or close to 99,000 prisoners, are held in privately operated facilities that incarcerate the state and federal overflow (BJS, 2005a,c). In six states, all in the West, at least one-quarter of all persons in prisons are in private facilities (BJS, 2005a). Several other alternatives to prisons and jails that constrain liberty, including restitution centers, camps, treatment facilities, and electronic monitoring programs, are listed in Table 4-1 (see Chapter 4); specific options within the state of California are provided in Table 4-2 (see Chapter 4). Parole and probation are two other settings in which individuals have restricted liberties by virtue of involvement in the criminal justice system. Parole is used for offenders

---

[1]U.S. District Court for the Northern District of California. Findings of Fact and Conclusions of Law Re Appointment of Receiver, *Marciano Plata, et al. vs. Arnold Schwarzenegger, et al.*, October 3, 2005, page 2.

who are conditionally released from prison to community supervision. An offender is required to observe the conditions of parole and is under the supervision of a parole agency. Parole differs from probation, which is determined by judicial authority and is usually an alternative to initial confinement.

The Prisoner Population

The Incarcerated Population Has Grown Enormously

The total estimated correctional population in the United States in 2004 was very close to 7 million, according to the Bureau of Justice Statistics (2005a). Table 2-1 indicates that the majority of these individuals were on probation (4 million), followed by confinement in prison (1.4 million), on parole (765,355), and confinement in jail (713,990). Overall, the population in 2004 was more than 4.5 times larger than it was in 1978.

By the end of 2004, the nation's prisons and jails incarcerated 2.1 million persons (BJS, 2005a) compared with 216,000 in 1974 (BJS, 2003a). Today, two-thirds of inmates are housed in federal and state prisons, and the other third are in local jails.

The numbers in Table 2-1 are point-in-time figures. Annual flow in and out of jail, where incarceration time is comparatively short, provides a useful picture as well. Nearly a quarter (23 percent) of all jail inmates spend 14 days or less in jail, 29 percent are held from 2 to 6 months, 7 percent are held for a year or more (BJS, 2004c). The transitory nature of jail confinement can have an impact on research participation, as discussed in Chapter 4.

Using Department of Justice statistics and trends, the Justice Policy

TABLE 2-1 Persons Under Adult Correctional Supervision, 1978–2004 Total Estimated

Year	Correctional Population	Probation	Parole	Jail	Prison
1978	1,531,596	899,305	177,847	158,394	296,050
1980*	1,840,400	1,118,097	220,438	82,288	319,598
1995	5,342,900	3,077,861	679,421	507,044	1,078,542
2000	6,445,100	3,826,209	723,898	621,149	1,316,333
2001	6,581,700	3,931,731	732,333	631,240	1,330,007
2002	6,758,800	4,024,067	750,934	665,475	1,367,547
2003	6,936,600	4,144,782	745,125	691,301	1,392,796
2004	6,996,500	4,151,125	765,355	713,990	1,421,911

*1980 figures from BJS, 2003c.
SOURCES: U.S. Census, 1998, 1994; BJS, 1997, 2000a, 2003c, 2004b, 2005a,f,g,h.

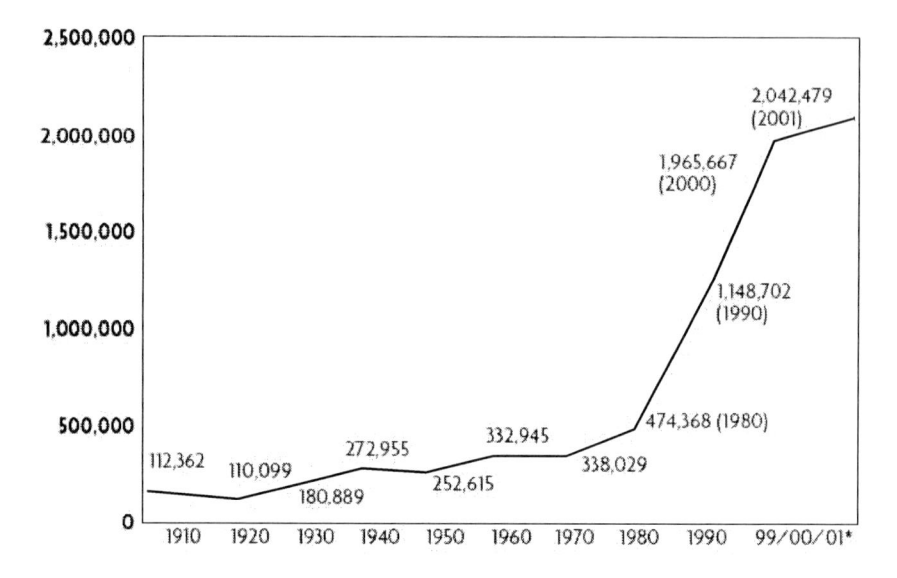

FIGURE 2-1 The punishing decade: number of prison and jail inmates, 1910–2000.
SOURCE: JPI (2002).

Institute (JPI) based in Washington, D.C., estimated in 2000 that the United States had the world's largest incarcerated population and highest incarceration rate. Just 6 weeks into the new millennium, America had one-quarter of the world's prison population, despite having less than 5 percent of the world's population (JPI, 2002). The U.S. incarceration rate was highest, with 686 per 100,000 of the national population (Walmsley, 2003), followed by the Cayman Islands (664), Russia (638), Belarus (554), Kazakhstan (522), Turkmenistan (489), and Belize (459). More than 62 percent of countries worldwide have rates below 150 per 100,000. By 2004, the U.S. rate had risen to 724 per 100,000 (BJS, 2005a).

Calling the 1990s "the punishing decade," JPI noted that the imprisoned population grew at a faster rate during the 1990s than during any decade in recorded history (see Figure 2-1). The prison growth during the 1990s dwarfed the growth in any previous decade; it exceeded the prison growth of the 1980s by 61 percent and is nearly 30 times the average prison population growth of any decade before the 1970s (JPI, 2002). This growth has led to serious overcrowding. According to BJS data for 2004 (BJS, 2005a), 24 state departments of corrections and the federal prison system are operating above capacity. The federal prison system is operating at 40 percent above capacity.

The population of prisoners under jail supervision who are confined in

TABLE 2-2 Persons Under Jail Supervision, by Confinement Status and Type of Program, Midyear 1995, 2000, and 2002–2004

Confinement Status and Type of Program	Number of Persons Under Jail Supervision				
	1995	2000	2002	2003	2004
Total	541,913	687,033	737,912	762,672	784,538
Held in jail	507,044	621,149	665,475	691,301	713,990
Supervised outside of jail facility[a]	34,869	65,884	72,437	71,371	70,548
Weekender programs	1,909	14,523	17,955	12,111	11,589
Electronic monitoring	6,788	10,782	9,706	12,678	11,689
Home detention[b]	1,376	332	1,037	594	1,173
Day reporting	1,283	3,969	5,010	7,965	6,627
Community service	10,253	13,592	13,918	17,102	13,171
Other pretrial supervision	3,229	6,279	8,702	11,452	14,370
Other work programs[c]	9,144	8,011	5,190	4,498	7,208
Treatment programs[d]	NA	5,714	1,256	1,891	2,208
Other/unspecified	887	2,682	9,663	3,080	2,513

NOTE: NA, not available.

[a]Excludes persons supervised by a probation or parole agency.

[b]Includes only those without electronic monitoring.

[c]Includes persons in work-release programs, work gangs, and other work alternative programs.

[d]Includes persons under drug, alcohol, mental health, and other medical treatment.
SOURCE: BJS, 2005c.

settings outside of a jail facility has doubled since 1995 (see Table 2-2). This point is important for the Chapter 4 discussion regarding the definition of the term *prisoner*. In 2004, jail authorities supervised 70,548 men and women in the community in work-release, weekend reporting, electronic monitoring, and other alternative programs.

Why Has the Prisoner Population Grown?

The exponential growth of prison and jail populations in the last two decades has many causes. Some relate to changes in federal and state sentencing policies, and some reflect the actions of American society in those years as it engaged in a war against drugs. BJS reports that, in 1997, 21 percent of state prisoners and more than 60 percent of federal prisoners were incarcerated for drug offenses (BJS, 1999c). Between 1995 and 2003, 49 percent of the total growth in the federal prison population was from drug offenses (BJS, 2005a). Michael Jacobson, former Commissioner of the

New York City Departments of Correction and Probation, argues in his book, *Downsizing Prisons* (2005), that mandatory minimum sentencing, parole agencies intent on sending people back to prison, three-strike laws (defined below), for-profit prisons, and other changes in the legal system have contributed to the spectacular rise of the general prison population. The Sentencing Project (TSP) came to the same conclusion, stating that rigid sentencing formulas such as mandatory sentencing and truth in sentencing often result in lengthy incarceration (TSP, 2001). According to Human Rights Watch (2003), the U.S. rate of incarceration soared to the highest in the world for the reasons stated previously: "Championed as protecting the public from serious and violent offenders, the new criminal justice policies in fact yielded high rates of confinement for nonviolent offenders. Nationwide, nonviolent offenders account for 72 percent of all new state prison admissions."

Three-strikes laws impose mandatory life terms or extremely long prison terms without parole for criminals who have been convicted of three felonies involving violence, rape, use of a deadly weapon, or molestation. In some states, such as California, the third felony does not even have to be a violent crime. California's three-strikes law is considered the toughest in the country, because it can be invoked when a third felony conviction is for a nonviolent crime—even one that could have been charged as a misdemeanor if the prosecutor had wanted to [JPI, 2004; TSP, 2001].) Nationally, half of the states have enacted some form of three-strikes legislation, but only a handful have convicted more than 100 individuals using the statute, led by a wide margin by California, according to the Justice Policy Institute and the Sentencing Project (JPI, 2004; TSP, 2001). "As of mid 1998, only California (40,511 individuals), Georgia (942), South Carolina (825), Nevada (304), Washington, (121), and Florida (116) had been using the three-strikes legislation to any significant extent" (TSP, 2001). Moving into 2004, three strikes was most heavily used in three states, with 42,322 persons incarcerated under the three-strikes law in California, 7,631 in Georgia, and 1,628 in Florida (JPI, 2004).

Reported rates of recidivism for adult offenders in the United States are extraordinarily high, as noted in a report by the Open Society Institute (OSI, 1997): "The national rearrest rate is around 63 percent, and the reimprisonment rate averages around 41 percent." Among probationers and parolees, recidivism is lower but still occurs. In 2003, 16 percent of probationers were incarcerated because of a rule violation or a new offense (BJS, 2004b). That same year, 38 percent of parolees were incarcerated because of violations of parole conditions (26 percent) or committing a new crime (11 percent) (BJS, 2004b). Parole officers are spending more time on policing whether conditions are violated (with more drug tests, more track-

TABLE 2-3 Prisoners Under the Jurisdiction of State or Federal Correctional Authorities, by Gender, 1995, 2003, and 2004

Variable	Men	Women
All inmates		
1995	1,057,406	68,468
2003	1,363,813	100,384
2004	1,391,781	104,848
Average annual change, 1995–2004	3.1%	4.8%
Sentenced to > 1 year		
2003	1,315,790	92,571
2004	1,337,668	96,125
Percent change, 2003–2004	1.7%	3.8%
Incarceration rate[a]		
1995	789	47
2004	920	64

[a]Total number of prisoners with a sentence of more than 1 year per 100,000 U.S. residents on December 31.
SOURCE: BJS, 2005a.

ing of movement, and so on) and less on promoting reintegration (Petersilia, 2000).

Finally, admissions to state and federal prisons are outpacing releases (BJS, 2005c). There was also a large increase in parole violators returning to prison between 1990 and 1998. The number of returned parole violators increased 54 percent between 1990 and 1998 (from 133,870 to 206,152) and has since slowed to a 2 percent annual increase (BJS, 2005a,c).

Who Is in Prison and Jail?

Men far outnumber women in prisons and jails. Men make up 93 percent of all inmates (BJS, 2005a). By the end of 2004, 104,848 women and 1,391,781 men were in state or federal prisons. The female prisoner population has been rising at a faster rate than the male prisoner population (Table 2-3). The overall increase since 1995 for male prisoners is 32 percent and for female prisoners, 53 percent (BJS, 2005a).

More women are entering the correctional system Between 1980 and 1998, the number of female inmates under the jurisdiction of federal and state correctional authorities increased more than 500 percent, from about 13,400 in 1980 to roughly 84,400 by the end of 1998, according to the U.S.

TABLE 2-4 Jail Populations by Gender, 1990–2004 (1-Day Count)

Year	Adult Males	Adult Females
1990	365,821	37,190
1991	384,628	39,501
1992	401,106	40,674
1993	411,500	44,100
1994	431,300	48,500
1995	448,000	51,300
1996	454,700	55,700
1997	498,678	59,296
1998	520,581	63,791
1999	528,998	67,487
2000	543,120	70,414
2001	551,007	72,621
2002	581,411	76,817
2003	602,781	81,650
2004	619,908	86,999

SOURCE: BJS, 2005e.

General Accounting Office (GAO, 1999). In 2004 (BJS, 2005a), that number had risen to 104,848 (Table 2-3). A large percentage of these women (85 percent) were on parole or probation (BJS, 1999b).

Within jails specifically (Table 2-4), between 1990 and 2004, the female inmate population grew 134 percent, whereas the male inmate population grew by 70 percent.

Not only is the female population becoming larger, but it is also becoming more diverse. Increasingly, incarcerated women are older and more likely minority and drug abusers than earlier populations of women prisoners (BJS, 2005a; GAO, 1999, 2000).

In *Gender-Responsive Strategies for Women Offenders* (2005), the National Institute of Corrections (NIC) staff characterize women in the criminal justice system: "Women offenders typically have low incomes and are undereducated and unskilled. They have sporadic employment histories and are disproportionately women of color. They are less likely than men to have committed violent offenses and more likely to have been convicted of crimes involving drugs or property. Often, their property offenses are economically driven, motivated by poverty and by the abuse of alcohol and other drugs." Women prisoners in general have poorer health than men, with higher rates of mental illness (BJS, 1999a) and HIV infection (BJS, 1999b). Women prisoners also are more likely to report medical problems after admission than men (BJS, 2001b). These data and the rising rates of incarceration among women make health care for women in prison a pressing issue (Young and Reviere, 2001).

Women offenders have needs that are different from those of men, stemming in part from their disproportionate victimization from sexual and physical abuse and their responsibility for children, according to the authors of *Women Offenders: Programming Needs and Promising Approaches* (BJS, 1998b). In an *American Journal of Public Health* editorial, Braithwaite et al. (2005) noted that the diverse needs of women are forgotten and neglected in the criminal justice system. Medical concerns that relate to reproductive health and to the psychosocial matters that surround imprisonment of single female heads of households are often overlooked. The authors state that "Women in prison complain of a lack of regular gynecological and breast examinations and say their medical concerns are often dismissed." They also note the poor physical health of women as they enter the correctional system, with higher than average risk for high-risk pregnancies, HIV/AIDS, hepatitis C, and human papillomavirus infection, a risk factor for cervical cancer. Nearly 6 in 10 women in state prisons had experienced physical or sexual abuse in the past (BJS, 1999b).

"Women have more severe substance abuse histories by the time they come to the attention of the criminal justice system," said Nena P. Messina, Ph.D., a criminologist at University of California, Los Angeles Integrated Substance Abuse Programs. *"That means they are using drugs on a daily basis. They are more likely to be injecting drugs, using multiple drugs, and trading sex for drugs and money. Their histories and their paths to substance abuse and crime are very different than men's."* Messina described her experience with women prisoners at the July 2005 meeting of this Institute of Medicine (IOM) committee.

In a survey of prisoners in New Jersey (Blitz et al., 2005), researchers found that women were more likely to be classified as special needs inmates (those with behavioral health disorders) than men (37 percent versus 16 percent). An active addiction disorder was present in one-half to three-quarters of women with behavioral health disorders. National data collected by the BJS in 1998 also showed more women than men (20 percent versus 16 percent) are diagnosed with mental disorders (BJS, 1999a).

Although substance abuse is common, drug rehabilitation programs are not common in these institutions (Braithwaite et al., 2005). Consequently, when women prisoners are released, they are at high risk of falling

TABLE 2-5 Children of Women Under Correctional Supervision, 1998

Variable	Women Offenders	Women Offenders with Minor Children	Minor Children
Total	869,600	615,500	1,300,800
Probation	721,400	516,200	1,067,200
Jail	63,800	44,700	105,300
State prisons	75,200	49,200	117,100
Federal prisons	9,200	5,400	11,200

NOTE: Only children under age 18 are counted.
SOURCE: BJS, 1999b.

back into addiction with exposure to the environmental pressures that led them there in the first place.

Women are also more likely than men to be solely responsible for their children. Two-thirds of incarcerated women have children younger than 18 years (BJS, 1999b). Approximately 1.3 million children in the United States have mothers under correctional supervision (Table 2-5). Just under a quarter million children have mothers who are serving time in prison or jail (BJS, 1999b).

Racial and ethnic disparities Blacks and Hispanics are disproportionately represented in prison and jail populations. At midyear 2004, an estimated 12.6 percent of all black males in their late 20s were in prisons or jails compared with 3.6 percent of Hispanic males and 1.7 percent of white males (BJS, 2005c). Young black men are particularly hit hard. One in eight black men in their late 20s is incarcerated on any given day (Mauer & King, 2004). A report of the National Center on Institutions and Alternatives (Lotke, 1997) indicated that in the District of Columbia, 50 percent of young black men ages 18 to 35 were under criminal justice supervision (in prison, jail, probation, parole, out on bond, or being sought on a warrant). Table 2-6 shows jail incarceration rates by race and ethnicity from 1990 through 2004.

Educational level and reading skills of prisoners Often individuals come into the correctional system with little education and, therefore, poor reading, writing, math, and oral communication skills (Haigler et al., 1994; Spangenberg, 2004). Poor reading and communication skills pose a challenge to informed consent, which is often handled through written documents, and points to the importance of ensuring that informed consent procedures are monitored to determine that prisoners truly understand what they are consenting to. The BJS (2003b) reported on the poor educa-

TABLE 2-6 Jail Incarceration Rates by Race and Ethnicity, 1990–2004[a]

Year	White Non-Hispanic	Black Non-Hispanic	Hispanic of Any Race
1990	89	560	245
1991	92	594	247
1992	93	618	251
1993	94	633	262
1994	98	656	274
1995	104	670	263
1996	111	640	276
1997	117	706	293
1998	125	716	292
1999	127	730	288
2000	132	736	280
2001	138	703	263
2002	147	740	256
2003	151	748	269
2004	160	765	262

NOTE: U.S. resident population estimates for sex, race, and Hispanic origin were made using a U.S. Census Bureau Internet release, December 23, 1999, with adjustments for census undercount. Estimates for 2000–2004 are based on the 2000 Census and then estimated for July 1 of each year.

[a]Per 100,000 U.S. residents.
SOURCE: BJS, 2005a.

tion level of prisoners. Forty-one percent of inmates in the nation's state and federal prisons and local jails and 31 percent of probationers had not completed high school or its equivalent (Table 2-7). In comparison, 18 percent of the general population age 18 or older had not finished the twelfth grade. Minority prisoners had lower education levels than whites (53 percent of Hispanics, 44 percent of blacks, and 27 percent of whites had no diploma or general equivalency diploma). The same report indicates that less educated prisoners were less likely to have jobs before they entered prison and more likely to have a prior sentence, to be sentenced as juveniles, and to return to prison after release.

Prisoners tend to leave the system poorly educated as well. According to a 1997 report by the OSI, *Education As Crime Prevention: Providing Education to Prisoners*, in the shift from rehabilitation to punishment and the exponential population growth, educational and vocational programs, which, OSI notes, correlate positively with the ability to remain out of prison, have been substantially reduced. Despite evidence supporting the connection between higher education and lowered levels of recidivism, the

TABLE 2-7 Educational Attainment for Correctional Populations and the General Population, 1997

Education	Total Incarcerated	Prison Inmates		Local Jail	Probation	General Population
		State	Federal			
≤ Some high school (%)	41.3	39.7	26.5	46.5	30.6	18.4
GED (5)	23.4	28.5	22.7	14.1	11.0	NA
High school diploma (%)	22.6	20.5	27.0	25.9	34.8	33.2
Postsecondary (%)	12.7	11/4	23/9	13.9	23.6	48.4

NOTE: GED, general equivalency diploma; NA, not available; Gen. Pop., general population.
SOURCE: BJS, 2003b.

Violent Crime Control and Law Enforcement Act of 1994 ended access to federal Pell Grants for undergraduate education to all prisoners. At least 25 states cut back on vocational and technical training programs since the Pell Grants were cut. In 1990, there were 350 higher education programs for inmates; by 1997, only 8.

Eight in 10 state prisons offer basic education and high school courses (BJS, 2003b). Fewer than one in three offer college classes. College, vocational, and high school courses are most common in federal prisons and least common in private prisons. For example, college courses are offered by 80 percent of federal prisons and 27 percent of private prisons. However, less than 20 percent of prisoners participated in college courses while incarcerated; this percentage dropped between 1991 and 1997 (Table 2-8). Vocational courses are more popular, taken by about one in three inmates in state and federal prisons.

Age of inmates The U.S. prison population is aging (BJS, 2004d). By year end 2003, 28 percent of all inmates were ages 40 to 54 (up from 22 percent in 1995). Inmates age 55 and older have experienced the largest percent change—an increase of 85 percent since 1995. However, they are still a small group, relative to inmates in other age groups, accounting for 4.3 percent of all inmates in 2003, up from 3.0 percent in 1995 (BJS, 2004d; TSP, 2005). According to the Sentencing Project, California's three-strikes law contributed to a rapid aging of the California prison population in the

TABLE 2-8 Participation in Educational Programs Since Most Recent Incarceration or Sentence, for State and Federal Prison Inmates, 1997 and 1991, for Local Jail Inmates, 1996, and for Probationers 1995

Variable	State 1991	State 1997	Federal 1991	Federal 1997	Local Jail Inmates 1996	Probationers 1995
Educational programs						
Total (%)	56.6	51.9	67.0	56.4	14.1	22.9
Basic	5.3	3.1	10.4	1.9	0.8	0.4
GED/high school	27.3	23.4	27.3	23.0	8.6	7.8
College courses	13.9	9.9	19.9	12.9	1.0	6.1
ESOL	NA	1.2	NA	5.7	NA	NA
Vocational	31.2	32.2	29.4	31.0	4.8	7.0
Other	2.6	2.6	8.4	5.6	2.1	3.4
Number of inmates	709,042	1,046,136	53,753	87,624	501,159	2,055,942

NOTE: Detail may not add to total because of rounding or inmates' participation in more than one program. NA, not available; GED, general equivalency diploma; ESOL, English speakers of other languages.
SOURCE: BJS, 2003b.

first 7 years since it was instituted (King and Mauer, 2001). The authors projected that, in 2026, 30,000 three-strikes prisoners will be serving sentences of 25 years to life. In California, new felony admissions of prisoners older than 40 increased from 15.3 percent in 1994 to 23.1 percent in 1999.

A survey by the *New York Times* (Liptak, 2005) found that 132,000 of the nation's prisoners are serving life sentences. The number of "lifers" has almost doubled in the last decade, far outpacing the overall growth of the prison population. About one-third of the lifers sentenced between 1988 and 2001 are serving time for crimes other than murder, including burglary and drug crimes. Fewer lifers have a chance of parole. In 1993, the *New York Times* survey found that about 20 percent of lifers had no chance of parole. In 2004, that number rose to 28 percent. As a result, the United States has a large and permanent population of prisoners who will die of old age behind bars. According to the Sentencing Project (Mauer et al., 2004), the increase in life sentences reflects changes in state policies, not continuous increases in violent crimes.

These figures on the graying of the prison population indicate that a small, but growing segment of today's prisoners face chronic diseases, such as diabetes and heart disease.

Health Status of Inmates

A highly disproportionate number of inmates suffer from infectious diseases, chronic diseases, and mental illness compared with the rest of the nation's population. According to a 3-year study requested by Congress and delivered in May 2002 by the National Commission on Correctional Health Care (*The Health Status of Soon-to-Be-Released Inmates*), tens of thousands of inmates are being released into the community every year with undiagnosed or untreated communicable disease, chronic disease, addiction, and mental illness (NCCHC, 2002). The report paints a picture of a large and concentrated population at high risk for communicable and chronic diseases.

Communicable diseases During 1996, about 3 percent of the U.S. population spent time in a prison or jail; however, between 12 and 35 percent of the total number of people with certain communicable diseases in the nation passed through a correctional facility during that same year (NCCHC, 2002). There were an estimated 107,000 to 137,000 cases of sexually transmitted diseases (STDs) among inmates in 1997 and at least 465,000 STD cases among releasees.

Hepatitis Hepatitis B and C are viral diseases that attack the liver. Both can cause lifelong infection, cirrhosis of the liver, cancer, liver failure, and death (BJS, 2004a; National Institutes of Health [NIH], 2002). Both viruses are spread through infected blood, most commonly via shared needles used to inject illegal drugs and through sexual contact. Nearly 2 percent of the U.S. population is chronically infected with hepatitis C virus (Hammett et al., 2002), while studies in prison populations in California, Virginia, Connecticut, Maryland, and Texas have found evidence of hepatitis C infection in 29 to 42 percent of prisoners (Centers for Disease Control and Prevention [CDC], 2002). Across the country, hepatitis C infection rates for prisoners are estimated at 15 to 30 percent. Between 1.3 and 1.4 million prisoners released from prison or jail in 1996 were infected with hepatitis C (NCCHC, 2002). The prevalence of hepatitis B infection among incarcerated individuals has been reported to range from 8 to 43 percent (Khan et al., 2005), while the rate in the U.S. population as a whole is 4.9 percent. In a state correctional facility in Georgia (housing up to 1,340 male inmates, one-third of whom are transferred or released each year), and within Rhode Island's prison system, there was a high prevalence of hepatitis B, and a high rate of ongoing HBV transmission (Khan et al., 2005).

Antiviral therapies for chronic hepatitis B and C are complicated, have limited effectiveness, and are not appropriate for everyone (CDC, 2002). Hepatitis B vaccination is recommended for incarcerated individuals (CDC, 2003). Although vaccination is offered to some inmate populations in state and federal correctional settings, universal immunization is not common (Khan et al., 2005).

HIV/AIDS At year end 2003, there were 23,659 inmates in state and federal prisons known to be infected with HIV (BJS, 2005d). Female prisoners were more likely to be HIV positive than male prisoners. Overall, 1.9 percent of male inmates and 2.8 percent of all female inmates were known to be HIV positive. In two states, more than 10 percent of the female inmate population was HIV positive (New York State: 14.6 percent; Maryland: 11.1 percent).

The overall rate of confirmed AIDS cases among the prison population (0.51 percent) was more than three times the rate in the U.S. general population (0.15 percent). In 2002 the percentage of deaths from AIDS was more than two times higher in the prison population than in the U.S. general population among individuals ages 15 to 54 years. About 1 in every 11 prisoner deaths were attributable to AIDS-related causes compared with 1 in 23 deaths in the general population. AIDS is the second leading cause of death in prisons (BJS, 2003d).

Tuberculosis Tuberculosis (TB) is an airborne disease that thrives among people who live in close quarters (Restum, 2005). About 12,000 people who had active TB during 1996 served time in a correctional facility during that year (NCCHC, 2002). More than 130,000 inmates tested positive for latent TB infection in 1997. An estimated 566,000 inmates with latent TB infection were released in 1996. More recent data (MacNeil et al., 2005) indicate that TB rates remain higher in prison systems than in the general population, and that prisoners with TB are less likely than noninmates to complete treatment. From 1993 to 2003, the percentage of TB cases among local jail inmates increased from 42.8 percent to 53.5 percent. Cases among federal inmates increased from 2.9 percent to 11.8 percent. Inmates with TB were more likely to be coinfected with HIV than noninmates with TB. Outbreaks of multidrug-resistant TB related to HIV coinfection have been documented in correctional facilities. The authors note: "Correctional systems, especially jails, offer distinct logistical obstacles to screening and treatment; inmates are moved frequently or are released, making evaluation and completion of therapy difficult at best."

Chronic diseases The National Commission on Correctional Health Care report (NCCHC, 2002) provided 1995 prevalence estimates for certain chronic diseases among federal, state, and local inmates: Asthma was estimated at 8 to 9 percent, diabetes at 5 percent, and hypertension at 18 percent. Figures on federal prisoners alone (BJS, 2001b) are somewhat lower: asthma at about 4 percent, diabetes at 4 percent, and hypertension at 8 percent. BJS (2001b) noted that inmate self-reported data may underestimate the prevalence of some medical conditions, especially those problems that require more sophisticated diagnosis and those that are more sensitive in nature. For many conditions, inmate self-reports are the only source of information.

Most state prison systems lack comprehensive and accessible data on the health status of their prisoners. A 1998 inventory of state and federal correctional information systems found that 20 states had electronic information systems that could identify offenders with physical disabilities at admission, 22 had systems that could identify inmates with mental or emotional problems, and 22 could identify inmates with specialized medical conditions. Eighteen states had this information electronically on current medical conditions for more than 75 percent of their inmates (BJS, 1998c).

Mental illness "Prisons are the largest mental health institutions in our country," stated Darrel A. Reiger, M.D., M.P.H., deputy medical director of the American Psychiatric Association, in his October 19, 2005, remarks to the committee. More than a quarter-million mentally ill individuals were incarcerated in a prison or jail at midyear 1998 (BJS, 1999a). In 1998, more than 179,000 offenders in state prisons, 7,900 in federal prisons, 96,700 in local jails, and almost 548,000 probationers were identified as mentally ill (Table 2-9). In this BJS survey, prisoners were counted as mentally ill if they

TABLE 2-9 Inmates and Probationers Identified as Mentally Ill, by Gender, Race/Hispanic Origin, and Age, Midyear 1998

Offender Characteristic	Inmates	State Inmates	Federal Inmates	Jail Probationers
Total	179,200	7,900	96,700	547,800
Gender (%)				
Male	15.8	7.0	15.6	14.7
Female	23.6	12.5	22.7	21.7
Race/Hispanic Origin (%)				
White*	22.6	11.8	21.7	19.6
Black*	13.5	5.6	13.7	10.4
Hispanic	11.0	4.1	11.1	9.0
Age (%)				
24 or younger	14.4	6.6	13.3	13.8
25–34	14.8	5.9	15.7	13.8
35–44	18.4	7.5	19.3	19.8
45–54	19.7	10.3	22.7	21.1
55 or older	15.6	8.9	20.4	16.0

*Excludes Hispanics.
SOURCE: BJS, 1999a.

answered *yes* to either of two questions, "Do you have a mental or emotional condition?" or "Because of emotional or mental condition, have you ever been admitted to a mental hospital, unit, or treatment program where you stayed overnight?" Mental illness is identified more often in women and whites, and the incidence increases with age. Mentally ill prisoners tend to serve longer sentences and experience more disciplinary problems while in prison. In addition, approximately 75 percent of people with serious mental illnesses in the criminal justice system have a co-occurring substance abuse disorder (New Freedom Commission on Mental Health [NFCMH], 2004).

Anxiety disorders and major depression were the most common mental illness diagnoses in jails and state prisons (Table 2-10). The prevalence of mental illnesses appears to rise when moving from local jails to state prisons.

Six in 10 mentally ill prisoners received treatment while incarcerated in a state or federal prison. Only 4 in 10 in local jails received treatment (BJS, 1999a). Women were more likely than men to receive mental health services while incarcerated (Table 2-11). Whites were more likely than blacks and Hispanics to receive mental health services (NFCMH, 2004). Mental health treatment is lacking for probationers and parolees as well. In 1998, probationers serving their current sentence had less exposure to mental

TABLE 2-10 Estimated Prevalence of Mental Illness, 1999

Illness	Jail Inmates (%)	State Prison Inmates (%)
Schizophrenia	1	2–4
Major depression	8–15	13–19
Bipolar disorder	1–3	2–5
Dysthymia	2–5	8–14
Anxiety disorder	14–20	22–30
Post-traumatic stress disorder	4–9	6–12

SOURCE: NCCHC, 2002.

health treatment compared with confined prisoners. Specifically, mentally ill probationers were less likely than state and federal prisoners to have taken a psychiatric medication, to have received any mental health service, or to have been hospitalized for their condition, although they were just as likely to have received counseling or therapy (BJS, 1999a). Furthermore, less than half of the probationers (43 percent) who were required to engage in mental health treatment had actually participated (BJS, 1999a).

Human Rights Watch (2003) has called prison mental health services "woefully deficient." Too often, they state, seriously ill prisoners are neglected, accused of malingering, or treated as disciplinary problems.

> Without the necessary care, mentally ill prisoners suffer painful symptoms and their conditions can deteriorate. They are afflicted with delusions and hallucinations, debilitating fears, extreme and uncontrollable mood swings. They huddle silently in their cells, mumble incoherently, or yell incessantly. They refuse to obey orders or lash out without apparent prov-

TABLE 2-11 Percent of Mentally Ill Receiving Mental Health Services While Incarcerated, 1998

Variable	State Prison	Federal Prison	Local Jail
Gender (5)			
Male	59.9	57.4	38.4
Female	67.3	76.5	56.2
Race/ethnicity (%)			
White	64.1	65.4	44.7
Black	56.4	50.0	34.2
Hispanic	59.9	62.5	40.6

SOURCE: BJS, 1999a.

ocation. They beat their heads against cell walls, smear themselves with feces, self-mutilate, and commit suicide. Prisons were never intended as facilities for the mentally ill, yet that is one of their primary roles today. Many of the men and women who cannot get mental health treatment in the community are swept into the criminal justice system after they commit a crime. In the United States, there are three times more mentally ill people in prisons than in mental health hospitals, and prisoners have rates of mental illness that are two to four times greater than the rates of members of the general public.

Substance abuse Drug and alcohol use and abuse play major roles in the lives of prisoners. Overall, three of four state prisoners and four of five federal prisoners are characterized as alcohol- or drug-involved offenders, according to a BJS report (BJS, 1999c). A history of drug and alcohol use and abuse was also common among probationers and parolees. In 1995, a U.S. Department of Justice survey found that 70 percent of probationers reported drug use in the past, 32 percent during the month before the crime, and 14 percent at the time of the crime (BJS, 1998a). A large number of parolees were also involved with drugs and alcohol. In 1991, more than half of parolees (54 percent) had used drugs in the month preceding their most recent crime, and 41 percent reported daily use during the same time period (BJS, 1995).

Injury, violence, rape, and suicide Prisoners face violence and injury within correctional settings. More than one-quarter of state and federal inmates reported being injured since admission to prison (Table 2-12). The likeli-

TABLE 2-12 Reason for Injury During Incarceration, 1999

Injury	Number	Percent[a]
Assault/fight	3,134	2.7
Accidental, total	25,975	22.1
Occupational	6,844	5.8
Recreational	11,141	9.5
Accidental, other[b]	7,859	6.7

[a]Percentages are based on the average daily population. If they were based on the total who had spent any time in prison in 1999, they would be lower.
[b]U.S. Bureau of Prisons distinguishes occupational and recreational injuries from accidental injuries.
SOURCE: BJS, 2001b.

TABLE 2-13 Likelihood of Injury Based on Time in Prison, 1999

Time Since Admission	Injured (%)	Medical Problem (Excluding Injury) (%)
Less than 12 months	13.2	15.8
12–23 months	19.8	19.1
24–47 months	26.7	20.4
48–71 months	36.8	20.3
72 months or more	45.9	30.4

SOURCE: BJS, 2001b.

hood of injury increases with time served in prison, as does the likelihood of a medical problem (Table 2-13).

In 2000, there were 34,355 assaults by state and federal prisoners against other inmates, and 51 prisoners died as a result of those violent actions (BJS, 2003d). These numbers do not capture assaults against officers and others who work in the nation's jails.

In 1999, nearly 22 percent of state inmates had a history of being injured while in prison (BJS, 2001b). Overall, 7 percent of state inmates were injured in a fight while in prison.

According to the 2003 Prison Rape Elimination Act,[2] more than 1 million people have been sexually assaulted in prisons over the past 20 years. The act also describes the devastating effects of sexual assault in this context: an increase in other types of violence, including murder, involving inmates and staff, and long-lasting trauma, which makes it even more difficult for people to succeed in the community after release.

In 2005, the BJS completed the first-ever national survey of administrative records on sexual violence in adult and juvenile correctional facilities (BJS, 2005b). This covers only reported incidents and thus provides just a partial picture. The survey included 2,700 adult and juvenile facilities. Nationwide in 2004, there were 8,210 allegations of sexual violence reported: 42 percent of allegations involved staff sexual misconduct; 37 percent were inmate-on-inmate nonconsensual sexual acts; 11 percent, staff sexual harassment; and 10 percent, abusive sexual contact. Correctional authorities reported 3.15 allegations of sexual violence per 1,000 inmates held in 2004. Ninety percent of victims and perpetrators of inmate-on-inmate nonconsensual sexual acts in prison and jail were male.

---

[2] Pub. L. No. 108-79 (2003).

Where Are Prisoners Incarcerated and How Are They Provided Services?

Since 1995, the federal system has grown at a much faster rate than state systems, peaking at 6 percent growth in the first 6 months of 1999 (BJS, 2005a). In 2004, the number of federal inmates increased 4.2 percent, more than twice the rate of state growth (1.6 percent). In 2004, private facilities held 6.6 percent of all state and federal inmates. However, six states, all in the West, had at least one-quarter of their prisoners in private facilities (BJS, 2005a). This does not account for the much larger population of prisoners on probation and parole and those who can be found in a wide variety of "alternative to incarceration" or community settings (see Tables 4-1 and 4-2).

Dislocation of inmates from local to distant jurisdictions Many states are outsourcing their prisoners to other state institutions away from urban areas and to a growing for-profit correctional business. In October 1999, according to a GAO (1999) report, about 30 percent of female inmates and 24 percent of male inmates in federal prisons were assigned to facilities more than 500 miles from their release residences. In situations in which prisoners are housed great distances from their homes, prisoners can lose total contact with their families. Because 64 percent of federal inmates have minor children, this is a great hardship for them and a burden for their children (BJS, 2000b). Schafer (1994) conducted a survey of visitors to two men's prisons and found that maintenance of family ties during incarceration is significantly related to successful completion of parole.

Increased use of isolation in punishment of inmates The United States has more than 60 supermaximum confinement facilities, housing well over 20,000 people (NIC, 1997). Rhodes (2005) describes the fortresslike facilities that force complete isolation and says that U.S. reliance on isolation is due to many factors, including political pressure for harsh sentencing, population pressure inside prison systems, and the internal architectural and staffing features of general population units. A study in Washington State (Lovell et al., 2000), which provides medium- and maximum-security psychiatric facilities, noted that the number of mentally ill inmates far exceeds available beds. As a consequence, some disturbed prisoners are held in supermaximum units. They found that 20 to 25 percent of supermaximum inmates showed strong evidence of mental illness.

Human Rights Watch (HRW, 2000) described life in isolation in supermaximum confinement in its 2000 report, *Out of Sight: Super-Maximum Security Confinement in the United States*:

> Prisoners in [supermaximum] facilities typically spend their waking and sleeping hours locked in small, sometimes windowless, cells sealed with

solid steel doors. A few times a week they are let out for showers and solitary exercise in a small, enclosed space. Supermax prisoners have almost no access to educational or recreational activities or other sources of mental stimulation and are usually handcuffed, shackled and escorted by two or three correctional officers every time they leave their cells. Assignment to supermax housing is usually for an indefinite period that may continue for years. Although supermax facilities are ostensibly designed to house incorrigibly violent or dangerous inmates, many of the inmates confined in them do not meet those criteria.

Quality of health care provided The U.S. Supreme Court ruled in *Estelle v. Gamble* (429 U.S. Part 97 [1976]) that "deliberate indifference to serious medical needs of prisoners constitutes the 'unnecessary and wanton infliction of pain' proscribed by the Eighth Amendment." The court in *Estelle v. Gamble* made clear, however, that a right to adequate medical care did not mean that "prisoners will have unqualified access to health care."

Coleman et al. (2005) noted that inadequacies of health care in most correctional settings existed in the 1970s and continue today: "Federal court decisions have documented continuing and severe health deprivations in many states."

> *"I have litigated my whole life about health care in prisons, seeing that it needs improvement," said Jack Beck, director of the Prison Visiting Project at the Correctional Association of New York at an October 2005 meeting of this committee. "However, it is an overstatement to say that no appropriate health care occurs in prisons throughout the United States. I think there are some places where it does occur. Is it a minority? Absolutely. But I think it does occur in some places." Mr. Beck is a member of the committee's Prisoner Liaison Panel.*

Model programs exist, however, NCCHC states that "many correctional agencies are doing too little to address communicable disease, chronic disease, and mental illness" (NCCHC, 2002). Few prison or jail systems have implemented comprehensive HIV-prevention programs in all their facilities. About 10 percent of state and federal prisons and 50 percent of jails do not adhere to CDC standards for screening and treating latent TB infection and active disease. Most prisons and jails fail to conform to nationally accepted health-care guidelines for mental health screening and treatment. Finally, of 41 state correctional systems responding to a survey

> **BOX 2-1**
> **California Prison Systems Medical Care System in Receivership**
>
> By all accounts, the California prison medical care system is broken beyond repair. The harm already done in this care to California's prison inmate population could not be more grave, and the threat of future injury and death is virtually guaranteed in the absence of drastic action. The Court has given defendants every reasonable opportunity to bring its prison medical system up to constitutional standards, and it is beyond reasonable dispute that the State has failed. Indeed, it is an uncontested fact that, on average, an inmate in one of California's prisons needlessly dies every six to seven days due to constitutional deficiencies in the CDCR's (California Department of Corrections and Rehabilitation's) medical delivery system. This statistic, awful as it is, barely provides a window into the waste of human life occurring behind California's prison walls due to the gross failures of the medical delivery system.
>
> It is clear to the Court that this unconscionable degree of suffering and death is sure to continue if the system is not dramatically overhauled. Decades of neglecting medical care while vastly expanding the size of the prison system has led to a state of institutional paralysis. The prison system is unable to function effectively and suffers a lack of will with respect to prisoner medical care.
>
> SOURCE: Findings of Fact and Conclusions of Law Re Appointment of Receiver, *Marciano Plata, et al. vs. Arnold Schwarzenegger, et al.*, U.S. District Court for the Northern District of California, October 3, 2005, p. 2.

conducted for the NCCHC report, just over half (24) reported having protocols for diabetes, 25 for hypertension, and 26 for asthma.

In July 2005, a federal judge ordered that a receiver take control of California's prison health-care system and correct what he called deplorable conditions that led to 64 unnecessary inmate deaths each year because of poor medical care (see Box 2-1). California houses approximately 164,000 inmates at 33 state prisons. The state expects to spend $1.1 billion on prison health care this year (Sterngold, 2005). Many U.S. state systems have been sued over the quality of their health care (Metzner, 2002; Sturm, 1993).

Health care for profit does not always offer a better alternative, according to a blistering series published in 2005 in the *New York Times*. The entry of Prison Health Services at Rikers Island in January 2001 made New York State's jail system the largest in the nation to entrust its health care to a commercial enterprise (Von Zielbauer, 2005b). Since then, state regulators have faulted Prison Health Services in several deaths (Von Zielbauer, 2005d).

> *"Medical care within the Federal Bureau of Prisons (FBOP) is symbolic, with minimal expectations of improving prisoners' health,"* writes Daniel S. Murphy, a member of the committee's prisoner liaison panel who experienced prison medical care firsthand and then obtained a doctorate degree and completed an in-depth analysis of medical directives and policies and the realities of medical care (2005). His article contains several firsthand accounts from prisoners whose medical needs were not met. He concludes: *"Many prisoners are condemned to death due to a lack of fundamental medical care."*

A year-long examination of Prison Health [Services] by the *New York Times* revealed repeated instances of medical care that was flawed and sometimes lethal. The company's performance around the nation provoked criticism from judges and sheriffs, lawsuits from inmates' families and whistle-blowers, and condemnations by federal, state, and local authorities. The company has paid millions of dollars in fines and settlements. Despite a tarnished record, Prison Health has sold its promise of lower costs and better care and become the biggest for-profit company providing medical care in jails and prisons. It has amassed 86 contracts in 28 states, and now cares for 237,000 inmates, or about one in every 10 people behind bars (Von Zielbauer, 2005a).

> *"They put you out of the prison at midnight, to save a day of expenses. If you are lucky, you get a month's worth of medications, but maybe only 10 days. Unless you live in Rhode Island, Connecticut, and maybe Massachusetts, you don't get discharge planning,"* explained David P. Paar, M.D., director, AIDS Care and Clinical Research Program, University of Texas Medical Branch in Galveston. *"They put you out of the prison into another traumatic situation. 'Where are my drugs coming from? Where am I going to get medical care? Who is going to take care of my kids.' You immediately go back to substance use and you miss the opportunity to change your life. That is the linkage between post-traumatic stress disorder, acquisition of blood-borne diseases, prison, and recidivism."* Dr. Parr spoke to the committee at its July 2005 meeting.

The New York City Department of Health and Mental Hygiene, which oversees the work of Prison Public Health Services Inc. at Rikers Island and at a jail in Lower Manhattan, found that during the first quarter of 2005, Prison Health failed to earn a passing grade on 12 of 39 performance standards the city sets for treating jail inmates. Some of the problems, like incomplete medical records or slipshod evaluations of mentally ill inmates, have been evident since 2004 but have not been corrected, according to health department reports. The company did not meet standards on practices ranging from HIV and diabetes therapy to the timely distribution of medication to adequately conducting mental health evaluations (Von Zielbauer, 2005c)

Public health implications of inadequate health care for prisoners The high recidivism rate in state and federal prisons, poor screening[3] and treatment for prisoners, and inferior follow-up health care on their release are a growing threat to U.S. rates of deadly communicable diseases, such as HIV/AIDS, hepatitis B and C, and TB (NCCHC, 2002; Restum, 2005). Prisoners are leaving prisons and jails and returning to their communities with a plethora of unaddressed health issues (NCCHC, 2002), including mental health and substance abuse problems. In 1992, prisoners who were expecting to be released to the community without supervision by 1999 had the following mental health and substance abuse problems: 14 percent were mentally ill, 25 percent were alcohol dependent, 42 percent reported the use of alcohol at the time of the offense, 59 percent reported drug use in the month before the offense and 45 percent at the time of the offense, 25 percent reported intravenous drug use in the past, and 12 percent were homeless when they were arrested (BJS, 2001a).

Mental illness and addiction disorders amplify the difficulties that prisoners face on release (Pogorzelski et al., 2005). In a study including adult women returning home from New York City jails (Freudenberg et al., 2005), annual incomes were well below poverty level, anxiety and depression increased in the postrelease period (from 15 percent to 25 percent), and rearrest rates were high (39 percent for adult women at 15 months

---

[3]For example, 21 percent of state prison facilities do no testing for hepatitis C (BJS, 2004a). Macalino et al. (2005) argue that following risk-based screening guidelines, such as those on hepatitis C from the CDC may not be enough. CDC issued recommendations in 2003 to screen all inmates with a history of injection drug use or other risk factors for hepatitis C. A study in the Rhode Island Department of Corrections indicated that 66 percent of prisoners who were hepatitis C positive did not report injection drug use (Macalino et al., 2005) and, therefore, would not have been screened. Therefore, risk-based testing underestimates hepatitis C virus prevalence in the correctional setting and is a missed opportunity for diagnosis and prevention of hepatitis C infection.

after release). The authors concluded that public policies created a class of people who are perpetually labeled as unqualified for public support, limiting or precluding access to health insurance, public housing, and employment opportunities.

History of Research with Prisoners

In 1997, Hornblum detailed the history of prisoners as research subjects in 20th-century America, stating that "From the early years of this century, the use of prison inmates as raw material for medical experiments became an increasingly valuable component of American scientific research. Postwar American research grew rapidly, as prisoners became the backbone of a lucrative system predicated on utilitarian interests. Uneducated and financially desperate prisoners "volunteered" for medical experiments that ranged from tropical and sexually transmitted diseases to polio, cancer, and chemical warfare." By the 1960s, new drug-testing regulations mandated by the Food and Drug Administration permitted increased human experimentation as large pharmaceutical companies sought stronger relationships with penal institutions. This article references earlier work by Jessica Mitford (1974), plus reports of prisoner involvement in studies of treatments for malaria, syphilis vaccines, radiation experiments, and more. In his 1998 book, *Acres of Skin: Human Experiments at Holmesburg Prison*, Hornblum details the medical experimentation that went on in one facility, Holmesburg Prison, a county facility in Philadelphia, which he says became a "supermarket of investigatory opportunity," where an array of studies explored everything from simple detergents and diet drinks to dioxin and chemical warfare agents. Sponsors included major pharmaceutical houses, RJ Reynolds, Dow Chemical, and the U.S. Army. From 1962 to 1966, a total of 33 pharmaceutical companies tested 153 experimental drugs at Holmesburg Prison alone, including Retin-A. After the national commission's 1976 report, medical research in prisons was sharply curtailed.

Echoes of Tuskegee and Retin-A Attitudes of blacks toward medical care in general and medical care within the prison system are extremely complicated and have become even more so since the emergence of AIDS. In communities of color, among some community members and advocates there was, and still is, a suspicion that AIDS was created in some form or fashion by sinister forces, either government or otherwise as a part of a scourge on black persons (Dalton, 1989). This suspicion was grafted onto an existing and ongoing refusal to participate in research, which is considered in the black communities, as "being used as guinea pigs." Much of this is the legacy of Tuskegee and of Retin-A. In the first, the Tuskegee experiments, black men in Tuskegee, Alabama, in the 1930s were enrolled in a research project designed and funded by the U.S. Public Health Service and intended to gather data on the natural history of syphilis, although the subjects were not told the real purpose. They were lied to and thought that they were gaining some sort of access to medical care and to funding for a burial on death. In the years after the project's funding, treatments were developed but were not offered to this cohort. Indeed, if the men moved from the Tuskegee site they were followed and a nurse was charged with ensuring that they did not gain access to care at another location.

After having been discussed in the scholarly literature for decades, the study was finally exposed in the popular press. The public was horrified by the conduct, planning, and execution of the study. This study, revealed in 1972 (Jones, 1993), was still alive in the consciousness of communities of color in the early 1980s when AIDS was identified and treatments began to be developed. A set of realities then converged: All treatment for AIDS during the 1980s was under protocols through the 1980s; a disproportionate number of persons of color and inmates had AIDS because needle sharing was one of the main routes of transmission; the war on drugs placed drug users in prison; and the only available treatment was provided under the label of research.

Retin-A was developed in Holmesburg Prison in Pennsylvania (Hornblum, 1998). In these experiments, it appears that prisoners were not told the possible immediate and long-term consequences of their participation and were not adequately treated for pain and suffering. Paradoxically, however, the AIDS epidemic was the occasion for some prisoner advocacy groups to contest the categorical restrictions of Subpart C. Inmates told prisoners' rights groups that they wanted "access to, not protection from" protocols offering treatments for AIDS. Despite the fact that these protocols described research and not treatment, they were sought as the only alternative to certain death. However, even in these requests, the mix of treatment and research, the lack of quality medical treatment in general, the history of mistreatment of prisoners in medical research (such as the Retin-A studies), and the epidemiology of AIDS made discussions of research in prisons fraught with emotion.

Implications of Demographics for the Ethical Conduct of Research

The limitations on personal freedoms and inadequacies in health care carry important challenges for the ethical conduct of research involving prisoners. (A more complete discussion of an ethical framework for research with prisoners is contained in Chapter 5.) Two areas in which the impact is clear are informed consent and privacy.

The ability of prisoners to provide ethically adequate informed consent Obtaining informed consent is a challenge because of several factors discussed in this chapter. Many prisoners have poor reading and communication skills (Haigler et al., 1994; Spangenberg, 2004), yet informed consent documents are often written for college-level readers (Sharp, 2004). In addition, correctional institutions are closed facilities that are designed to confine and punish. Medical care is designed to diagnose, comfort, and cure. These are mutually incompatible purposes from which flow many of the ethical dilemmas of care and, secondarily, of research in these settings (Anno and Dubler, 2001). Over the last three decades, the goal of rehabilitation has largely been replaced by goals of confinement and punishment. During the same period, despite the Supreme Court's holding that a constitutional right to health care exists for prisoners, problems remain in healthcare delivery (NCCHC, 2002; Restum, 2005).

When correctional health care services are inadequate, voluntary informed consent becomes a greater challenge (Anno and Dubler, 2001). The absence of adequate health care arguably creates a coercive influence on prisoners, who may feel compelled to join investigative trials to access decent medical treatment available only through research protocols. Within correctional settings, the problem of dual loyalty—conflicts between the ethic of undivided loyalty to patients and pressure to use clinical methods and judgment for social purposes and on behalf of third parties—is a particular challenge (Bloche, 1999; Physicians for Human Rights [PHR], 2003). Although NCCHC standards require an independent medical staff, to the extent that the medical staff is part of the prison, their role as patient advocates may be discouraged. For example, prison physicians have been asked to medicate prisoners to quell physical resistance, to restore competence to stand trial, or to prepare for execution. Some states have put a stop to these practices, for example, forbidding psychiatrists from medicating condemned prisoners to make them competent for execution (Bloche, 2006); others have not.

Barriers to privacy and right to consent or refuse care The sanctity of the provider-patient relationship, the right to privacy and confidential care, and the voluntary informed decision whether to consent to or refuse care can be compromised in correctional settings. Maintaining privacy can be a monumentally difficult task. Confidential health information may be surmised from factors as simple as in an inmate's movement, a cell search, or a pattern of scheduled visits. It is a given, even in an independent medical service, that information that might be relevant to correctional officials will be shared for the good of the community, such as for the purpose of avoiding danger to the inhabitants (Dubler and Sidel, 1989).

> It is but just that the public be required to care for the prisoner, who cannot, by reason of the deprivation of his liberty, care for himself.
>
> *Spicer v. Williamson*,
> Supreme Court of North Carolina (1926)[4]

Because of incarceration, the legal context of providing medical, dental, and mental health services is different in prisons and jails from that in the outside community. In no other setting are such services constitutionally guaranteed. Drawing upon the prohibition against "cruel and unusual punishment" in the Eighth Amendment to the Constitution (and the due process clauses of the Fifth and Fourteenth Amendments for juveniles, pretrial detainees, and federal prisoners), the courts require that institutions with custody of human beings provide for their basic necessities, including health care.

The legal framework was established in the 1976 landmark decision of *Estelle v. Gamble*,[5] in which the Supreme Court ruled that prisoners have a right to be free of "deliberate indifference to their serious health-care needs." In the hundreds of published cases following *Estelle*, three basic rights have emerged: the right to access to care, the right to care that is ordered, and the right to a professional medical judgment. The failure of correctional officials to honor these rights has resulted in protracted litigation and the issuance of injunctions regarding the delivery of health-care services (Winner, 1981).[6,7,8]

A mentally competent adult has a constitutional right to refuse medical treatment, including the direction that life-saving or other extraordinary measures be withdrawn in terminal cases (*Cruzan v. Missouri Department of Health*).[9] As Judge Cardozo stated almost 80 years ago: "Every human being of adult years and sound mind has a right to determine what shall be done with his own body" (*Schloendorff v. Society of New York Hospitals*).[10] This right extends to prisoners as well (*White v. Napoleon*).[11] The right to refuse is based on the concept of informed consent:

> A prisoner's right to refuse treatment is useless without knowledge of the proposed treatment. Prisoners have a right to such information as is reasonably necessary to make an informed decision to accept or reject pro-

---

[4]*Spicer v. Williamson*, 132 E.E. 291, 293 (N.C. 1926).
[5]*Estelle v. Gamble*, 429 U.S. 97, 97 S.Ct. 285 (19760.
[6]*Todaro v. Ward*, 431 F.Supp. 1129 (S.D.N.Y.), aff'd, 565 F.2d 48 (2d Cir. 1977).
[7]*Martinez v. Mancusi*, 443 F.2d 1192 (2d Cir. 1970).
[8]*Williams v. Vincent*, 508 F.2d 541, 544-5 (2d Cir. 1974).
[9]*Cruzan v. Missouri Department of Health*, 497 U.S.261, 110 S.Ct. 2841 (1990).
[10]*Schloendorff v. Society of New York Hospitals*, 211 N.Y. 125, 129 (1914).
[11]*White v. Napoleon*, 897 F.2d 103 (3d Cir. 1990).

posed treatment, as well as a reasonable explanation of the viable alternative treatments that can be made available in a prison setting.

White v. Napoleon[12]

The right has never been regarded as absolute, however, (see *Comm'n of Correction v. Myers*);[13] and it may be overridden if there are strong public health reasons to administer treatment, as when the Supreme Court upheld mandatory smallpox vaccination in 1905, despite the patient's religious objections *(Jacobson v. Massachusetts)*.[14] Inmates have been required, for example, to submit to blood and tuberculosis tests and to diphtheria and tetanus injections (*Thompson v. City of Los Angeles; Zaire v. Dalsheim; Ballard v. Woodard*).[15] Involuntary administration of antipsychotic medication has also been upheld when accompanied by appropriate clinical findings and procedural protections for the inmate patient (*Washington v. Harper*).[16]

Summary of Findings on Changing Demographics and Health Issues

- The correctional population has expanded more than 4.5 fold between 1978 and 2004—from 1.5 million to almost 7 million. Prisons and jails house 2.1 million prisoners; an additional 4.9 million are on probation and parole.
- Distrust of the AIDS/HIV movement in the 1990s within some minority communities resulted in more skepticism about physicians and researchers. This means that there is now, compared with the 1970s, a more compelling need for collaboration among all parties (details on collaborative responsibility are presented in Chapter 5).
- The aging of the prisoner population, the high number of prisoners with mental illness, and the poor reading and communication skills among prisoners means that there are now increased concerns about prisoners' capability to give informed consent, calling for a greater focus than before on the informed consent process and validation of prisoner consent to test their comprehension of research disclosures (see Chapter 6).
- Because the possibility of poor health-care delivery exists in correctional settings, new regulations should include instructions that IRBs con-

---

[12] *White v. Napoleon*, 897 F.2d 103, 113 (3d Cir. 1990).
[13] *Commission of Correction v. Myers*, 399 N.E.2d 452 (Mass. 1979).
[14] *Jacobson v. Massachusetts*, 197 U.S. 11 (1905).
[15] *Thompson v. City of Los Angeles*, 885 F.2d 1439 (9th Cir. 1989); *Zaire v. Dalsheim*, 698 F.Supp. 57 (S.D.N.Y. 1988); *Zaire v. Dalsheim*, 698 F.Supp. 57 (S.D.N.Y. 1988).
[16] *Washington v. Harper*, 494 U.S. 210, 110 S.Ct. 1028 (1989).

sider the adequacy of health care in considering whether to approve biomedical protocols in the correctional setting (see Chapter 6).

CURRENT RESEARCH ENVIRONMENT

Current Status of Prisoner Research

As the committee approached its task of addressing possible ethical considerations for revisions to the U.S. Department of Health and Human Services (DHHS) regulations for the protection of prisoners involved in research, it faced a dearth of information as to the recent and current landscape of research involving prisoners as participants. There were no comprehensive reviews[17] and no central repository of information about the amount and different types of research involving prisoners. To better describe the volume and scope of contemporary research with prisoners, the committee undertook these three activities:

1. An extensive survey, conducted by telephone or face-to-face interviews with key personnel from the departments of corrections (DOC) in four large states (California, Florida, New York, Texas) and two smaller states (Iowa, Utah). The questions were designed to reveal policies and procedures that govern research activities in those organizations and yield estimates of the volume of research activities over the past 2 years.[18]

2. A similar survey of somewhat more limited scope conducted by e-mail with key DOC informants from the remaining 44 states (42 responded).

3. A review of a random sample of articles published from 1999 to 2005 that involved prisoners as research participants.

The committee also considered several commissioned papers (see Box A-1). Because of the wide array of research objectives, methodologies, and designs, a brief typology of research was developed to describe relevant types of research (see Appendix A).

---

[17]Reviews of limited scope were identified and reviewed. See, for example, Tewksbury and Mustaine (2001).

[18]For both surveys the committee confined its efforts to state DOCs. Information on policies, procedures, and practices related to research in other settings that fit into a broader definition of prisoner sites (e.g., jails, juvenile justice detention facilities, residential community programs that may serve as alternatives to traditional incarceration or transitional facilities) was not solicited.

Results from the Surveys with Key DOC Personnel

This section summarizes key findings from the surveys of key DOC personnel (from in-depth interviews with personnel from six states plus e-mail survey responses by 42 additional state DOCs). See Appendix A for additional details of this survey.

Types of Research Permitted and Research Personnel

- The vast majority of states permit research that involves administrative records reviews and DOC program evaluations (46 of 48).
- Social/behavioral studies of a nontherapeutic nature involving minimal risk designs (e.g., survey, questionnaire, or nonintervention correlational studies [36 of 48]) are also commonly permitted.
- Just about half of the states permit social or behavioral studies of a therapeutic intervention implemented by an outside investigator (i.e., not a standing DOC program).
- Few states permit nontherapeutic social or behavioral studies that involve greater than minimal risk (5 of 48).
- Therapeutic biomedical research is permissible in 15 of 48 state DOCs. Some states prohibit this research by legislation and others by DOC policy.
- Three states permit biomedical studies of a nontherapeutic nature.
- Many research activities (mainly records reviews and program evaluations) are initiated by in-house staff, according to the six state DOCs that responded to the more in-depth interviews. Each receives applications from external investigators as well, most commonly institutions of higher learning (university faculty and graduate students), federal agencies (e.g., National Institute on Drug Abuse), and private research groups (e.g., Rand Corporation). Given that most states in this sample prohibit, either by state law or DOC policy, medical and biomedical studies, pharmaceutical companies were not commonly mentioned as sources of extramural research applications.

Policies and Procedures for Application Review and Study Implementation

- About 30 state DOCs require IRB review before research can commence. Certain states (e.g., California, Iowa, New York, and Utah) only require external IRB review for applications from external investigators.
- Eighteen state DOCs use an internal IRB for proposal review. Just five of those include a prisoner or prisoner representative as a member of the IRB.

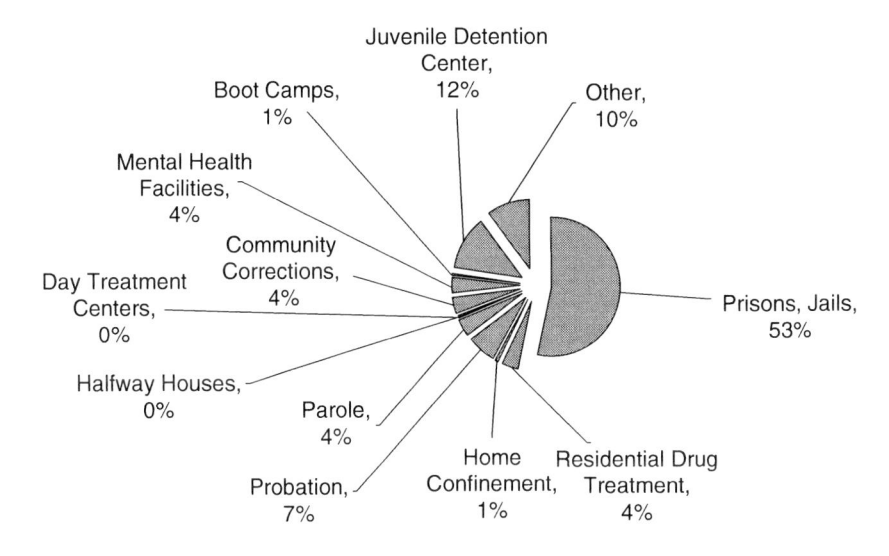

FIGURE 2-2 Facilities/location of studies.

- Financial or other incentives to inmates for research participation are prohibited by five of the six state DOCs interviewed in depth. In some cases, this prohibition has been waived on a case-by-case basis.
- Fewer than half of the states have a procedure in place for reporting adverse events associated with research activity.

Published Literature: A Review of Selected Prisoner Studies[19,20]

Key findings from the literature survey include the following:

Locus of research activity Just over half of the prisoner studies were conducted in higher-security confinement settings, including jails and prisons (see Figure 2-2). More than one-third occurred in alternatives to incarceration, which included, in order of importance, juvenile detention centers,

---

[19]The committee would like to thank John Weir and James Ray, graduate students at the University of South Florida, who reviewed the articles and provided the codings on which these data are based.

[20]See Appendix A for a description of the literature selection strategy and additional findings.

probation, residential drug treatment programs, parole, mental health facilities, community corrections, home confinement, and boot camps.

Types of research Very little research in the published literature involves medical clinical trials or other biomedical studies (see Figure 2-3). The majority of published studies were minimal risk, nontherapeutic social and behavioral studies (41 percent), DOC program evaluations (26 percent), administrative records review (21 percent), or social or behavioral therapeutic studies (6 percent).

Study content/design Prisoner research is dominated by epidemiological studies (e.g., surveys, 39 percent) and correlational designs (27 percent).

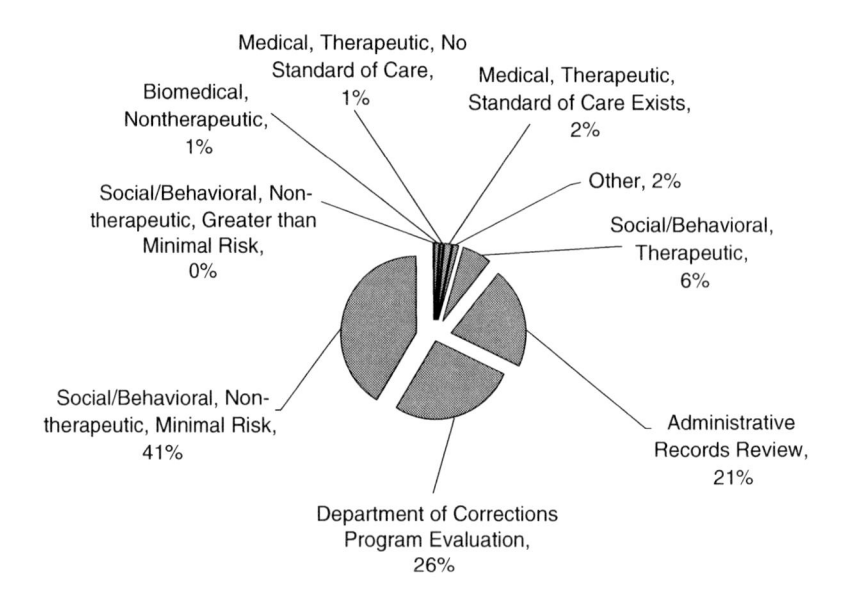

FIGURE 2-3 Type of study.
NOTE: Greater than minimal risk included any biomedical (nontherapeutic) study; any medical therapeutic study (regardless of the existence of a standard of care); any social/behavioral therapeutic study; and any nontherapeutic study involving a manipulation that the research assistant (RA) judged to involve potentially serious physical or emotional stress (e.g., long sleep deprivation). Not greater than minimal risk included any study based on review of administrative records; any program evaluation study; any nontherapeutic social/behavioral study that involved either no manipulation (e.g., innocuous questionnaires and surveys) or involved a manipulation that the RA judged not to involve potentially serious physical or emotional stress (e.g., long sleep deprivation).

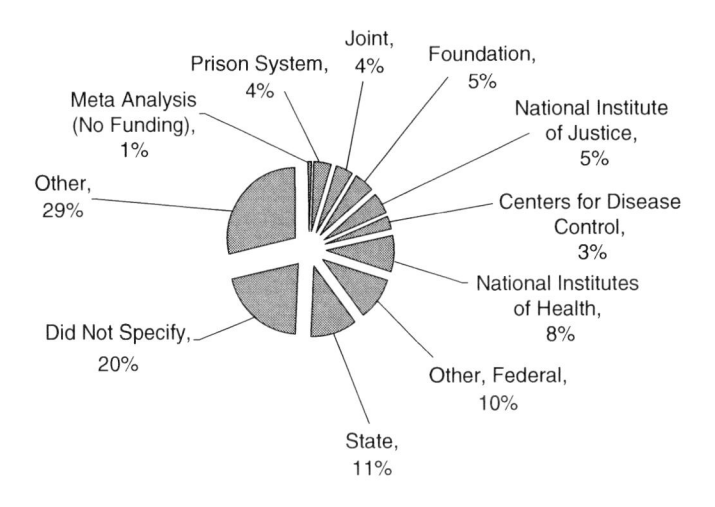

FIGURE 2-4 Source of funding.

Other studies are described as examining behavioral issues (14 percent), medical outcomes (5 percent), case studies (6 percent), nonmedical experiments (1 percent), or "other" (8 percent). An alternative classification of study content reveals that health status questions (43 percent) and personality characteristics (19 percent) are the focus of most research. Other studies deal with aspects of being confined (10 percent) or reentry into the community (11 percent) or bear no clear relationship to prisoner status (9 percent).

Sources of funding It was sometimes challenging to determine or to categorize the source of funding for prisoner research from published reports. Approximately 20 percent of the studies reviewed did not indicate the source of support (see Figure 2-4), and another 29 percent fit the "other" coding category (e.g., a medical school grant; university small grants; a study supported by a Veterans Affairs office). Prisoner research is funded by a wide variety of state and federal entities. Federal resources cited in the present sample included two DHHS agencies (NIH, 8 percent and CDC, 3 percent), National Institute of Justice (5 percent), and "other" federal (10 percent). Also mentioned were state funds (11 percent), foundation grants (5 percent), and prison system funding (4 percent).

Mechanisms of research approval For 15 percent of the studies, a statement in the report indicated that the investigators had obtained IRB approval for the research; for another 19 percent of studies, the approval of some other reviewing body (e.g., a research committee) was referenced. For most studies (66 percent), the reports did not indicate whether, or by whom, the research was approved (in terms of human subjects protections).[21]

A review of 10 years of correctional and scientific literature on HIV/AIDS studies involving prisoners (Farley, unpublished, 2005) yielded similar findings. The studies reviewed lacked transparency. Fewer than one-third of the studies mentioned review by an IRB, and nearly one-half made no mention of informed consent.

Data Retrieval Needs Improving

"[Prisoners'] only single armor against being subjected to experimental abuse hangs on a single thread, on a single federal regulation in federally funded research only," said Vera Hassner Sharav, founder and president of the Alliance for Human Research Protection. "Chimpanzees, by contrast, are protected by mandatory rules, oversight, and enforcement mechanisms since the Animal Welfare Act of 1966. The U.S. Department of Agriculture (USDA) must submit annual reports to Congress documenting the disposition of every chimp, dog, rabbit, and hamster. No one keeps track of how many human beings have died or been harmed in clinical research." Sharav painted this stark comparison of protections for prisoners with protections for animals in research at the committee's July 2005 meeting.

The dearth of information regarding the contemporary landscape of prisoner research led the committee to gather systematic information concerning the frequency and types of prisoner research currently being conducted and the research-related policies and procedures of state agencies that house large numbers of prisoners. It was conceded at the outset that the scope of the committee's efforts in this regard would be limited. For example, the surveys of key personnel in prisons were limited to state DOCs and did not include the federal prison system or the myriad city, county, and municipal jails in which offenders may be at least temporarily

---

[21] This does not necessarily mean, however, that human subjects reviews were not conducted or that appropriate approvals were not obtained. Journals and journal editors vary considerably in their requirements for reporting (or not) that the research had prior IRB or other human subjects review and approval.

> *Jeffrey Ian Ross, an associate professor in the Division of Criminology, Criminal Justice, and Social Policy at the University of Baltimore, and a member of the committee's Prisoner Liaison Panel, agreed at the committee's October 2005 meeting that a registry is needed. "I would make it a point to have some sort of clearinghouse that actually tracks this kind of research on a regular basis so we know if it is increasing, decreasing, and whether it is more behavioral, social science, criminologic, or medical."*

housed. Similarly, the review of published literature was of limited scope and was not supplemented with efforts to uncover, sample, and review unpublished reports in the possession of state, federal, or private agencies or research institutions.

There is no central repository of information about the amount and type of research involving prisoners. For the same reason that registries of clinical research on drugs and biologics exist and have recently garnered strong support (DeAngelis et al., 2004; IOM, 2006), a national database would bring clarity to the currently murky landscape of research involving prisoners.

Recommendation 2.1: *Maintain a public database of all research involving prisoners.* The Department of Health and Human Services, in cooperation with the Department of Justice, should systematically and comprehensively document all human subjects research with prisoners.[22]

The establishment of a national registry of research involving prisoners should include data, such as who is conducting research, with what support, what kind of research, on what populations, and the nature and extent of ethical oversight provided. There is currently no central repository of information about the amount and type of research involving prisoners, however a government-run registry of clinical research does exist (www.Clinicaltrials.gov) and could be a starting point and leveraging mechanism to make this endeavor feasible and not cost prohibitive. A national registry would shed light on the totality of research taking place on prisoners and the quality of ethical oversight provided for each protocol. To enable consideration of questions of justice, it could be used to examine

---

[22]The term *prisoner* is defined by the Committee in Chapter 4 and used throughout this report in a broader way that it is commonly used. In this report, the term *prisoner* refers to all persons, including parolees and probationers, whose liberty has been restricted by decisions of the criminal justice system.

the magnitude and volume of prisoners in different types of research to determine the allocation of benefits and burdens of research among prisoners. A registry would also enhance the application of research findings to prisoner populations. In the absence of such a registry, the committee was unable to accurately determine the nature and extent of prisoners' participation as subjects of research.

Cost is always a consideration when suggesting a database be developed. The director of Clinicaltrials.gov, the federal government's public database of clinical research, indicated that the annual costs for that database, which is maintained at the National Library of Medicine, is $3.2 million per year (Deborah Zarin, personal communication, May 17, 2006). She noted, however, that there may not be a reason to start a new registry for research involving prisoners. The existing clinicaltrials.gov could add a field that indicated if prisoners were included in a study, and then users could customize the view to see only those studies. At present, clinicaltrials.gov does not include social/behavioral research, but it could be a starting point and leveraging mechanism to make Recommendation 2.1 feasible and not cost prohibitive.

Summary of Findings on Current Research Environment

Findings from the surveys of DOC personnel and the literature review shed light on the possible impact of the national commission's *Report and Recommendations—Research Involving Prisoners* (NCPHSBBR, 1976) and indicate practical and political complexities that may hamper efforts to create a uniform and comprehensive system of protections for prisoners as research participants. Findings and implications from these data include the following:

- The reach of the Subpart C regulations to protect prisoners involved in research does not extend to the vast majority of prisoner research participants. The current regulations are binding only with respect to research supported by DHHS or in those institutions that voluntarily extend the regulations to non-DHHS funded studies involving prisoners (currently the Central Intelligence Administration and Social Security Administration; see Chapter 3). Survey responses from key DOC personnel reveal that a significant amount of research with prisoners is initiated and conducted internally, and that extramural research applications come from a wide variety of investigators, some (perhaps many) of whom may not be supported by DHHS funding, and thus not bound by the regulations. Similarly, the review of published prison research studies indicates that only about 11 percent of studies are DHHS funded, through NIH and the CDC (the percentage may be slightly higher given that NIH and CDC may jointly fund some studies coded as having multiple funding sources).

- It is not clear that all studies involving prisoners are being conducted with IRB review and approval. Also, prison research committees, which may serve some type of proxy IRB role, only infrequently include prisoners or prisoner representatives among their membership.
- Biomedical research involving prisoners, particularly that of a nontherapeutic nature, is rare, perhaps as a consequence of the national commission's 1976 report. Across the two surveys, one-third of respondents indicated that therapeutic medical studies might be permissible, and only 5 percent (two states) indicated that nontherapeutic biomedical research might be permissible. Several DOCs report that biomedical research, including potentially therapeutic research, is prohibited by state law or DOC policy. Further, medical studies with the potential for therapeutic outcome make up only 2 percent of the published prisoner research studies. Although the current regulations permit therapeutic medical studies with prisoners under certain circumstances, little such research appears to be taking place.
- Some DOC research implementation policies may preclude potential remedies that some have suggested to ensure fair and equitable research participation by prisoners. For example, some have suggested the prisoner participants be allowed to receive incentives that, if not equal, are at least proportional to those available to nonprisoner participants in the community. Five of the six state DOCs interviewed in depth prohibit prisoner participants from receiving financial or other incentives for research participation.

REFERENCES

Anno BJ, Dubler N. 2001. *Correctional Health Care: Guidelines for the Management of an Adequate Delivery System.* Chapter 4. Chicago: National Commission on Correctional Health Care.

BJS (Bureau of Justice Statistics). 1995. *Probation and Parole Violators in State Prison, 1991.* [Online]. Available: http://www.ojp.usdoj.gov/bjs/pub/pdf/ppvsp91.pdf [accessed December 16, 2005].

BJS. 1997. *Jail Inmates in Custody, by Gender, Federal and State By State, 1973, 1983, 1988, 1993.* [Online]. Available: http://www.ojp.usdoj.gov/bjs/jails.htm#selected [accessed April 4, 2006].

BJS. 1998a. *Substance Abuse and Treatment of Adults on Probation, 1995.* [Online]. Available: http://www.ojp.usdoj.gov/bjs/pub/pdf/satap95.pdf [accessed December 16, 2005].

BJS. 1998b. *Women Offenders: Programming Needs and Promising Approaches.* Washington, DC: U.S. Department of Justice.

BJS. 1998c. *State and Federal Corrections Information Systems.* [Online]. Available: http://www.ojp.usdoj.gov/bjs/pub/pdf/sfcis.pdf [accessed December 21, 2005].

BJS. 1999a. *Mental Health and Treatment of Inmates and Probationers.* [Online]. Available: http://www.ojp.usdoj.gov/bjs/pub/pdf/mhtip.pdf [accessed December 16, 2005].
BJS. 1999b. *Women Offenders.* [Online]. Available: http://www.ojp.usdoj.gov/\bjs/pub/pdf/wo.pdf [accessed October 13, 2005].
BJS. 1999c. *Substance Abuse and Treatment, State and Federal Prisoners, 1997.* [Online]. Available: http://www.ojp.usdoj.gov/bjs/pub/pdf/satsfp97.pdf. [accessed October 15, 2005].
BJS. 2000b. *Incarcerated Parents and Their Children.* Washington, DC: U.S. Department of Justice.
BJS. 2001a. *Trends in State Parole, 1990-2000.* [Online]. Available: http://www.ojp.usdoj.gov/bjs/pub/pdf/tsp00.pdf [accessed December 16, 2005].
BJS. 2001b. *Medical Problems of Inmates, 1997.* [Online]. Available: http://www.ojp.usdoj.gov/bjs/pub/pdf/mpi97.pdf [accessed October 14, 2005].
BJS. 2003a. *Prevalence of Imprisonment in the U.S. population, 1974-2001.* [Online]. Available: http://www.ojp.usdoj.gov/bjs/pub/pdf/piusp01.pdf [accessed December 30, 2005].
BJS. 2003b. *Education and Correctional Populations.* Washington, DC: U.S. Department of Justice.
BJS. 2003c. *Sourcebook of Criminal Justice Statistics. Adults on Probation, in Jail or Prison, and on Parole.* [Online]. Available: http://albany.edu/sourcebook/pdf/sb2002/sb2002-section6.pdf [accessed January 2, 2006].
BJS. 2003d. *Census of State and Federal Correctional Facilities, 2000.* [Online]. Available: http://www.ojp.usdoj.gov/bjs/pub/pdf/csfcf00.pdf [accessed January 3, 2006].
BJS. 2004a. *Hepatitis Testing and Treatment in State Prisons.* [Online]. Available: http://www.hcvinprison.org/docs/hep_stateprisons_04.pdf [accessed January 3, 2006].
BJS. 2004b. *Probation and Parole in the United States, 2003.* [Online]. Available: http://www.ojp.usdoj.gov/bjs/pub/pdf/ppus03.pdf [accessed December 16, 2005].
BJS 2004c. *Profile of Jail Inmates,* 2002. [Online]. Available: http://www.ojp.usdoj.gov/bjs/pub/pdf/pji02.pdf [accessed April 5, 2006].
BJS. 2004d. *Prisoners in 2003.* [Online]. Available: http://www.ojp.usdoj.gov/bjs/pub/pdf/p03.pdf. [accessed April 6, 2006].
BJS. 2005a. *Prisoners in 2004.* [Online]. Available: http://www.ojp.usdoj.gov/bjs/abstract/p04.htm [accessed January 23, 2006].
BJS. 2005b. *Sexual Violence Reported by Correctional Authorities, 2004.* [Online]. Available: http://www.ojp.usdoj.gov/bjs/pub/pdf/svrca04.pdf [accessed October 14, 2005].
BJS. 2005c. *Prison and Jail Inmates at Midyear 2004.* Washington, DC: U.S. Department of Justice.
BJS. 2005d. *HIV in Prisons, 2003.* [Online]. Available: http://www.ojp.usdoj.gov/bjs/pub/pdf/hivp03.pdf [accessed October 14, 2005].
BJS. 2005e. *Key Facts at a Glance, Demographic Trends in Jail Populations.* [Online]. Available: http://www.ojp.usdoj.gov/bjs/glance/tables/jailagtab.htm [accessed March 20, 2006].
BJS. 2005f. *Prisoners in Custody, 1977-98.* [Online]. Available: http://www.ojp.usdoj.gov/bjs/prisons.htm#selected [accessed April 4, 2006].
BJS. 2005g. *Adults on Probation, Federal and State by State, 1977-2004.* [Online]. Available: http://www.ojp.usdoj.gov/bjs/pandp.htm#selected [accessed April 4, 2006].
BJS. 2005h. *Adults on Parole, Federal and State by State, 1977-2004.* [Online]. Available: http://www.ojp.usdoj.gov/bjs/pandp.htm#selected [accessed April 4, 2006].
Blitz CL, Wolff N, Pan KY, Pogorzelski W. 2005. Gender-specific behavioral health and community release patterns among New Jersey prison inmates: Implications for treatment and community reentry. *American Journal of Public Health* 95(10):1741–1746.

Bloche MG. 1999. Clinical loyalties and the social purposes of medicine. *Journal of the American Medical Association* 281(3):268–274.

Bloche MG. 2006. The supreme court and the purposes of medicine. *The New England Journal of Medicine* 354(10):993–995.

Braithwaite RI, Treadwell HM, Arriola KRJ. 2005. Health disparities and incarcerated women: A population ignored. *American Journal of Public Health* 95(10):1679–1680.

CDC (Centers for Disease Control and Prevention). 2002. *Viral Hepatitis and the Criminal Justice System.* [Online]. Available: http://www.cdc.gov/idu/hepatitis/viralhepcrimhaljust.pdf [accessed January 3, 2006].

CDC. 2003. Prevention and control of infections with hepatitis viruses in correctional settings. *Morbidity and Mortality Weekly Report* 52(RR-1):1–44.

Coleman CH, Menikoff JA, Goldner JA, Dubler NN. 2005. *The Ethics and Regulation of Research with Human Subjects.* Dayton, OH: Lexis/Nexis.

Dalton H. 1989. AIDS in blackface. *Daedalus: Proceedings of the American Academy of Arts and Sciences* 118(3):205–228.

DeAngelis CD, Drazen JM, Frizelle FA, Haug C, Hoey J, Horton R, Kotzin S, Laine C, Marusic A, Overbeke AJ, Schroeder TV, Sox HC, Van Der Weyden MB. 2004. Clinical trial registration: A statement from the International Committee of Medical Journal Editors. *Journal of the American Medical Association* 292(11):1363–1364.

Dubler N, Sidel V. 1989. On research on HIV infection and AIDS. *The Milbank Quarterly* 67(2):171–207.

Farley JE. 2005. *10 Years of HIV/AIDS Research Behind Bars: Time for Change.* Unpublished manuscript.

Freudenberg N, Daniels J, Crum M, Perkins T, Richie BE. 2005. Coming home from jail: The social and health consequences of community reentry for women, male adolescents, and their families and communities. *American Journal of Public Health* 95(10):1725–1736.

GAO. 1999. *Women in Prison: Issues and Challenges Confronting U.S. Correctional Systems.* [Online]. Available: http://www.gao.gov/archive/2000/gg00022.pdf [accessed November 23, 2005].

GAO. 2000. *State and Federal Prisoners: Profiles of Inmate Characteristics in 1991 and 1997.* Washington, DC: U.S. Government Printing Office.

Haigler KO, Harlow C, O'Connor P, Campbell A. 1994. *Literacy Behind Prison Walls: Profiles of the Prison Population from the National Adult Literacy Survey National Center for Education Statistics* [Online]. Available: http://nces.ed.gov/pubsearch/pubsinfo.asp?pubid=94102 [accessed October 15, 2005].

Hammett TM, Harmon MP, Rhodes W. 2002. The burden of infectious disease among inmates of and releasees from US correctional facilities, 1997. *American Journal of Public Health* 92:1789–1794.

Hornblum AM. 1997. They were cheap and available: Prisoners as research subjects in twentieth century America. *British Medical Journal* 315:1437–1441.

Hornblum AM. 1998. *Acres of Skin: Human Experiments at Holmesburg Prison.* New York: Routledge.

HRW (Human Rights Watch). 2000. *Out of Sight: Super-Maximum Security Confinement in the United States* [Online]. Available: http://www.hrw.org/reports/2000/supermax/ [accessed October 13, 2005].

HRW. 2003. *Ill-Equipped: U.S. Prisons and Offenders with Mental Illness.* [Online]. Available: http://www.hrw.org/reports/2003/usa1003/index.htm (accessed October 13, 2005).

IOM (Institute of Medicine). 2006. *Developing a National Registry of Pharmacologic and Biologic Clinical Trials: Workshop Report.* Washington, DC: The National Academies Press.

Jacobson M. 2005. *Downsizing Prisons: How to Reduce Crime and End Mass Incarceration.* New York: New York University Press.

Jones JH. 1993. *Bad Blood: The Tuskegee Syphilis Experiment.* New York: The Free Press.

JPI (Justice Policy Institute). 2002. *The Punishing Decade: Prison and Jail Estimates at the Millennium.* [Online]. Available: http://www.cjcj.org/pubs/punishing/punishing.html [accessed October 14, 2005].

JPI. 2004. *An examination of 3-Strike Laws 10 years after their Enactment* [Online]. Available: http://www.justicepolicy.org/article.php?id=450 [accessed May 9, 2006].

Khan AJ, Simard EP, Bower WA, Wurtzel HL, Khristova M, Wagner KD, Arnold KE, Nainan OV, LaMarre M, Bell BP. 2005. Ongoing transmission of hepatitis B virus infection among inmates at a state correctional facility. *American Journal of Public Health* 95(10): 1793–1799.

King RS, Mauer M. 2001. *Aging Behind Bars: "Three Strikes" Seven Years Later.* [Online]. Available: http://www.sentencingproject.org/pdfs/9087.pdf [accessed October 14, 2005].

Liptak A. 2005, October 2. To more inmates, life term means dying behind bars. *The New York Times*, p. 1.

Lotke E. 1997 *Hobbling a Generation: Young African American Men in D.C.'s Criminal Justice System Five Years Later.* National Center on Institutions and Alternatives. [Online]. Available: http://66.165.94.98/stories/hobblgen0897.html [accessed April 6, 2006].

Lovell D, Cloyes C, Allen DG, Rhodes LA. 2000. Who lives in supermaximum custody? A Washington State study. *Federal Probation* 61(3):40–45.

Macalino GE, Dhawan D, Rich JD. 2005. A missed opportunity: Hepatitis C screening of prisoners. *American Journal of Public Health* 95(10):1739–1740.

MacNeil JR, Lobato MN, Moore M. 2005. An unanswered health disparity: Tuberculosis among correctional inmates, 1993 through 2003. *American Journal of Public Health* 95(10):1800–1805.

Mauer M, King RS. 2004. *Schools and Prisons: Fifty Years After Brown V. Board of Education* [Online]. Available: http://sentencingproject.org/pdfs/brownvboard.pdf [accessed January 2, 2006].

Mauer M, King RS, Young MC. 2004. *The Meaning of "Life": Long Prison Sentences in Context.* [Online]. Available: http://www.sentencingproject.org/pdfs/lifers.pdf [accessed October 17, 2005].

Metzner JL. 2002. Class action litigation in correctional psychiatry. *Journal American Academy of Psychiatry and the Law* 30:19–29.

Mitford J. 1974. *Kind and Usual Punishment.* New York: Vintage.

Murphy D. 2005. Health care in the federal bureau of prisons: Fact or fiction. *California Journal of Health Promotion* 3(2):23–37.

NCCHC (National Commission on Correctional Health Care). 2002. *The Health Status of Soon-to-Be Released Inmates: Executive Summary.* [Online]. Available: http://www.ncchc.org/stbr/Volume2/ExecutiveSummary.pdf [accessed October 10, 2005].

NCPHSBBR (National Commission for the Protection of Human Subjects of Biomedical and Behavioral Research). 1976. *Report and Recommendations: Research Involving Prisoners.* Washington, DC: NCPHSBBR.

NFCMH (New Freedom Commission on Mental Health). 2004. *Subcommittee on Criminal Justice Background Paper.* DHHS Pub. No. SMA-04-3880, Rockville, MD. Available: http://www.mentalhealthcommission.gov/papers/CJ_ADACompliant.pdf [accessed March 20, 2006].

NIC (National Institute of Corrections). 1997. *Supermax Housing: A Survey of Current Practice.* Longmont, CO: U.S. Department of Justice.

NIC. 2005. *Gender-Responsive Strategies for Women Offenders: A Summary of Research, Practice, and Guiding Principles for Women Offenders*. Washington, DC: U.S. Department of Justice.
NIH (National Institutes of Health). 2002. *Management of Hepatitis C: 2002*. [Online]. Available: http://consensus.nih.gov/2002/2002Hepatitisc2002116html.htm [accessed January 23, 2006].
OSI (Open Society Institute). 1997. *Education as Crime Prevention. Providing Education to Prisoners* (Research Brief No. 2). New York: Chesapeake Institute.
Petersilia J. 2000. Challenges to prisoner reentry and parole in California. *California Policy Research Center Brief Series*. [Online]. Available: http://www.ucop.edu/cprc/parole.html [accessed April 4, 2006].
PHR (Physicians for Human Rights). 2003. *Dual Loyalty & Human Rights in Health Professional Practice: Proposed Guidelines and Institutional Mechanisms*. [Online]. Available: http://www.phrusa.org/healthrights/dl_intro.html [accessed May 17, 2006].
Pogorzelski W, Wolff N, Pan KY, Blitz CL. 2005. Behavioral health problems, ex-offender reentry policies, and the "second chance" act. *American Journal of Public Health* 95(10): 1718–1724.
Restum ZG. 2005. Public health implications of substandard correctional health care. *American Journal of Public Health* 95(10):1689–1691.
Rhodes LA. 2005. Pathological effects of the supermaximum prison. *American Journal of Public Health* 95(10)1692–1693.
Schafer NE. 1994. Exploring the link between visits and parole success: A survey of prison visitors. *International Journal of Offender Therapy and Comparative Criminology* 38(1): 17–32.
Sharp, SM. 2004. The problem of readability of informed consent documents for clinical trials of investigational drugs and devices: United States considerations. *Drug Information Journal* 38:353–359.
Spangenberg, G. 2004. *Current Issues in Correctional Education: A Compilation & Discussion*. [Online]. Available: http://www.caalusa.org/correct_ed_paper.pdf [accessed October 14, 2005].
Sterngold, J. 2005, July 1. U.S. seizes state prison health care: Judge sites preventable death of inmates, depravity of system. *San Francisco Chronicle*, p. A-1.
Sturm SP. 1993. The legacy and future of corrections litigation. *University of Pennsylvania Law Review* 142:638–738.
Tewksbury R, Mustaine EE. (2001). Where to find corrections research: An assessment of research published in corrections specialty journals, 1990–1999. *The Prison Journal* 81:419–435.
TSP (The Sentencing Project). 2001. *Aging Behind Bars: "Three Strikes" Seven Years Later*. [Online]. Available: http://www.sentencingproject.org/pdfs/9087.pdf [accessed October 14, 2005].
TSP. 2005. *New Incarceration Figures: Growth in Population Continues*. Available: http://www.sentencingproject.org/pdfs/1044.pdf [accessed April 6, 2006].
U.S. Census. 1998. Table no. 377: federal and state prisoners: 1970 to 1996. In: *Statistical Abstracts of the United States: 1998*. [Online]. Available: http://www.census.gov/prod/3/98pubs/98statab/sasec5.pdf [accessed December 23, 2005].
U.S. Supreme Court. 1976. *Estelle v. Gamble*, 429 U.S. 97. [Online]. Available: http://www.justia.us/us/429/97/case.html [accessed January 2, 2006].
Von Zielbauer P. 2005a, February 27. As health care in jails goes private, 10 days can be a death sentence. *New York Times*, p 1.
Von Zielbauer P. 2005b, February 28. In city's jails, missed signals open way to season of suicides. *New York Times*, p. 1.

Von Zielbauer P. 2005c, June 10. Inmates' medical care at Rikers fails in evaluation. *New York Times*, p. B-1.

Von Zielbauer P. 2005d, August 1. A company's troubled answer for prisoners with HIV. *New York Times*, p. 1.

Walmsley R. 2003. *World Prison Population List* (4th edition). [Online]. Available: http://www.homeoffice.gov.uk/rds/pdfs2/r188.pdf [accessed January 2, 2006].

Winner, 1987. An introduction to the constitutional law of prison medical care. *Journal of Prison Health* 1(1):67–84.

Young VD, Reviere R. 2001. Meeting the health care needs of the new woman inmate: A national survey of prison practices. *Journal of Offender Rehabilitation* 34(2):31–48.

3

Federal Regulatory Landscape

The current regulatory scheme for research with human subjects is a patchwork of regulations and enforcement mechanisms that do not lend themselves to broad or easy application, particularly with regard to research involving prisoners. The environment when the existing regulations were adopted resulted in a set of regulations promulgated by the U.S. Department of Health and Human Services (DHHS) that were intended to be restrictive with respect to research involving prisoners: The default position is that no such research should occur, and the four or five categories of research allowed under the regulations are essentially exceptions to that general rule. The Office for Human Research Protections (OHRP) applies these regulations with the assumption that if the research described does not appear to fit into any given category, it cannot be approved, even if it otherwise seems beneficial and appropriate.

The restrictiveness of the DHHS regulations regarding prisoners may have had the unintended effect of creating widely varying regulatory schemes applicable to research involving prisoners, because of the unwillingness of other federal agencies to adopt the same set of regulations. Under the current framework, although they can voluntarily agree to more, research institutions are only required to abide by DHHS-promulgated regulations when they conduct research funded by the DHHS (including DHHS agencies such as the National Institutes of Health [NIH], the Food and Drug Administration [FDA], the Centers for Disease Control and Prevention [CDC], and the Substance Abuse and Mental Health Services Administration, which is actually a very small portion of all research involving prisoners conducted in the United States). For the regulations to apply to other federally funded research, absent the consent of research institutions, it was necessary for every other department or agency funding such research to incorporate the DHHS-promulgated regulations into that department or agency's own regulations. Sixteen other departments and agencies of the federal government adopted the generally applicable Common Rule regarding research with human subjects, thus partially accomplishing a goal of uniformity in the ethical regulations applicable to federally funded research.

However, perhaps because of the restrictiveness of the regulations, nearly all of the same departments or agencies did not adopt the additional protections for prisoners. At least one of the departments adopting the Common Rule, the Bureau of Prisons (BOP) at the Department of Justice (DOJ), instead adopted its own regulations that apply to all research with prisoners in BOP custody (not merely research that is funded by the DOJ). Additionally, the FDA promulgated its own rules, consistent to the extent practical with the Common Rule, governing clinical research associated with the products it regulates. However, the FDA's attempt to adopt parallel regulations that were essentially the same as DHHS's prisoner protections[1] was the subject of a lawsuit brought by prisoners wishing to participate in such research. Therefore, the FDA does not have provisions comparable to DHHS Subpart C for prisoner populations.

Outside of DHHS and its agencies, only the Central Intelligence Agency (CIA) and the Social Security Administration (SSA) have adopted the DHHS's prisoner protections (Figure 3-1).

In sum, regarding research involving prisoners as human research subjects, the applicable regulations are far from uniform and range from no protection at all (for research that is not funded by one of the 17 agencies that have adopted the Common Rule), to basic Common Rule protection, to heightened, overlapping, and possibly inconsistent regulations (e.g., for persons in BOP custody participating in therapeutic clinical trials). This chapter describes the components of the patchwork of regulations: the Common Rule, Subpart C (the DHHS's protections for prisoners as research subjects), and the alternative regulations applied by other departments.

ADOPTION OF DHHS HUMAN SUBJECTS PROTECTION REGULATIONS

The first federal protections for human subjects were issued in 1966 by the NIH. This document, *Clinical Investigations Using Human Subjects*, served as the Public Health Service's policy and was an initial attempt to

---

[1] 45 C.F.R. Part 46, Subpart C.

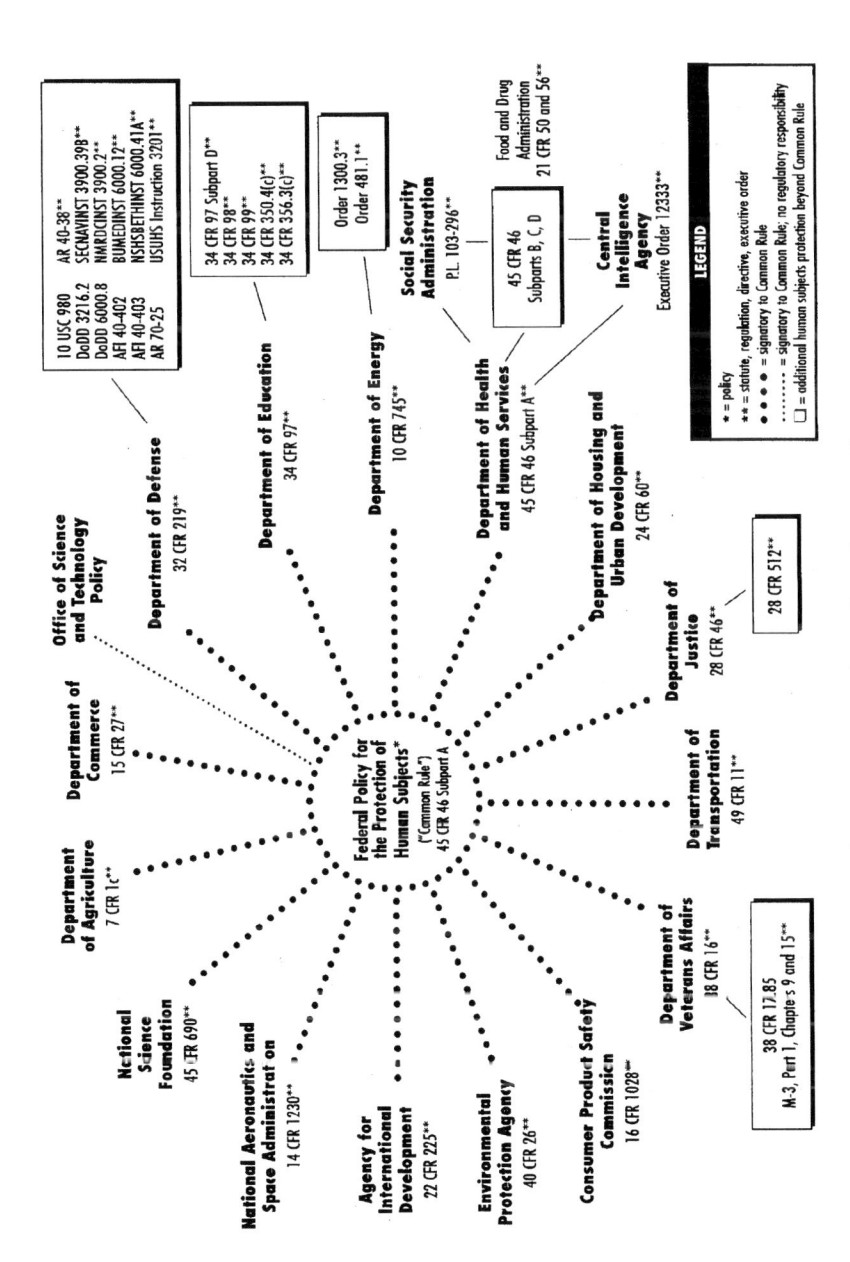

FIGURE 3-1 Chart of applicable regulations to research involving human subjects.
SOURCE: National Bioethics Advisory Commission (NBAC) (2001).

protect human subjects. It required prospective review of human subjects research, focusing on the rights of potential participants by balancing risks and benefits while ensuring appropriate informed consent procedures (Public Health Service [PHS], 1966).

These NIH policies, which initially applied only to extramural research, were later raised to regulatory standards for the entire Department of Health, Education, and Welfare (DHEW) in 1974. These regulations were later modified in 1981 and codified as Title 45 Part 46 of the Code of Federal Regulations. Revisions have occurred several times since then; the most recent changes took effect in 1991 with the development of the Federal Policy for the Protection of Human Subjects, also known as the Common Rule.

The Common Rule

The Common Rule is incorporated as Subpart A of 45 C.F.R. Part 46, the basic DHHS regulations for the protection of human research subjects. The regulatory framework outlined in the Common Rule applies to 17 federal agencies that are involved in conducting or funding human subjects research.[2] The Common Rule provides guidelines on conducting certain types of research with human subjects. Specifically, it discusses issues such as review by institutional review boards (IRBs), informed consent, balancing risks and benefits, protecting privacy, and additional requirements for approval. Failure to adhere to these regulations can result in sanctions. Agency or department support of the research can be suspended or terminated, or additional conditions can be imposed on the individual project or on the research organization or institution.

Human subjects are defined as persons about whom a research investigator obtains either (1) identifiable private information or (2) data as a result of an intervention or interaction with the person.[3] The Common Rule defines research as any "systematic investigation, including research development, testing and evaluation, designed to develop or contribute to generalizable knowledge."[4]

The Common Rule also identifies certain categories of research that are exempt. Notably, these exemption categories cannot be applied to any research involving prisoners; therefore, both the general protections (Subpart A) and the heightened protections (Subpart C) provided under 45 C.F.R. Part 46 still apply.[5]

---

[2]See Figure 3-1. The FDA adopted a modified version of the Common Rule applicable to research involving all products it regulates.
[3]45 C.F.R. § 46.102(f).
[4]45 C.F.R. § 46.102(d).
[5]45 C.F.R. § 46.101(i), n.1.

IRBs

A number of protections for human subjects involved in research are specified in the Common Rule. IRBs are required to review and approve any nonexempt research that involves human subjects, with its membership specified, functions defined, and review processes outlined.[6] The Common Rule also includes criteria for IRB approval of research and identifies certain categories of research that can be approved on an expedited basis.[7] It also specifies that, when "some or all of the subjects are likely to be vulnerable to coercion or undue influence," the IRB must find that "additional safeguards have been included to protect the rights and welfare of those subjects."[8] IRBs are empowered to suspend or terminate research that has been approved and are required to maintain records that document all IRB activities.[9]

In some cases, IRB review of individual research projects can be expedited if the project involves no more than minimal risk and fits certain categories (e.g., collection of small amounts of blood, analysis of existing materials) or involves minor changes to a previously approved research project. Minimal risk for the Common Rule is defined as:

> The probability and magnitude of harm or discomfort anticipated in the research are not greater in and of themselves than those ordinarily encountered in daily life or during the performance of routine physical or psychological examinations or tests.[10]

Under expedited procedures that bypass the full IRB process, the IRB chair or one or more experienced IRB members who is designated by the chair can review and approve the research. Although regulations do not preclude the use of expedited review for research involving prisoners, the OHRP recommends that such research be reviewed by the full committee.

Informed Consent

Informed consent processes are also defined in the Common Rule. The basic disclosure requirements for obtaining informed consent are (1) a description of the study and its purposes; (2) identification of any foreseeable risks or discomforts to the participant; (3) a description of any benefits that could be expected; (4) disclosure of alternative treatments that may

---

[6] 45 C.F.R. § 46.107–109.
[7] 45 C.F.R. § 46.110–111.
[8] 45 C.F.R. § 46.109(b).
[9] 45 C.F.R. § 46.113.
[10] 45 C.F.R. § 46.102(i).

also be beneficial; (5) a description of how confidentiality of records will be maintained; (6) for treatment involving more than minimal risk, an explanation of the potential consequences resulting from participation in the research; (7) contact information for answering questions; and (8) a statement that the individual's participation in the research must be voluntary, that refusal to participate will not result in a penalty or loss of benefits to which the individual is otherwise entitled, and that the individual may withdraw at any time.[11] Additional information may also be required, depending on the specific nature of the research.[12] The investigator must document that the person agreed to participate in the research project by obtaining the individual's signature or the signature of an authorized representative.[13]

Institutional Assurances

Generally, the Common Rule requires that the departments or agencies applying the Common Rule obtain some form of written assurance from all research institutions engaging in covered research that the research complies with the regulations.[14] If a research organization frequently conducts research supported by one of the signatory federal agencies, it may apply for a federal-wide assurance (FWA), a special kind of assurance process administered by the DHHS. The research organization seeking an FWA certifies that (1) all research will be performed in accordance with the ethical principles in the Belmont Report and (2) for any research that the organization conducts for which it receives any federal funds,[15] certain procedures will be followed that ensure compliance with the Common Rule and any other applicable subparts the organization chooses to sign on to.

In lieu of requiring its own form of written assurance, a department or agency other than DHHS may accept the FWA.[16] In that case, once the FWA is approved by the DHHS, it allows individual research proposals to be approved by the organization and its local IRB rather than by the individual federal department or agency that is funding the research, and any reports required are made both to the department or agency and the OHRP.[17] Note that most organizations that conduct federally funded research hold an FWA.

---

[11] 45 C.F.R. § 46.116(a).
[12] 45 C.F.R. § 46.116(b).
[13] 45 C.F.R. § 46.117.
[14] 45 C.F.R. § 46.103.
[15] If the organization voluntarily extends its assurance to all research regardless of funding source, the organization's certification extends to that research as well.
[16] 45 C.F.R. § 46.103(a).
[17] 45 C.F.R. § 103(a).

Subpart C: Prisoners as Research Subjects

Beyond the Common Rule contained in Subpart A, additional subparts of 45 C.F.R. Part 46 provide further and more specific protection for certain particularly vulnerable populations: pregnant women, fetuses, and neonates (Subpart B); prisoners (Subpart C); and children (Subpart D). Subpart C, "Additional Protections Pertaining to Biomedical and Behavioral Research Involving Prisoners as Subjects," the focus of this project, was first finalized in 1978. These additional protections were developed in response to the National Commission's *Report and Recommendations: Research Involving Prisoners* (NCPHSBBR, 1976). They represent further safeguards that must be met when conducting research with this vulnerable population group. To date, Subpart C has only been adopted by the DHHS, the CIA, and the SSA.

Key Definitions Within Subpart C

Subpart C defines a prisoner as any person who is "involuntarily confined or detained in a penal institution" as a result of violating a criminal or civil statute, a person who is committed to other facilities as an alternative to criminal prosecution or incarceration, or someone who is detained pending arraignment, trial, or sentencing.[18] Research with this population must present no more than minimal risk. Here, that is defined as:

> The probability and magnitude of physical or psychological harm that is normally encountered in the daily lives, or in the routine medical, dental, or psychological examination of healthy persons.[19]

Subpart C identifies four categories of research that are permitted with prisoners.

1. Study of the *possible causes, effects, and processes of incarceration* and of criminal behavior, provided that the study presents no more than minimal risk and no more than inconvenience to the subjects;

2. Study of *prisons as institutional structures or of prisoners as incarcerated persons*, provided that the study presents no more than minimal risk and no more than inconvenience to the subjects;

3. Research on conditions *particularly affecting prisoners as a class* (for example, vaccine trials and other research on hepatitis which is much more prevalent in prisons than elsewhere; and research on social and psychologi-

---

[18] 45 C.F.R. § 46.303(c).
[19] 45 C.F.R. § 46.303(d).

cal problems such as alcoholism, drug addiction, and sexual assaults) provided that the study may proceed only after the Secretary has consulted with appropriate experts, including experts in penology, medicine, and ethics, and published notice in the *Federal Register*, of the intent to approve such research; or

4. Research on practices, both innovative and accepted, which have the *intent and reasonable probability of improving the health or well-being of the subjects*. In cases in which those studies require the assignment of prisoners in a manner consistent with protocols approved by the IRB to control groups which may not benefit from the research, the study may proceed only after the Secretary has consulted with appropriate experts, including experts in penology, medicine, and ethics, and published notice in the *Federal Register* of the intent to approve such research.[20]

There has been confusion among researchers and correctional departments regarding the exact meaning of the categories stated previously and the specific circumstances in which they should be applied (See later discussion on the Subpart C Subcommittee of Secretary's Advisory Committee on Human Research Protections [SACHRP] on page 81). In October 2002, the secretary of the DHHS published a notification in the *Federal Register* proposing to waive certain provisions of Subpart C to epidemiological research involving prisoners that involved no more than minimal risk and no more than inconvenience to potential subjects.[21] The regulations, which became final in June 2003, allow for epidemiological research on specific diseases that describes the prevalence or incidence of the disease by identifying all cases, including prisoner cases, or studies of potential risk factor associations for these diseases in which prisoners were included in the population of interest but were not the sole study group.[22]

Implementation of an epidemiological research project involving prisoners requires that an IRB must approve the research, document that one of the two conditions described previously has been met, and determine that the research involves minimal risk and no more than inconvenience to the prisoner-subjects.[23]

Additional Requirements for IRBs

When research is proposed that involves prisoners, IRBs must approve each individual project. IRBs for prisoner research are not only required to

---
[20] 45 C.F.R. § 46.306(a)(2) (emphasis added).
[21] 67 Fed. Reg. 62432 (October 7, 2002).
[22] 68 Fed. Reg. 36929 (June 20, 2003).
[23] 68 Fed. Reg. 36930 (2003).

meet the conditions of the Common Rule (outlined previously) but also must have among its membership a prisoner or prisoner representative.

Further, the IRB must find that the research proposal meets both the Common Rule requirements as well as additional requirements specific to the prisoner setting. These additional requirements are as follows:

- the research is within one of the four permissible categories of research for prisoners;
- benefits that accrue as a result of the prisoner's participation should not be so great in comparison to what is available in the correctional environment that the ability to provide informed consent is impaired;
- risks are commensurate with those that would be accepted by nonprisoner volunteers;
- selection procedures are fair and not subject to arbitrary intervention by either prison authorities or other prisoners;
- the consent form is written in language that is easily understood by the prisoner;
- the person's participation in the research project will not be a consideration in parole or probation decisions; and
- adequate provisions are made for follow-up care, should it be needed, once the research study ends.[24]

OHRP Certification

Once the IRB has found that the research meets the criteria described previously and approves the study, OHRP certification must be obtained for research in Categories i through iv and for epidemiological waivers as well (Table 3-1). If the OHRP certifies that the category is appropriate and that the criteria have been met, the research is approved. This certification step adds an average of 3–4 weeks to the review process.

Report of the SACHRP Subcommittee

In 2003, the SACHRP asked its Subpart C Subcommittee to review the text and application of Subpart C, primarily to determine whether the current DHHS interpretation and application of Subpart C's requirements should be modified. Among the topics the subcommittee addressed were:

- the definition of the term *prisoner* under Subpart C;

---

[24] 45 C.F.R. § 46.305(a).

TABLE 3-1 Approximate OHRP Prisoner Certifications January 2000–October 12, 2005

Subpart C Category	2000	2001	2002	2003	2004	2005	Total
46.306(a)(2)(i)	12	26	18	23	53	56	18
46.306(a)(2)(ii)	1	1	6	4	5	3	20
46.306(a)(2)(iii)	0	2	1	1	0	0	4
46.306(a)(2)(iv)	12	35	20	34	27	31	159
Epidemiology waiver				2	11	2	15
Disapproved				2	1	3	6
Not DHHS				1	4	11	16
Total	25	64	45	67	101	106	408

NOTE: OHRP, Office for Human Research Protections; DHHS, Department of Health and Human Services.
SOURCE: Gorey, 2005.

- the application of research protections to those who become incarcerated after agreeing to participate in a nonprisoner study;
- issues with identifying a prisoner representative for prisoner-research IRBs and particularly in multisite studies;
- conduct of expedited review in prisoner research;
- the definition of minimal risk under Subpart C (which is different from the Subpart A definition); and
- the requirement of secretarial review when prisoners in the control group are merely provided the standard of care (SACHRP, 2005).

Definition of Prisoner

The subcommittee recommended that a modified Subpart A analysis apply when a subject who is enrolled in a study may not be fully within the definition of prisoner for the duration of the study. First, the subcommittee affirmed that the interpretation of the term *prisoner* should remain defined by the words of the regulation and not be expanded to include other individuals whose liberty is restricted, such as those in community correctional facilities or on probation or parole. Although these individuals deserve heightened protection, the subcommittee recommended that the DHHS rely on Subpart A's protections for individuals "vulnerable to coercion or undue influence" without including them as prisoners under Subpart C. Likewise, when an individual is incarcerated after enrolling in a study, the concerns about coercion and undue influence are not as great, and it may be difficult to modify the research protocol to comply with Subpart C. Therefore, the subcommittee suggested that Subpart A's general requirement of heightened protection instead apply. The subcommittee recommended that an IRB should review a researcher's request to continue the research when an individual subsequently becomes incarcerated, taking into account the new conditions of incarceration but without fully engaging in a new Subpart C approval process.

Prisoner IRB Representative

The subcommittee discussed a variety of problems with identifying a representative who would be skilled and knowledgeable enough to be effective but not so unlike the rest of the IRB as to be marginalized. The subcommittee recommended that the OHRP should assist IRBs in searching for an appropriate prisoner representative, which might include family members of prisoners, former prisoners (especially people in recovery from substance addiction who have also had experience as prisoners), and service providers who assist in the correctional process. The OHRP should provide functional criteria that might help IRBs (and investigators, who are also responsible for the composition of an IRB that will properly evaluate ethical issues) identify persons who can be an effective voice for prisoners within the IRB. With respect to multisite studies, the subcommittee recommended that, although Subpart C only requires one prisoner representative on a central IRB for multisite research, the IRB must nevertheless consider the individual circumstances of each prison site, which can vary widely. With respect to expedited review, the subcommittee recommended that, if expedited review of a protocol is required, a prisoner representative be one of the reviewers.

Defining Minimal Risk and Benefit to Participant

The subcommittee considered two issues regarding the distinction between using other healthy prisoners as the ethical baseline as opposed to other healthy persons generally. First, the subcommittee affirmed that the different definition of minimal risk in the Subpart C regulations compared with Subpart A regulations was appropriate. The Subpart C regulations specify that the determination of minimal risk must be in comparison to the ordinary experience of a healthy person, interpreted as meaning a healthy person outside the prison environment. The subcommittee cautioned that the greater situational risk in the prison setting should not influence the baseline for the IRB's decision; rather, the minimal risk should be compared with the risk to a healthy person in a safe environment. The OHRP should provide guidance, using examples, of how the minimal risk might be viewed in different protocols.

At the same time, the subcommittee viewed the current OHRP interpretation of when a protocol does not provide a benefit to the participant as overly restrictive. The OHRP's position is that using standard of care as a control arm does not provide any benefit to the participant and thus requires secretarial review and expert panel consideration. The subcommittee's view is that, because the participant receives the standard of care and does ultimately benefit from the results of the research, even if not immediately, such a control arm should not require heightened review. The subcommittee recommended that only when the control group is placebo only (and thus deviating from the standard of care) should the protocol be considered to include an arm not benefiting from the research.

The subcommittee also pointed out the problems with the jurisdiction of Subpart C. Because it has been adopted by so few agencies, it has limited application to federally funded research. In addition, it does not automatically apply to institutions that have signed an FWA unless they specifically request that it be part of their obligation. Because of these two enormous gaps in coverage, most research involving prisoners does not fall under the special protections of Subpart C.

Recommendations for Further Consideration by the IOM

In addition to its recommendations on these issues, the subcommittee noted with approval that the IOM had been charged with studying the human research protections for prisoners. The subcommittee recommended the IOM committee's consideration of:

- the need for a requirement that research only be conducted in prisons providing standard of care to the general population (and how best to get such services in place);
- the interpretation of the requirement that follow-up care be provided when the prisoner has been released from confinement; and
- the limited jurisdiction of Subpart C (i.e., to DHHS-supported research only).

OTHER FEDERAL HUMAN SUBJECTS PROTECTIONS

The full panoply of DHHS protections for prisoners in Subpart C presently apply only to research funded by the DHHS, the CIA, and the SSA. Some of the other 14 departments and agencies that have adopted the Common Rule accept the OHRP-approved FWA as assurance of compliance with ethical regulations regarding human research subjects. However, those departments and agencies have not adopted Subpart C, so the assurance will only require certification of compliance with the Common Rule (Subpart A).[25] Although institutions holding an FWA and engaging in re-

---

[25] One exception is the Department of Education, which has adopted Subpart D but has not adopted Subparts B or C of the DHHS regulations.

search funded by one of those other departments or agencies may voluntarily extend their protections to include those under the other subparts (including Subpart C), the OHRP estimates that only about 60 percent of institutions holding an FWA have done so.

Moreover, prisoner research that is funded by another department or agency (other than DHHS) falls outside of the protections of OHRP oversight even if the institution has requested in its FWA that Subpart C apply, because the OHRP does not monitor the institution's compliance with a voluntary assurance regarding Subpart C. Additionally, an organization that does not receive its funding from any of these sources generally will not hold an FWA and would not be required to comply with the Common Rule or any of the subparts.[26]

In evaluating the effectiveness of Subpart C, it is useful to compare other human research subjects protections to these regulations. In particular, Subpart D contains DHHS's regulations regarding children, and provides a different framework for assessing the risks and benefits (and according appropriate protections). Within the DHHS, the FDA has promulgated additional human subjects protections regarding research conducted on drugs and medical devices (but has not succeeded in attempting to regulate such research in the prison context). In contrast, the BOP has established a set of regulations regarding all research conducted with the prisoners in its custody.

Subpart D

Recall that there are four categories of permissible research established in Subpart C: (1) study of the possible causes, effects, and processes of incarceration (presenting no more than minimal risk); (2) study of prisons as institutional structures or of prisoners as incarcerated persons (presenting no more than minimal risk); (3) research on conditions particularly affecting prisoners as a class (after consultation with experts and notice in the *Federal Register*); and (4) research on practices, both innovative and accepted, that have the intent and reasonable probability of improving the health or well-being of the subjects, when there is a control group that is nontherapeutic, after consultation with experts and notice in the *Federal Register*.[27] If biomedical or behavioral research does not fall into one of these categories as described, it is not permitted.[28]

Subpart D, although similar in some ways to Subpart C, takes a different approach to the definition of categories of permissible research involv-

---

[26]See Figure 3-1. However, various human subjects protections may still apply, independently of the funding source, as discussed in more detail below. See Table 3-3.
[27]45 C.F.R. § 46.306(a)(2).
[28]45 C.F.R. § 46.306(b).

ing children (IOM, 2004). Specifically, Subpart D gradually increases the protections as the risk-benefit scale tilts more toward risk and, at the top end of the scale, has a case-by-case escape clause for research that is not otherwise approvable but that presents an exceptional opportunity to learn about a problem particularly affecting children.[29]

As to the risk-benefit analysis, the protection is tailored as shown in Table 3-2.

Thus, the scheme gradually steps up the requirements for approval as the risk increases and the prospect of direct benefit to the individual decreases.

Moreover, this scheme allows for appropriate research that might fall through the cracks under the Subpart C framework. First, IRBs may find Subpart D's descriptions of categories easier to understand than those of Subpart C because they specify how the risks and benefits are to be analyzed and how the protections should be increased to match. Second, the framework is more flexible in that 45 C.F.R. § 46.407 allows for research that does not neatly fit into one of the previous three categories, if, after expert consultation and public review and comment, the secretary finds it is both sufficiently important and well designed and is conducted in accordance with sound ethical principles.

Overall, the Subpart D framework is a more natural fit with the overarching ethical framework. Rather than determining in advance that certain kinds of research appropriately balance risks and benefits and forbidding all others, as in Subpart C, Subpart D allows the IRB discretion to determine the balance of risk to the individual with the prospect of benefit (direct or indirect) to the individual, requires appropriate assurance of informed and voluntary participation and draws a line when the risk outweighs the benefit to such an extent that it can be presumed that individuals would not consent if their consent was completely voluntary.

Other DHHS Agencies: FDA Regulations

As noted previously, the FDA has adopted a modified form of the Common Rule in 21 C.F.R. Part 50, Subpart A, as well as regulations regarding research with children as subjects in Subpart D. Apart from the FDA's definition of the scope of its regulations, the differences between these and the Common Rule are, for present purposes, minimal.[30] Rather,

---

[29] 45 C.F.R. § 46.404–407.

[30] The primary difference is in the regulations governing informed consent, which provide specific exceptions to informed consent for (1) emergent care treatments for life-threatening conditions in which the subjects cannot be identified in advance (e.g., treatments for stroke or heart attack victims) and (2) certain Department of Defense treatments of armed forces personnel, if authorized by the President, but which otherwise forbid any waiver or exception to informed consent.

TABLE 3-2 Subpart D Framework

Risk-Benefit	IRB Finding/Protection
No greater than minimal risk (§ 46.404)[a]	1. Adequate provision made for informed consent, minimizing risks, and protecting privacy and confidentiality
More than minimal risk but either 1. An intervention with prospect of direct benefit for the individual or 2. A monitoring procedure likely to contribute to individual's well-being (§ 46.405)	1. Risk justified by benefit 2. Relation of risk to benefit is at least as favorable to subjects as in alternative approaches 3. Adequate provision made for informed consent, minimizing risks, and protecting privacy and confidentiality
More than minimal risk and no prospect of direct benefit but likely to yield generalizable knowledge about the subject's disorder or condition (§46.406)	1. Risk is a minor increase over minimal 2. Intervention or procedure is "reasonably commensurate with those inherent in their actual or expected situations" 3. The generalizable knowledge is "of vital importance for the understanding or amelioration of the subjects' disorder or condition" 4. Adequate provision made for informed consent, minimizing risks, and protecting privacy and confidentiality
Research not otherwise approvable but presents an "opportunity to understand, prevent, or alleviate a serious problem affecting the health or welfare of children" (§ 46.407)	*IRB finds:* 1. The research does, in fact, provide such an opportunity: *If the Secretary, after consultation with experts and opportunity for public review and comment, finds:* 1. Research will be conducted in accord with sound ethical principles 2. Adequate provision is made for informed consent, minimizing risks, and protecting privacy and confidentiality

[a] Note that minimal risk is defined in the same manner in Subpart D as in Subpart A (the Common Rule). The definition of minimal risk in Subpart C is different, as noted previously.
SOURCE: 45 C.F.R. Part 46, Subpart D.

the FDA regulations on protection for human research subjects are interesting primarily because of their scope and secondarily because of the reason why they do not contain a Subpart C.

Unlike DHHS as a whole, which only enforces its requirements in DHHS-funded research, the FDA has the authority to regulate a broad category of research governing medical treatments and devices regardless of the source of funding or the FDA's ability to control the subjects or direct the research. Specifically, the FDA's regulations apply to "all clinical investigations regulated by the [FDA][31] . . . as well as clinical investigations that support applications for research or marketing permits for products regulated by the [FDA]."[32] Thus, the FDA's regulations reach all research regarding the application, safety, and effectiveness of any drug, medical device, biological product, nutritional supplement, food or color additive, or other product subject to FDA approval. Moreover, because compliance with the FDA standards is required of all research that will be used to support an effort to gain FDA approval, it is in the interest of the research sponsor who intends to use the research to support an FDA application to use care in developing research protocols that comply with these regulations; supportive research can be rendered worthless because of noncompliance.

Nevertheless, although FDA regulations contain a Subpart D governing children as research subjects that is similar to Subpart D of the DHHS regulations, the FDA regulations do not contain a Subpart C governing research with prisoners as subjects. The FDA developed such regulations and posted them in the *Federal Register* in 1978, and it adopted a final rule on the regulations applicable to prisoner research in 1980.[33] Before the regulations became effective, however, a group of prisoners brought suit in federal court to have these regulations declared invalid as violating the prisoners' rights to participate in medical research. The FDA decided to delay the effective date of the regulations until five months after the court's decision in the case, and it ultimately settled the case by declaring the regulations indefinitely suspended. According to the notices posted in the *Federal Register,* research was being conducted on a small number of persons in a small number of prisons, so it was not worth the FDA's time and expense to litigate the suit to uphold the validity of the regulations.[34] Since then, the indefinitely suspended regulations have been removed from the Code of Federal Regulations, and Subpart C of 21 C.F.R. Part 50 is simply "reserved."

---

[31]The clinical investigations regulated by the FDA are those involving drugs and medical devices approved solely for investigational use because their safety and effectiveness cannot otherwise be reasonably ensured.

[32]Given the different scope of the FDA regulations compared with the Common Rule, the clinical investigation covered by the FDA regulations is limited to "any experiment that involves a test article and one or more human subjects" that is either regulated by the FDA or the results of which is intended to be submitted to the FDA, and it does not apply to nonclinical laboratory studies [Electronic Records; Electronic Signatures. 21 C.F.R. § 50.1(c), (2000)]. *Human subject* is also defined differently as "an individual who is or becomes a participant in research, either as a recipient of the test article or as a control" (Electronic Records; Electronic Signatures 21 C.F.R. § 50.1[g]).

[33]45 Fed. Reg. 36386 (May 30, 1980).

[34]46 Fed. Reg. 18951 (March 27, 1981); 46 Fed. Reg. 35085 (July 7, 1981).

DOJ Regulations

As a general matter, the DOJ (including its research and development arm, the National Institute of Justice) has adopted the Common Rule at 28 C.F.R. Part 46 (NIJ).[35] With respect to research involving prisoners in the custody of the BOP, however, the DOJ was concerned that Subpart C did not adequately address the level of risk in the third category of Subpart C (research on conditions particularly affecting prisoners as a class) and did not fully consider the difficulty in ensuring confidentiality of prisoners' personal information in the prison environment. For those reasons, as well as to conform the review process to other BOP and local prison procedures, the department developed its own regulations that apply to prisoners in BOP custody. The resulting BOP policy is found in two separate program statements: PS 1070.07 regarding research (BOP, 1999)[36] and PS 6031.01 regarding patient care (BOP, 2005).

Addressing the DOJ's concern about the kinds of research allowed, the BOP regulations forbid nontherapeutic medical research or pharmaceutical trials and cosmetic research. However, they do allow the following:

- therapeutic medical research, including clinical trials, "that may be warranted for a specific inmate's diagnosis or treatment" if the research is (1) approved by the prison's medical director, (2) conducted with prior written consent, and (3) "conducted under conditions approved by the Department of Health and Human Services," which presumably means that it is conducted in accordance with Subpart C;
- research regarding disease prevalence, response to accepted therapeutic interventions, behavioral, and other nonmedical research pursuant to the program statement on research. (See Table 3-3.)

Thus, research of medical treatments, including clinical trials of pharmaceuticals and medical devices, is either not permitted or, at least in theory, is conducted in compliance with Subpart C requirements. Research involving federal prisoners is conducted pursuant to regulations other than Subpart C only when it involves behavioral, epidemiological, or other nonmedical research.[37] Of course, prisoners in BOP custody account for less than 10 percent of the total incarcerated population, so the remainder of

---

[35] According to the Bureau of Justice Statistics (2005), federal prisons have not housed any inmates under age 18 since 1999, and accordingly, there are no separate regulations dealing with juvenile prisoners.

[36] This policy is codified, minus interpretive commentary, as a regulation at 28 C.F.R. Part 512.

[37] It is not clear from the BOP program statement whether nonpharmacological treatments for mental illness are considered medical research.

TABLE 3-3 Summary of Regulations Applicable to Research Even If It Is Not Federally Funded by Any Agency

Variable	Federal		State	
	Adult	Juvenile	Adult	Juvenile
Medical treatment Nontherapeutic/Cosmetic	Not permitted	Not permitted	FDA Subpart A	FDA Subpart A, FDA Subpart D, state policy
Pharmaceutical/medical device—therapeutic (for specific inmate's condition)	DOJ Subpart A [Applicable DHHS regulations incorporated by reference in BOP policy] FDA Subpart A	DOJ Subpart A [Applicable DHHS regulations incorporated by reference in BOP policy] FDA Subpart A FDA Subpart D	FDA Subpart A, state policy	FDA Subpart A, FDA Subpart D, state policy
Non-FDA-regulated medical treatment—therapeutic	DOJ Subpart A [Applicable DHHS regulations incorporated by reference in BOP policy]	DOJ Subpart A [Applicable DHHS regulations incorporated by reference in BOP policy]	Varies by state	Varies by state
Nonmedical Research	DOJ Subpart A BOP research policy	DOJ Subpart A BOP research policy	Varies by state	Varies by state

NOTE: FDA, Food and Drug Administration; DOJ, Department of Justice; DHHS, Department of Health and Human Services; BOP, Bureau of Prisons.

SOURCES: 28 C.F.R. Part 46, Subpart A; BOP, 1999; 21 C.F.R. Part 50, Subparts A, D; 45 C.F.R. Part 46, Subparts A, C.

incarcerated persons (of whom nearly two-thirds are housed in state prisons and over one-third in local jails) are not covered by these regulations.[38]

The BOP program statement on research contains many protections similar to those in Subparts A and C but with more detail on the subject of confidentiality, some differences in informed consent, and more concern that the research protocol be approved by all levels of prison administration.

Confidentiality

The BOP research program statement specifically provides that personal identifiable information may not be released without the subject's prior written consent and, in particular, may not be admitted as evidence or used for any other purpose in any judicial, administrative, or legislative proceeding. At the same time, as part of the process of informed consent, the subject must be told that confidentiality may not be guaranteed as to information that the subject intends to commit a crime, harm him- or herself or someone else, or leave a facility in which he or she is incarcerated.

The concern for confidentiality of records also places specific limits on the researcher. Records that contain information that may be traced to an individual generally must not be placed on any electronic retrieval system. Additionally, nonemployee researchers can only have access to BOP records if the information does not identify the individual and will only be used "as a statistical research or reporting record," unless the information is available under the Freedom of Information Act.

Informed Consent

BOP policies relating to informed and voluntary consent appear to have been tailored to their assessment of the requirements of the prison setting. First, the disclosures that are required for informed consent are modified slightly from the Common Rule requirements. In some cases, the disclosure is required to be more specific. For instance, where the Common Rule requires disclosure of "which procedures are experimental," the BOP regulations require a somewhat more specific disclosure of "the purpose of each procedure" and further require "identification of the principal investigator(s)," which is not specifically required by the Common Rule. As noted previously, the program statement regarding confidentiality contains an exception for when an inmate threatens to harm him- or herself or others, or to leave the facility. Certain other information that is required

---

[38]Additionally, all 2,477 prisoners under age 18 in custody of the BOP are housed in state facilities, where no uniform set of regulations governs protections of human research subjects.

under the Common Rule's informed consent disclosure requirement, such as alternative treatments and information regarding treatment for research-related injury, is not expressly required to be disclosed under the BOP program statement on research,[39] perhaps because such disclosures are less relevant in a setting in which medical treatment is controlled by the institution. Nevertheless, the BOP program statement allows the possibility that other information might be required "as needed to describe adequately the nature and risks of the research."

More striking on the issue of informed (and voluntary) consent is the BOP program statement's treatment of incentives for participating in research. Where Subpart C provides a standard against which to measure incentives—that incentives should not be "of such a magnitude that his or her ability to weigh the risks of the research against the value of such advantages in the limited choice environment of the prison is impaired"[40]— BOP policy simply forbids any incentives for research subjects in BOP custody. However, "soft drinks and snacks to be consumed at the test setting may be offered," and steps may be taken to avoid prisoners being put at a disadvantage (e.g., because of work schedule) by participating in the research.

Review of Research Protocols

Review under the BOP research program statement reflects further BOP control over the research protocol and review process. The review is conducted at three levels. First, an application meeting the detailed informational requirements set forth in the policy is submitted to the warden, who convenes a local research review board (LRRB).[41] The LRRB not only reviews the proposal for compliance with the research policy but also consults with prison operational staff and evaluates the research protocol's compliance with prison policies. The warden takes the LRRB review, formulates recommendations, and forwards the application to the regional director, who then sends the application to a central IRB, called the Bureau Research Review Board (BRRB). After BRRB review and recommendations, the chief of the Office of Research and Evaluation (ORE), who chairs

---

[39]Because DOJ's adoption of the Common Rule renders the informed consent requirements applicable to all research conducted by, supported by, or subject to regulation by DOJ, the Common Rule's informed consent requirements should nevertheless control (28 C.F.R. § 46.101[a]; *cf.* 28 C.F.R. § 46.116–117).

[40]45 C.F.R. § 46.305(a)(2).

[41]If the request is for multisite research, the request goes to the Office of Research and Evaluation, which administers all BOP research, for determination of a proper review process.

the BRRB, sends the proposal to the director of the BOP, who has the final authority to approve or disapprove all research proposals. Finally, the warden has the opportunity to review the project in its final form, consult with the LRRB, and request reconsideration if necessary. Furthermore, each research project is reviewed on an annual basis, and the director has the authority to terminate a project at any time if it violates the policy or "may prove detrimental to the inmate population."

Perhaps in recognition of the difficulty of convening a fully qualified local IRB, and because the LRRB's decision is always reviewed by the BRRB, membership requirements for LRRBs are not as strict as in Subpart C and, in fact, need not necessarily meet the requirements of an IRB as set out in Subpart A. As a general rule, the LRRB "is encouraged, but not required" to meet the membership requirements set forth in the Common Rule. However, the program statement specifies that the LRRB must have the chief psychologist at the prison as the chairperson, and representatives of departments that will be involved with the project must serve as consultants to the LRRB. When the facility allows more than one research project per year, it is "specially encouraged" to require membership, including a prisoner's representative, that would comply with DHHS's Subpart C.

The BRRB is necessarily an IRB and, as described by the research policy requirements, meets Subpart C requirements. The BRRB is composed of the chief of the ORE, who serves as the chair; at least four other members; and one alternate, who serves in the event of a conflict of interest of a member. A majority cannot be BOP employees, and the membership must include an individual with legal expertise (usually someone from the BOP general counsel's office) and "a representative for inmates whom the Director determines is able to identify with inmate concerns and evaluate objectively a research proposal's impact on, and relevance to, inmates and to the correctional process" (who is generally a prison chaplain). The implementation guidelines further specify that the members shall have varying backgrounds, genders, and racial/cultural makeup, shall not be associated with the conduct of the research, and shall include at least one scientist and one nonscientist. Thus, the research program statement's description of the BRRB meets Subpart C requirements and also sets out a few additional requirements not contained in Subpart C.

Overall, the BOP guidelines are a useful tool for comparison with Subpart C because they govern all research involving prisoners in federal custody, whether or not it is funded by the DOJ (or DHHS). Moreover, they reflect the BOP's decisions regarding which aspects of Subpart C are not feasible or are unnecessary and which aspects are inadequate, because they either do not provide enough protection for subjects in the prison environment or are not specific enough about what is required.

ANALYSIS

The SACHRP Subpart C Subcommittee requested that the IOM consider the limited reach of the DHHS regulations under the current regime. The committee agrees that the limited reach of the regulations, combined with the patchwork of different regulatory schemes, inhibits the impact of the regulations to the detriment of prisoners involved in research.

Recommendation 3.1 *Establish uniform guidelines for all human subjects research involving prisoners.* **Congress should mandate a uniform set of guidelines for human research participant protection programs[42] for research involving prisoners.**

All human subjects research involving prisoners should be regulated by the same ethical standards irrespective of the source of funding, the supporting agency, or the type of correctional facility (federal, state, local, or private) or program that houses the prisoner. Under the current system of research regulation, this would mean that all 17 federal agencies that are signatories to the Common Rule, any additional federal agencies, and any nonfederal sponsors of research would be required to comply with a newly drafted subpart C.[43] All research involving prisoners, therefore, would be registered with the OHRP. There is no justification for variability across agencies and facilities regarding their approaches to protecting the rights, health, and dignity of prisoners participating in human subjects research, individuals who are among the most vulnerable human subjects of research.

The primary policy forming the basis of the DHHS regulations regarding the protection of human subjects is at 42 U.S.C. § 3515b (Prohibition on Funding Certain Experiments Involving Human Participants):

> None of the funds appropriated by this Act or subsequent Departments of Labor, Health and Human Services, and Education, and Related Agencies Appropriations Acts shall be used to pay for any research program or project or any program, project, or course which is of an experimental nature, or any other activity involving human participants, which is determined by the Secretary or a court of competent jurisdiction to present a

---

[42] The term *human research participant protection program* (HRPPP) is used throughout this report to mean the network of entities with direct responsibility for the safety of those enrolled in the studies carried out under its purview. The HRPPP most often includes the research organization, the study sponsor, investigator, IRB, and, when relevant, the data safety monitoring board (IOM, 2003). In the contexts described in this report, prison research subject advocates would be an important part of this network as well.

[43] Federal regulation of state and private research would be constitutionally permissible by using, e.g., the federal spending power. See, e.g., *South Dakota v. Dole*, 483 U.S. 203, 211 (1987), upholding the constitutionality of a federal statute conditioning states' receipt of federal funds on adoption of a minimum drinking age of 21.

danger to the physical, mental, or emotional well-being of a participant or subject of such program, project, or course, without the written, informed consent of each participant or subject, or a participant's parents or legal guardian, if such participant or subject is under eighteen years of age. The Secretary shall adopt appropriate regulations respecting this section.[44]

In addition, the Public Health Service Act contains more specific statutes requiring IRB review as a precondition to funding.[45] Because the primary statute is explicit about being limited to research funded by these departments, the comprehensive regulations promulgated by the DHHS regarding human participants are, in part, limited to research funded by the DHHS, which the secretary has full and unquestionable authority to regulate.

However, most of the Common Rule was also drafted to apply to research not funded by the DHHS but regulated by the department.[46] The catch is that the regulation defines research subject to regulation quite narrowly as "those research activities for which a federal department or agency has specific responsibility for regulating *as a research activity* (for example, investigational new drug requirements administered by the FDA)."[47] Regulation in such a narrow area is likewise on quite solid ground as a natural extension of its authority to regulate the research activity.

The jurisdictional limits of these regulations demonstrate a conservative approach to regulation, limiting the scope of the regulations to those areas where the DHHS's authority is unquestionable. Two issues remain: whether the DHHS presently has some implicit authority to regulate beyond these two narrow areas (if it were willing to go beyond the specific authorization) and, if not, whether Congress can grant it such authority.

Existing Authority for Broader Regulation

The authority for any regulation promulgated by an executive department such as the DHHS must be traced to a statute authorizing the DHHS to create regulations in that area. In turn, the statutory authority for the executive department to create rules and regulations in a certain subject area must be traced to a specific constitutional authority for the federal government to oversee that area, because the federal government has no general power to regulate. The DHHS authorizing statute is not entirely clear (although it does not foreclose the possibility of regulation), but it is

---

[44]Prohibition on Funding Certain Experiments Involving Human Participants. 42 U.S.C. § 3515(b).
[45]42 U.S.C. §§ 289, 289a–1.
[46]45 C.F.R. § 46.101(a)(2).
[47]45 C.F.R. § 46.102(e) (emphasis added).

clear that Congress could, if it so chose, expressly expand DHHS's authority to regulate human research subjects protection.

The DHHS's authorizing statute is actually an enactment of the 1953 reorganization plan transmitted by President Eisenhower, transferring the responsibilities of the Federal Security Agency to the newly created DHEW.[48] The DHEW was created "to improve the administration of the vital health, education, and social-security functions now being carried on in the Federal Security Agency."[49] The SSA and the Department of Education were originally agencies within the DHEW; the Department of Education was created in 1979 (at which point the department was renamed DHHS), and the SSA was separated from the DHHS in 1994. Thus, the remaining function of the DHHS is dedicated to various health- and safety-related activities.

Can the DHHS Be Granted Broader Authority?

Nevertheless, for reasons similar to why the FDA is constitutionally possible, it is possible for the DHHS to be given authority to regulate research involving human subjects.

The Constitution of the United States

The congressional spending power derives from the federal Constitution, Article I, Section 8, clause 1, which provides in pertinent part:

> Section 8. The Congress shall have power to lay and collect taxes, duties, imposts and excises, to pay the debts and provide for the common defense and general welfare of the United States; but all duties, imposts and excises shall be uniform throughout the United States. . . .

The Scope of the Congressional Spending Power

For generations, the "spending power" has provided the legal basis for legislation touching upon myriad subjects. The court has long recognized the broad authority conferred under the spending clause. "[W]hen money is spent to promote the general welfare, the concept of welfare or the opposite is shaped by Congress. . . ." *Helvering v. Davis*, 301 U.S. 619 (1937).

South Dakota v. Dole, 483 U.S. 203 (1987), remains the primary precedent for the authority of Congress to pass spending clause legislation. In

---

[48]Establishment of Department; effective date. 42 U.S.C. § 3501.
[49]Reorganization Plan No. 1 of 1953, 5 U.S.C. App. 1, 18 Fed. Reg. 2053, 67 Stat. 631 (March 12, 1953).

that case, the Supreme Court upheld a federal statute that reduced federal highway funding to states with a minimum drinking age below 21. The court found that the legislation was sufficiently related to the federal interest in promoting safe highway travel and concluded that the statute did not exceed Congress's spending power under the U.S. Constitution, Article I, Section 8, clause 1, *Id.* at 208–209. The Supreme Court affirmed the broad scope of the spending power, though it acknowledged that congressional authority is limited in the following ways:[50]

> The first of these limitations is derived from the language of the Constitution itself: the exercise of the spending power must be in pursuit of "the general welfare." In considering whether a particular expenditure is intended to serve general public purposes, courts should defer substantially to the judgment of Congress. Second, we have required that if Congress desires to condition the States' receipt of federal funds, it "must do so unambiguously. . . ., enabl[ing] the States to exercise their choice knowingly, cognizant of the consequences of their participation." Third, our cases have suggested (without significant elaboration) that conditions on federal grants might be illegitimate if they are unrelated "to the federal interest in particular national projects or programs." Finally, we have noted that other constitutional provisions may provide an independent bar to the conditional grant of federal funds.

South Dakota v. Dole, 483 U.S. 203, 207–208 (citations and footnote omitted). Considering the legislation at issue—limiting the drinking age—was considered sufficiently related not only to the general welfare and to the states' receipt of federal highway funds, these "limitations" are evidently not exceedingly rigorous. In sum, it is clear that Congress has well established and broad authority to condition federal funding upon acceptance of specified conditions that, in a general sense, pertain to the purpose of the legislation.[51]

---

[50]A more recent spending clause case is *Rumsfeld v. Forum for Academic and Institutional Rights (FAIR)*, WL 521237 (U.S. Sup. Ct. March 6, 2006). This case held, among other things, that universities that accept federal money could not refuse to allow the military to recruit on campus, even if military hiring and retention policy violated the university's own regulations on sexual orientation discrimination. However, this was based on both the spending power (Art. I Sec. 8, Cl 1), and the power to raise armies (Art. I, Sec. 8, Cl. 12). The Court held that Congress had the constitutional authority (i.e., in order to raise armies) to directly impose restrictions regarding access of military recruiters, regardless of funding, so it certainly had the power to do so as a condition of providing the funding. As such, it does not provide a good test of the limits of spending clause authority.

[51]In the recent assisted suicide case, *Gonzales v. Oregon*, 126 S. Ct. 904, 923 (2006), the United States Supreme Court acknowledged the power of Congress to "set uniform national standards in regulating health and safety," including (hypothetically) the practice of medicine. The Court ultimately rejected the federal government's argument that the Controlled Substances Act trumped the authority of doctors to prescribe lethal doses of medication under

The spending power is a familiar basis for congressional action. There are numerous examples of legislation—for example, Title VI of the Civil Rights Act, Title IX of the Education Amendments, § 504 of the Rehabilitation Act, and The Religious Land Use and Institutionalized Persons Act of 2000, 42 U.S.C. § 2000cc, *et seq.* (2000)—all of which contain conditions based on the spending clause power. One particularly pertinent example of spending power legislation is the Prison Rape Elimination Act of 2003 [PREA] (42 U.S.C. § 15601, *et. seq.*). Section 15605 (d) of PREA provides in pertinent part:

(d) Applications.

(1) In general. To request a grant under this section, the chief executive of a State shall submit an application to the Attorney General at such time, in such manner, and accompanied by such information as the Attorney General may require.

(2) Contents. Each application required by paragraph (1) shall—

(A) include the certification of the chief executive that the State receiving such grant—

(i) has adopted all national prison rape standards that, as of the date on which the application was submitted, have been promulgated under this Act [42 U.S.C. § 15601, et seq.] . . .

This legislation conditions the release of federal funds upon fairly demanding and relatively intrusive terms, but because of the conditional nature of spending power legislation, it likely would withstand a legal challenge under principles articulated by the U.S. Supreme Court.[52]

Spending power legislation could easily be used to require compliance with the DHHS regulations in state as well as federal institutions. Every state receives federal assistance for corrections (U.S. Census Bureau, 2006), and that assistance is itself based, at least in part, on Spending Clause legislation.[53] Hence, if Congress were so inclined, it could enact legislation (or amend the existing legislation) to require the state agency's adoption of a regulatory scheme governing the involvement of prisoners in research as a

---

state law because the federal statute did not reveal a congressional intent to override traditional state regulation of medical practice. *See also, Gonzales v. Raich*, 125 S. Ct. 2195 (2005) (noting that Congress can regulate the channels, the instrumentalities, and activities that substantially affect interstate commerce).

[52]No cases could be found in which Congress's authority to pass the PREA had been challenged.

[53]The legislation is the Edward Byrne Memorial State and Local Law Enforcement Assistance Program, PL 100-690 (BJS, 2001).

condition for receiving the federal funds. There are many rationales that would likely be sufficient justification for such legislation. For example, the federal government's interest in "set[ting] uniform national standards in regulating health and safety," as articulated in *Gonzales v. Oregon*, 126 S. Ct. 904, 923 (2006), and in particular, in ensuring reliable results from health sciences research, would be sufficient. This assisted suicide case addressed Congress's more limited authority to directly impose requirements, but the interest articulated by the Court would be sufficient to impose conditional requirements. Additionally, the PREA was based in part on the federal government's interest both in ensuring states do not violate prisoners' federal civil and constitutional rights by their deliberate indifference to the problem of prison rape, and its interest in ensuring the "effectiveness and efficiency" of federally funded research and grant programs relating to health care and other prisoner-related research, which (Congress stated) were compromised (directly and indirectly) by state officials' failure to monitor and address the problem of prison rape.[54] Clearly these rationales would also support legislation requiring states to impose (at a minimum) the ethical limitations on research required by the DHHS as a condition of receiving the same federal funding.

The regulations could only be imposed in this manner if the states did in fact accept the federal funding. However, because the federal government only seeks to require the states to establish the same ethical regulations as those promulgated by the DHHS, and not to spend money on any new programs, the committee is confident that the states would choose simply to enact the DHHS regulations rather than foregoing substantial federal monies to avoid compliance.

Alternatives to Comprehensive Regulation

If a change in the statutory authority for these regulations is not possible (either constitutionally or practically), the DHHS might, at a minimum, work with the FDA (and perhaps the BOP) to develop regulations for research involving prisoners, which the FDA might then consider adopting (either in whole or in a modified form) for all research within its jurisdiction. The result would be uniform regulation by the FDA of all research relating to pharmaceuticals, medical devices, and other products within the FDA's jurisdiction, both in state and federal prisons, supplemented by the DHHS's regulation of federally supported research. Although not ideal, this framework may still reduce the amount of patchwork regulation applicable to research involving prisoners and be a step toward uniformity of ethical

---

[54] 42 U.S.C. § 15601 (13–14).

standards used in biomedical research in the prison setting. However, the more desirable approach, which the committee recommends (i.e., to establish a uniform set of guidelines for all research involving prisoners), will require congressional action.

REFERENCES

BJS (Bureau of Justice Statistics). 2001. *Justice Variable Passthrough Data, 1997.* NCJ 190359. Washington, DC: U.S. Department of Justice.
BJS. 2005. *Prison and Jail Inmates at Midyear 2004.* NCJ 208801. Washington, DC: U.S. Department of Justice.
BOP (Bureau of Prisons). 1999. *Program Statement 1070.07.* [Online]. Available: http://www.bop.gov/DataSource/execute/dsPolicyLoc [accessed March 27, 2006].
BOP. 2005. *Program Statement 6031.01.* [Online]. Available: http://www.bop.gov/DataSource/execute/dsPolicyLoc [accessed March 27, 2006].
Gorey J. 2005. *Statement of Task: Committee on Ethical Considerations to DHHS Regulations for Protection of Prisoners Involved in Research.* Presented at the Institute of Medicine Meeting 4 (October 19, 2005) of the Committee on Ethical Considerations to DHHS Regulations for Protection of Prisoners Involved in Research, Washington, DC.
IOM (Institute of Medicine). 2003. *Responsible Research: A Systems Approach to Protecting Research Participants.* Washington, DC: The National Academies Press.
IOM. 2004. *The Ethical Conduct of Clinical Research Involving Children.* Washington, DC: The National Academies Press.
NBAC (National Bioethics Advisory Commission). 2001. *Ethical and Policy Issues in Research Involving Human Participants.* [Online]. Available: http://www.georgetown.edu/research/nrcbl/nbac/human/overvol1.pdf [access-ed March 27, 2006].
NCPHSBBR (National Commission for the Protection of Human Subjects of Biomedical and Behavioral Research). 1976. *Report and Recommendations: Research Involving Prisoners.* Washington, D.C. U.S. Department of Health, Education, and Welfare, Pub. No. (OS) 76-131.
NIJ (National Institute of Justice). *Introduction to Human Subject and Privacy Protections at the National Institute of Justice* [Online]. Available: http://www.ojp.usdoj.gov/nij/funding/humansubjects/hs_01.html [accessed April 11, 2006].
PHS (Public Health Service). 1966. Clinical investigations using human subjects. In: *Final Report* (Supplemental Vol. I). Washington, DC: U.S. Government Printing Office. Pp. 475–476.
SACHRP (Secretary's Advisory Committee on Human Research Protections). 2005. Report of the Subpart C Subcommittee to SACHRP, April 18, 2005 [Online]. Available: http://www.hhs.gov/ohrp/sachrp/mtgings/present/SubpartC.htm [accessed March 27, 2006].
U.S. Census Bureau. 2006. *Federal Aid to States for Fiscal Year 2004.* U.S. Government Printing Office, Washington, D.C.

4

Defining Prisoners and Correctional Settings

This chapter provides the committee's recommendation for a new definition of the term *prisoner*, which considers the contexts, or "places," relevant to research with prisoners. The goal of this definition is to expand the reach of the regulatory procedures and oversight mechanisms recommended in this report to the fuller population of individuals who are under restricted liberty and, therefore, face potentially greater risks than the general population when participating in research. It identifies the personal interests that may be violated because of research participants' status as prisoners[1] and the settings in which protections against such potential violations are required. As a point of departure, this chapter briefly reviews the ethical foundations that underpin research regulations and current regulatory language relevant to prisoner settings and notes the relevant ethical principles that led the committee to expand the definition of the term *prisoner* for purposes of protecting those involved in research.

ETHICAL FOUNDATIONS OF CURRENT RESEARCH REGULATIONS

The ethical foundations of research protections in the United States are based on two key ethical considerations identified by the National Com-

---

[1] Using the place-centric term *prisoner* to define individuals also found outside of the typical prison setting may be confusing to some readers. This definition is aimed, however, at a systemic approach to oversight of research involving those subject to restricted liberty through the criminal justice system.

mission for the Protection of Human Subjects of Biomedical and Behavioral Research (NCPHSBBR, 1976). They are respect for persons and justice. The principle of respect for persons invokes the protection of individuals' autonomy and personal dignity and requires that informed and voluntary consent be obtained from subjects before their involvement in research. This basic principle is often difficult to implement in a correctional setting because of the power dynamics and inherent deprivations within such a setting, especially with respect to voluntariness. Privacy and confidentiality play central roles within the principle of respect for persons as well. The principle of justice concerns the fair treatment of persons and groups. In the context of research involving prisoners, justice requires that prisoners not bear a disproportionate share of the research burden without a commensurate share of benefit, and also that prisoners have the freedom to decide questions of research participation for themselves. Justice becomes particularly important to encouraging research on a system that disproportionately affects the disadvantaged and racial and ethnic minorities (Chapter 2).

The competence and freedom of a prisoner to make a choice as well as the reality of privacy protection through confidentiality can be hampered in any of the correctional settings that restrict liberty, whether by the correctional officers or other prisoners within the prison walls or by probation officers, for example, in the community. If, for instance, researchers plan to study the effectiveness of electronic monitoring as compared with parole supervision, a system of oversight should be in place to protect the persons involved in the study—who currently are not covered under Subpart C protections. An expanded definition of prisoner is offered in this chapter. A fuller description of the ethical framework followed by the committee is found in Chapter 5.

CURRENT REGULATIONS PERTINENT TO PLACES OF PRISONER RESEARCH

In Subpart C of 45 C.F.R. § 46.303(c), the term *prisoner* is defined as:

Any individual involuntarily confined or *detained in a penal institution*. The term is intended to encompass individuals sentenced to an *institution* under a criminal or civil statute, individuals *detained in other facilities* by virtue of statutes or commitment procedures which provide alternatives to criminal prosecution or incarceration in a penal institution, and *individuals detained* pending arraignment, trial, or sentencing [emphases added].

The current regulations clearly emphasize custodial confinement as a consequence of the state's exercise of its power via the criminal justice system. The potential impact of confinement in highly controlled institutional settings on individual autonomy is explicitly recognized in other sections of the current regulations. For example, 45 C.F.R. § 46.305 (a)(2)–(7) includes the following regarding the issue of voluntariness to ensure that the subject's participation in the research is not coerced:

- any possible advantages accruing to the prisoner through his or her participation in research, when compared to the general living conditions, medical care, quality of food, amenities and opportunity for earnings in the prison are not of such magnitude that his or her ability to weigh the risks of the research against the value of such advantages in a limited choice environment of the prison is impaired;
- the risks involved in the research are commensurate with risks that would be accepted by nonprisoner volunteers; and
- adequate assurance exists that parole boards will not take into account participation in making parole decisions, and prisoners will be informed that participation will have no effect on parole.

Institutional review boards (IRBs), however, have received guidance from the Office for Human Research Protections (OHRP) that suggests the definition may include parolees but not probationers. There is clearly confusion as to the parameters of the definition as it stands today. The important issue, as noted by the commission is that "prisoners are, as a consequence of being prisoners, more subject to coerced choice and more readily available for the imposition of burdens which others will not willingly bear" (NCPHSBRR, 1976).

CORRECTIONAL SETTINGS ENCOMPASS MORE THAN PRISONS AND JAILS

Although this committee believes that research in correctional institutional settings should be subject to federal regulations, it also believes that the present emphasis on custodial detention is too narrow and results in depriving many other justice-involved individuals of human subjects protections appropriate to prisoner research participants. Several tables in Chapter 2 provide details relevant to this issue. Table 2-1 provides a broad snapshot of the number of individuals within the correctional population and notes that, as of December 2003, only 2.1 million of the 7 million total correctional population were in prisons and jails (Bureau of Justice Statistics [BJS], 2004). The rest had restricted liberties but outside the razor wire, in programs such as those listed in Table 4-1. These 4.9 million individuals (up from 1 million in 1978) require special protections when participating in research as well. Table 4-2 on pages 106–107 illustrates the vast array of incarceration options within the state of California and details a long list of alternatives to incarceration offered, including community service, electronic monitoring, and probation.

TABLE 4-1 Alternatives to Incarceration That May Be Available to Offenders

Program	Description
Bail supervision programs	While awaiting trial, the accused, rather than being held in custody, is supervised by a member of the community.
Alternative measures programs	The offender is diverted from the criminal justice system before or after being charged. The offender enters into a kind of contractual agreement to answer for the crime. The agreement can include community service work, personal service to the victim, charitable donation, counseling, or any other reasonable task or condition.
Restitution programs	The offender must pay back the victim for damages or loss.
Community service order	A condition on a probation order, or a separate disposition in the case of young offenders, that requires the offender to perform work in the community.
Probation	The offender is supervised in the community and follows the set of conditions (rules) set out in the probation order. Conditions of probation include keeping the peace, good behavior, obeying the law, and reporting regularly to a probation officer and may include a range of other, optional conditions.
Intensive supervision probation	An alternative to incarceration in the United States similar to probation but which involves more frequent surveillance and greater controls.
Electronic monitoring	Offenders are fitted with an anklet or bracelet that transmits signals of their whereabouts to the correctional officer, allowing offenders to continue with employment or education commitments in the community.
Parole	A period of conditional community supervision after a prison term. If the conditions of supervision are violated, the parolee can be returned to prison to serve any of the remaining portion of the sentence. • Discretionary parole exists when a parole board has authority to conditionally release prisoners based on a statutory or administrative determination of eligibility. • Mandatory parole generally occurs in jurisdictions using determinate sentencing statutes in which inmates are conditionally released from prison after serving a specified portion of their original sentence minus any good time earned.

SOURCE: Adapted from John Howard Society of Alberta, 1998.

According to the Bureau of Justice Statistics (BJS, 2001), among state parole discharges in 1999, 43 percent were returned to prison, a statistic relatively unchanged since 1990. This high rate of return to incarceration demonstrates that significant power dynamics continue for persons who are outside the prison walls but still under some form of community correction. Thus, the element of voluntariness in the informed consent process is conceptually very similar for persons incarcerated and those under some form of disposition alternative to incarceration.

A logical system of oversight would expand the definition of the term *prisoner* to include parole and probation. There is little logic in providing protections, as do the current regulations, to a person detained before trial and not yet convicted of a crime, but not to a person who has been convicted of a crime and is subject to incarceration because of violations of parole or probation conditions. The expanded definition is also supported by the findings of one researcher that policing whether conditions are violated (with more drug tests, more tracking of movement, and so on) is becoming more of a priority for parole officers than promoting reintegration (Petersilia, 2000).

DEFINITION OF PRISONER

This section articulates the committee's revised definition of prisoner, which places an emphasis on liberty restrictions resulting from the interactions with the criminal justice system. These restrictions include, but are not limited to, custodial confinement. The aim is to expand the reach of regulations to protect prisoners and others with restricted liberty.

Such an individual may be ordered to reside in settings in which freedom of movement is restricted (e.g., precinct holding pen, jail, prison, halfway house, or prerelease center) or in the community under constraints ordered by the criminal justice system (e.g., probation, parole or house arrest, or drug court sentence).

Recommendation 4.1 *Redefine the term* prisoners *to expand the reach of human subjects protections.* The Department of Health and Human Services and other relevant agencies that write, implement, or enforce regulations pertaining to research with prisoners should expand the definition of the term *prisoner* to include all settings, whether a correctional institution or a community setting, in which a person's liberty is restricted by the criminal justice system.

It is not custodial confinement alone that creates the potential for coercion and threatens an individual's right to autonomous decision mak-

TABLE 4-2 Descriptions of Various Criminal Justice Agencies and Facilities in California

Facility	Description	Reference
Facilities supervised by department of corrections or camps division		
State facilities		
State prisons	Provides housing for persons committed to DOC	California penal code § 2000–2048.7, 4504, welfare
City or county facilities		
City facilities	Facilities used to hold prisoners for examination or trial	California penal code § 4004.5
County jails, farms, camps	Persons committed on criminal process and detained for sentencing or already convicted	California penal code § 4000, 4050, 4100, 6031.4
Regional jail camps	Provides housing for persons sentenced to long jail terms	California penal code § 6300–6304
Youth correctional centers*	Provides treatment for young offenders assigned to CYA or DOC administration by the county	Penal code § 6250–6253, welfare and institutions code § 1850–1852
Community correctional centers*	Contact facilities providing housing for persons committed to DOC	Penal code § 6250–6253, welfare and institutions code § 3307–3310
Temporary emergency detention facilities*	CYA facilities for county commitments < 18 years of age	Welfare and institutions code § 1752.15
Conservation centers, forestry camps	Provides housing and work assignments for persons committed to DOC and CYA	Penal code § 6200–6203, welfare and institutions code § 1760.4
Restitution centers*	Provides housing for a select group of persons committed to DOC with restitution orders	Penal code § 6220–6228

Community treatment programs*	Prisoners mother program: houses women who have 1 or more children < 6 years of age	Penal code § 3410–3416
Facilities supervised by DOCs		
Community correctional reentry centers	Contract facilities for persons committed to DOC who have < 120 days left to serve	Penal code § 6258, 6259
Work furlough programs	Contract facilities for persons committed to DOC who are within 120 days of release	Penal code § 6260–6263
Halfway houses	Contract facilities in metropolitan areas used for persons committed to DOC who are addicted	Welfare and institutions code § 3153
Substance abuse correctional detention centers	Facilities operated jointly by the state and county with primary funding for construction from the state; persons committed to DOC will use ≥ 50% of total beds	Penal code § 6240–6242
Substance abuse treatment control unit	Provides housing for persons committed to DOC or CYA who are on parole and are addicted or in imminent danger of addiction; DOC and CYA facilities are separate; 90-day maximum stay; "dry-out beds"	Health and safety code § 11560–11563
Parole DOC	Authority and requirements related to DOC power to parole	Penal code § 3040–3071

NOTE: DOC, Department of Corrections; CYA, California Youth Authority.
*Facilities authorized by the California Penal Code for the placement of adult offenders, which provide additional community corrections alternatives.

ing (consent or refusal to participate in research). Rather, it is restrictions of freedom or the imposition of other sanctions by an agent of the criminal justice system who observes, scrutinizes, supervises or monitors, and ultimately determines the imposition of punishments for an individual's behavior. Persons on parole and others subject to limits on liberty or privacy are particularly vulnerable to the risk of reinstitutionalization based on decisions made by parole officers and other personnel of the criminal justice system. This threat to independence creates the potential for coercion and requires that prisoners be afforded additional levels of research protection as well. Note that persons who become prisoners while in a nonprisoner study must also be afforded special protections on entering a correctional setting.

A prisoner, for the purposes of this report, is any person whose liberty is restricted as a result of the interaction with the criminal justice system. Although the limitations on personal choice and control are perhaps most evident and oppressive in locked detention facilities (e.g., jails and prisons), the power differential between criminal justice agents and prisoners exists in many other contexts as well; the differences are a matter of degree. Individuals involved in a wide variety of community-based criminal justice programs, ranging from probation and parole to pre- or postadjudication diversions such as drug courts or mental health courts, are subject to coercion by the array of agents (e.g., parole or probation officers and diversion program counselors) who monitor the individuals' compliance with program requirements; such agents may also invoke further sanctions for program failure or noncompliance. Thus, one can fall within the protections recommended by this committee by virtue of being ordered by the criminal justice system to reside in a confined setting or, if living in the community, by virtue of the restrictions on individual decision making imposed by some part of the criminal justice system. To be a prisoner, there must be some nexus or connection between the setting or restricted liberty of the person and the action of the criminal justice system. For all individuals who meet this definition, regulations that govern research with prisoners should be applied. The current statutory or constitutional distinctions between the civil and criminal processes, which are evolving, are not sufficiently clear to allow an easy determination of whether the proposed systems of protection should apply. For instance, juveniles confined under orders of family court (or the equivalent, such as a juvenile court) likely require additional protections, but an analysis of their needs is beyond the scope of this report. If, however, they are transferred from the original jurisdiction of the family court (or the equivalent, such as a juvenile court) to the jurisdiction of a state or federal criminal court, then they would fall under this definition. Other types of confinement on the civil/criminal frontier that our definition encompasses include commitment by reason of an acquittal on the grounds

DEFINING PRISONERS AND CORRECTIONAL SETTINGS   109

of insanity and commitment as a sexual offender (e.g., so-called criminal sexual psychopaths or violent sexual predators) under various state laws. However, those persons whose confinement is the result of other civil proceedings, such as those designed to protect a mentally ill person from harming self or others, would not be covered by our system of protections. There are substantial ethical issues involved in conducting research with these populations that go beyond the scope of this report. Parallel studies, such as the ones undertaken by this committee, may be needed to explore ethical issues of research involving these groups.

DELINEATION OF SETTINGS

In the interest of clarity, the committee specifies an array of settings in which regulations governing research with prisoners should apply, as well as a brief listing of settings for which the recommended regulations are not considered necessary. Some cases may arise that are not specifically addressed, and these must be decided on a case-by-case basis. Further discussion of research gradation and level of risk, which determine the study design and monitoring safeguards required, is provided in Chapter 6.

When Proposed Regulations Should Apply

Settings and situations in which proposed regulations governing research with prisoners should apply are as follows:

- state or federal prisons (including, e.g., camps, farms, boot camps);
- any jail or detention facility (e.g., municipal, city, county, federal);
- any community-based criminal justice supervision program such as bail or bond supervision, parole, or probation; community correctional reentry centers; work furlough programs; halfway houses; or similar programs;
- any community-based alternative disposition program, including (but not limited to) restitution programs, community service programs, or participation in other activities deemed to constitute punishment or other mandatory activities resulting from being sentenced;
- inpatient or outpatient psychiatric treatment settings if an individual is involuntarily committed as a result of a finding of not guilty by reason of insanity;
- treatment settings for any person who, having served a sentence for a sex offense, is subsequently deemed to meet criteria for involuntary commitment under various criminal sexual psychopath or violent sexual predator (or equivalent) statutes in a civil proceeding;
- placement or participation in a community residential drug, alcohol,

or mental health treatment program, day program, or partial-day program if mandated by a criminal court as part of an order for conditional release or sentencing; and

- participation in a drug court, mental health court, or other criminal justice specialty court that functions to divert arrested or convicted individuals into substance abuse or mental health service programs.

When Proposed Regulations Should Not Apply

Settings and situation in which proposed regulations governing research with prisoners would not apply are as follows:

- individuals committed to involuntary inpatient psychiatric or substance abuse treatment, or to any form of mandated community treatment, by the order of a juvenile, civil, or probate court (as stated earlier in this chapter, juveniles likely need additional protections, but this committee was not equipped to address their specific needs);
- individuals living in a noncustodial community setting who meet the above definition of prisoner but whose status as a prisoner is not relevant or related to their enrollment in a particular community-based research project. This means that the criminal justice agent or agency having supervisory jurisdiction over the individual was not involved in the plans for study enrollment, and the study itself does not include prisoner status as a criterion for participation. This exclusion permits prisoners living in the community to enroll in research that is open to any citizen in the community (e.g., hospital or medical school-based clinical trials, survey studies) without imposing the restrictions of the proposed regulations on those research entities.

WHEN LIBERTY STATUS CHANGES

If the subject's liberty status changes through arrest or revocation of probation or parole, and the person is then confined in a custodial setting, do the provisions of Subpart C become applicable to the subject? The committee's answer was yes, regardless of the nature of the research. Upon entering a custodial setting, that person becomes formally and in every way a prisoner, subject to the same constraints and concerns that the committee has expressed in this report, and therefore needs the same safeguards. There is no ethical justification for providing fewer safeguards for a new entrant into prison than those already in prison.

This does not mean, however, that study participation would be automatically terminated. It means that continued participation requires a new review of that prisoner's participation in the study. The original IRB should review the impact of the correctional setting on the procedures, with input from the IRB affiliated with the correctional setting. It should be done in an expedient manner (e.g., within 30 to 45 days) to allow for continuation of study participation.

Continuity of care is an important issue, especially for treatment studies. If terminating prisoner participation would adversely affect the health of the subject, participation may continue until the IRB review takes place. The custodial official receiving the prisoner should be informed that the prisoner is enrolled in a research protocol, provided information on the protocol, and explained the potential risks of not allowing continued participation. The researcher would have an obligation to advocate for providing the appropriate care while seeking to comply with regulations applicable to that setting.

Certain social or behavioral studies that, for example, examine health and risk behaviors over several years, may see some participants move into correctional settings. If the researchers wish to continue study involvement for those individuals, review would be necessary to weigh the risks and benefits within the new setting. If the risks remain low, continuation may be approvable. However, if new risks are foreseen, but they are still low, the consent may need to be updated for the participant's continued involvement.

This need for review may not be an issue for many jailed detainees who are often incarcerated for just a few days if that short period does not affect participation in the protocol. In a related, but different situation, if a prisoner is participating in a study within a correctional setting and is transitorily confined to disciplinary segregation, the researcher will have to evaluate whether or not the potential interruption in access during the period of segregation would preclude continued participation.

Research studies lose participants for many reasons. There may be occasions in which participation in the study may not continue for the research participant who becomes incarcerated. For example:

- The IRB may determine that the risks outweigh potential benefits to remaining in the study.
- By statute, some states do not permit biomedical/clinical trials research in prisons.
- By Department of Corrections policy, some states do not permit biomedical/clinical trials research in prisons.

REFERENCES

BJS (Bureau of Justice Statistics). 2001. *Trends in State Parole, 2000.* [Online]. Available: http://www.ojp.usdoj.gov/bjs/pub/pdf/tsp00.pdf [accessed December 23, 2005].

BJS. 2004. *Probation and Parole in the United States, 2003.* [Online]. Available: http://www.ojp.usdoj.gov/bjs/pub/pdf/ppus03.pdf [accessed December 23, 2005].

John Howard Society of Alberta. 1998. *Community Corrections.* [Online]. Available: http://www.johnhoward.ab.ca/PUB/C29.htm [accessed June 27, 2005].

NCPHSBBR (National Commission for the Protection of Human Subjects of Biomedical and Behavioral Research). 1976. *Research Involving Prisoners.* DHEW Pub. No. (OS) 76-131. Washington, DC: U.S. Department of Health, Education, and Welfare.

Petersilia J. 2000. Challenges to prisoner reentry and parole in California. *California Policy Research Center Brief Series.* [Online]. Available: http://www.ucop.edu/cprc/parole.html [accessed April 4, 2006].

5

The Ethical Framework for Research Involving Prisoners

In 1976, the National Commission for the Protection of Human Subjects of Biomedical and Behavioral Research (NCPHSBBR) addressed the ethics of research with prisoners in a document entitled *Report and Recommendations: Research Involving Prisoners*. The commission focused on respect for persons and justice as the two key ethical considerations guiding their recommendations.

The intervening decades have offered few reasons to quarrel with the commission's identification of these two factors as fundamental ethical principles guiding the conduct and regulation of research with prisoners. The goal of this chapter is to demonstrate that the principles of justice and respect for persons, although having evolved in meaning over the past three decades, should still be the basis for determining whether to conduct research with prisoners.

As part of this ethical evolution, the committee suggests that collaborative responsibility should be added to an updated ethical framework as a derivative of the principle of justice. The national commission thought of justice as primarily a matter of the distribution of the benefits and burdens of research, and that is certainly a legitimate understanding. Recent scholarship has offered reason to elevate some other concerns under the heading of justice. In particular, attention to distributive justice should be complemented by attention to the needs and responsibilities of all parties who will be involved with or affected by a research endeavor.

This focus on collaboration will more effectively facilitate the implementation of ethical research. For research to be truly ethical, it must be tailored to the individual setting; a one-size-fits-all approach is inadequate. Every research setting and population presents unique challenges and concerns. Ethically appropriate subject protections in one institution may be grossly inadequate in another. Only through close cooperation and communication with all relevant parties, in every implicated setting, can researchers ensure that they are creating ethical conditions that are favorable for respect and unfavorable for exploitation in any research context.

THE 1976 COMMISSION'S ETHICAL FRAMEWORK

Historical Context

The commission's deliberations took place against a background that included the Nazi experiments with concentration camp prisoners followed by the adoption of a stringent standard of voluntary consent in the Nuremburg Code. Many interpreted the code's statement that potential subjects "be so situated as to be able to exercise free power of choice, without the intervention of any element of force, fraud, deceit, duress, overreaching, or other ulterior form of constraint or coercion" (U.S. GPO, 1953) as precluding participation by prisoners.

This thinking was reinforced by publicity about the realities of research in prisons. The late 1960s and early 1970s saw a series of exposés documenting abuses in connection with nontherapeutic research in U.S. prisons (Mitford, 1973a,b; Rugaber, 1969). Many of those who were most vocal about the plight of prisoners (i.e., journalists and prisoner advocacy and civil liberties groups) saw research with prisoners largely under the twin headings of coercion and exploitation (Mitford, 1973a,b; Rugaber, 1969). For the most part, these groups pushed for restriction rather than reform of the prison research enterprise.

Although the commission did not recommend a ban on all research with prisoners, their work and the subsequent scholarship and regulation have been described as tending toward that result: "The result of these regulations has been, as was their goal, the virtual elimination of biomedical research activity in prisons and jails" (Dubler and Sidel, 1989). According to one informed estimate, in the late 1990s only about 15 percent of institutions that engaged in clinical research in the United States included prisoners in their research protocols (Hoffman, 2000). In 1997, New York State had the largest estimated number of HIV-infected prisoners of any prison system (9,456), but only 8 (less than .001 percent) were enrolled in clinical trials (Lazzarini and Altice, 2000).

Justice and Respect for Persons

The commission's emphasis on limiting research involving prisoners was guided by its choice of ethical framework. Congress's charge to the commission concerning research with prisoners identified informed consent as the primary locus of ethical concern. In particular, Congress directed the commission to attend to three components of informed consent: (1) nature of the consent; (2) adequacy of the information given; and (3) competence and freedom of the prisoners or their legal representatives to make a choice.[1]

In carrying out this charge, the commission used elements of a principle-based ethical framework that would be more fully fleshed out in the Belmont Report. The commission identified two basic ethical dilemmas arising in connection with the use of prisoners as research subjects and linked these dilemmas to two basic ethical principles (NCPHSBBR, 1976). The first issue was whether prisoners bear a fair share of the burdens of research and receive a fair share of the benefits. The commission linked this dilemma to the principle of justice, specified as the fair treatment of persons and groups. The second issue was whether prisoners could give truly voluntary consent. The commission linked this dilemma to the principle of respect for persons, specified as involving the protection and promotion of personal autonomy. The principles of beneficence and nonmaleficence (providing benefit and doing no harm) were not discussed by the commission in its report on prison research; however, they were prominently featured in the Belmont Report, and both maintain an underlying importance in the ethics of human subjects research. These concepts have been well developed in other works (Beauchamp and Childress, 2001).

The commission then reviewed two possible perspectives on prisoner participation in research involving two very different interpretations of respect for persons and justice. According to the first perspective, the principles of respect for persons and justice require that prisoners not be deprived of the opportunity to volunteer for research. Here the emphasis is on the freedom of prisoners to decide questions of research participation for themselves and on the possible benefits of research participation.

According to the second perspective, the principles of respect for persons and justice require (1) that prisoners be protected from exploitation, safeguards be introduced to reduce elements of constraint, and, when that proves impossible, participation be prohibited; and (2) that prisoners as a group not bear a disproportionate share of research burdens without a commensurate share of benefits. Here the emphasis is on structural conditions that create special vulnerabilities in prison populations and the pos-

---

[1] National Research Act (Public Law 93-348 (1974); 88 Stat. 348), section 202(a)(2).

sible burdens of research participation. The commission adopted the second perspective.

The commission explicitly stated that its stance was influenced by its understanding of the realities of prison life, including conditions of social and economic deprivation and the possibility or even likelihood of manipulation or corruption on the part of prison authorities and prisoners in positions of privilege. Recognizing that they were inclining toward protectionism, the commissioners commented that "should coercion be lessened and more equitable systems for the sharing of burdens and benefits be devised, respect for persons and concern for justice would suggest that prisoners not be deprived of the opportunity to participate in research" (NCPHSBBR, 1976).

Flowing from this protectionist perspective, the commission's ethical framework and current federal regulations permit therapeutic research[2] with prisoners as long as multiple safeguards are in place, but they do not encourage or provide incentives for therapeutic research with prisoners. The perception that all forms of research involving prisoners are equally ethically problematic, or subject to blanket prohibition or to conditions so onerous that the research is not worth doing, may be responsible for the dwindling of prisoner research participation to the point that justice concerns have been expressed about the exclusion of prisoners from clinical trials.

AN UPDATED ETHICAL FRAMEWORK

The committee developed a new ethical framework that utilizes the ethical principles applied by the national commission in the 1976 report, with several new, important components. The framework builds on the principles of respect for persons and justice by shifting from a categorical approach to review to a risk-benefit analysis approach, and by adding a derivative of justice, called collaborative responsibility to research proposal development.

Ideas about justice and respect for persons have evolved over the past three decades. To construct a comprehensive ethical framework for thinking about research in prisons, this chapter explores recent research ethics scholarship.[3] Changes in the way these principles have been conceptualized have influenced the shape of our recommendations. However, before beginning to address how this new ethical framework is different than that of the

---

[2]The commission thought use of the term *therapeutic research* aided and abetted the therapeutic misconception and substituted the more precise but more unwieldy expression *research on practices which have the intent and reasonable probability of improving the health or well-being of the subject.*

[3]Other concepts, such as coercion, undue inducement, exploitation, and choice, remain important ethical considerations but will not be discussed in this chapter.

original commission, it is important to emphasize that it does not deviate from their core ethical principles.

Respect for persons requires that research subjects be treated as autonomous individuals. As discussed in Chapter 1, it is clear that prisoners are still an extremely vulnerable population, with severely restricted autonomy; thus, this issue requires special attention. Prisoners still need to be protected from the risk of coercion, undue inducement, and exploitation. The historical pattern of research abuses in prisons underscores the need to have an ethical framework that, first and foremost, is concerned with the welfare of prisoners. Similarly, justice still requires a careful consideration of the fair distribution of burdens and benefits. Prisoners, as a vulnerable population, are in jeopardy of receiving a disproportionate share of the risk associated with human subjects research. As stated by the National Bioethics Advisory Commission (NBAC), "In research involving human subjects, risk is a central organizing principle, a filter through which protocols must pass (NBAC, 1998). Like the original commission, our recommendations start with a baseline ethical concern for the protection of prisoners.

Respect for Persons

In this section, the committee expresses its support for a broadened view of the principle of respect for persons, to consider more than a narrow focus on informed consent issues, which are still vital but not the whole picture. It also suggests a shift from a categorical approach to research review to a risk-benefit approach.

An Expanded View of Respect for Persons

In accord with its emphasis on the principle of respect for persons, the original commission's report focused on informed consent. Although informed consent is still an ethically important means of ensuring respect for the right of persons to engage in autonomous decision making, recent scholarship has questioned the myopia caused by such a narrow focus.

Kahn, Mastroianni, and Sugarman (1998) are the editors of a volume that captures a major research ethics reform agenda in its title: *Beyond Consent: Seeking Justice in Research*. One question the editors raise is whether research ethics has been too concerned with informed consent to the neglect of other matters. There seems to be agreement from a variety of perspectives that informed consent forms have consumed too much time and energy. Critics of the preoccupation with forms are not necessarily interested in shifting attention away from informed consent. Rather, they may emphasize that documentation should be but a part of an informed consent process that involves opportunities for questions and answers and allows time for reflection before a decision is made, and that more attention should be paid to ameliorating basic power and knowledge differentials, which may undermine information sharing, understanding, and voluntariness. One proposal for reform advises simply raising the consciousness of investigators and ancillary personnel. Another suggests the use of external measures such as third-party monitoring to guard against deficiencies. This could be accomplished by the integration of third-party research subject advocates in the informed consent process, especially for studies that are considered unusually sensitive or risky or that involve subjects with impaired autonomy (see prison research subject advocate [PRSA] discussion in Chapter 6).

A more fundamental question is whether too much weight has been placed on informed consent in the framework of research ethics and research regulation. As noted previously, the National Research Act charge to the commission focused on informed consent issues, so the centrality of consent issues in the report is neither surprising nor necessarily indicative of a judgment on the part of the commissioners that the most compelling issues in research with prisoners are those of consent.

An alternate perspective, discussed by Emanuel et al. (2000), focuses on directing attention to risks and to risk-benefit analysis. According to this view, only health-related benefits derived from the research can be counted as benefits to individual subjects, meaning that extraneous benefits, such as payments or medical services unrelated to the research, are excluded in this analysis. Further, although the process of weighing risks against benefits is inherently subjective, the analysis should be based on data permitting identification of the types of potential harms and benefits, their probability of occurrence, and their long-term consequences. For example, a placebo-controlled trial of new antiemetic therapy for patients undergoing chemotherapy could be rejected because the investigators failed to give adequate weight to the discomfort associated with nausea and vomiting and failed to take steps to minimize this potential harm by using available antiemetic agents in the control group (Emanuel et al., 2000).

These questions about an undue focus on informed consent influence our recommendations. More attention needs to be paid to risks and risk-benefit analysis rather than the formalities of an informed consent document. The ethical risks associated with research involving prisoners cannot be solved by focusing only on the informed consent document.

The Role of Protectionism

A risk-benefit paradigm is necessarily more flexible than the current categorical approach. Although some might view this flexibility as opening the door for potential abuses, this new approach should actually increase the protection of prisoners involved in research.

This committee, like the original commission, is focused on the protection of prisoners as our core ethical concern. However, there are many approaches one can take to accomplish this goal, involving different levels of protective oversight mechanisms. One scholar outlines three types of protectionism:

> Weak protectionism is the view that this problem is best resolved through the judgment of virtuous scientists. Moderate protectionism accepts the importance of personal virtue but does not find it sufficient. Strong protectionism is disinclined to rely, to any substantial degree, on the virtue of scientific investigators for purposes of subject protection (Moreno, 2001).

The movement over time has been from weaker to stronger forms of protectionism as a means of addressing a fundamental problem, specifically, the tension between protecting the interests of subjects and promoting scientific progress. Strong protectionism sharply limits investigator discretion and demands external assurances through measures such as third-party monitors of consent, conflict-of-interest committees, and other procedures. These external assurances can be associated with costs, thus leading to an ethical critique of strong protectionism. For example, an emphasis on external assurances may weaken the sense of personal moral responsibility on the part of investigators. Similarly, rigid external assurances, like those seen in the current regulations, can direct attention away from an analysis of risks and benefits, where the key ethical issues can be found.

Simultaneously, there has been a countervailing force in the march toward strong protectionism, exemplified in the push by acquired immune deficiency syndrome (AIDS) activists for greater access to clinical trials and by progressives for the inclusion of women and children in research studies. More recently, there has been a similar movement to ensure that racial and ethnic minority groups are included in research. These tendencies form one basis for a somewhat different reading of the history. This reading indicates a trend away from viewing certain types of research participation (especially clinical trials) as mostly risky or burdensome toward viewing them as mostly beneficial.

This represents a change in thinking about distributive justice. The commission focused on the equitable distribution of risks and worried that prisoners would bear more than their fair share. However, an equally valid case can be made for attention to the distribution of benefits. For example, Mastroianni and Kahn (2001) wrote that, in the 1970s, federal "policies emphasized the protection of human subjects from the risks of harm in research, and justice was seen as part of this protection," but since the early 1990s "justice as applied in research ethics has emphasized the need to ensure access to the potential benefits that research has to offer" (Mastroianni and Kahn, 2001).

During the committee's October 2005 meeting, the prisoner liaison panel spent a great deal of time debating the appropriateness of including prisoners in research, with special concerns for biomedical research.

"We have 275 million people in this country. We have 2 million in prisons. What is the allure to this population, if it is not the fact that it is a controlled population?" asked Daniel Murphy, Ph.D., a former prisoner in the Federal Bureau of Prisons and now professor in the Department of Political Science and Justice Studies at Appalachian State University. In other words, why conduct studies with prisoners when there are many more people outside of prison who are potential participants?

Some fundamental changes in the nature of the research conducted with human subjects provide support for this account of the recent history of research practices. For example, although the paradigmatic studies with prisoners in the period leading up to the report were studies in which investigators induced disease to learn more about it, biomedical research is more likely now to be discussed in terms of clinical trials comparing alternative beneficial treatments. The last several years have also seen the publication of studies comparing the outcome between patients who participate in clinical trials and those who receive standard care outside such trials; the results have tended to favor the former (Agrawal and Emanuel, 2003).

The two accounts can be reconciled in several ways. Increased protectionism is quite visible over the past century, whereas movements demanding greater access to clinical trials are far more recent. Further, protectionism as distrust of individual investigators can coexist with a view that participation in research subject to external oversight can often offer benefits to individuals and groups. One can simultaneously believe that the piling on of more rules and oversight bodies at some point becomes counterproductive and that human subjects are presently inadequately protected. Indeed, many modern ethicists seem to hope for a reawakening of scientific conscience rather than additional fortifications to the citadel of regulations.

> "It is so much easier for indiscretions or bad intentions to take place behind those prison walls and razor wire. I have seen it in so many cases, where doctors who were sworn to save lives and do good have become so consumed by that intellectual scientific quest that they forget about the test subject. It is just so easy to abuse the situation," stated Allen Hornblum, author of Acres of Skin (Hornblum, 1998) and former member of the Philadelphia Prison System Board of Trustees.

This committee concurs. The critique of strong protectionism, combined with a new understanding of research as a potential benefit, requires a reexamination of the current regulations. Advances in ethical thinking about protectionism suggest a new regulatory model. In particular, the committee rejects strong protectionism because it discounts the notion that researchers can be trusted to act virtuously in the protection of subjects. Researchers have responsibility for protecting subjects in their studies, especially those who are most vulnerable. However, given the troubling history of research abuses in prisons, weak protectionism is not an option. The recommendations in this chapter, and throughout this report, reflect a moderate protectionist stance, acknowledging that robust protections are needed but that they need not be rigid or absolute.

This position should not be perceived as a call for the relaxation of prison research ethics. Justice and respect for persons are as vital today as they were three decades ago; research still must be constrained by these ethical principles. The prison continues to be a setting in which it may be difficult to avoid contamination through contact with what will often be a culture of, at best, deprivation and dysfunction and, at worst, corruption, brutality, and degradation (Hornblum, 1997, 1998; Murphy, 2005; Rhodes, 2005).

Perhaps some unease is appropriate about removing what prisoners themselves, given full information and understanding, might regard as acceptable or even desirable options in light of their circumstances, circumstances that are unlikely to be changed for the better by research bans. A prisoner's ability to participate in research need not be completely precluded.

The original commissioners talked to actual prisoner-subjects during a fact-finding visit to Jackson State Prison on November 14, 1975. The prison, in southern Michigan, was at the time home to one of the largest nontherapeutic biomedical research programs in the country. The report notes that commission members spoke with a representative sample of research participants and nonparticipants selected by commission staff from a master list of all prisoners and found that, overall, participants valued the opportunity to participate in research and felt they were sufficiently informed and free to enroll or withdraw at will, and nonparticipants did not object to this opportunity being available to others (NCPHSBBR, 1976).

> *"My experience has really been that prisoners want access to innovative intervention programs. They want to change. They want to have access to the things that are going to help them, and that is one reason why people become involved, at least in working with us,"* said Olga Grinstead, Ph.D., adjunct associate professor at the University of California, San Francisco's Center for AIDS Prevention Studies, when she spoke to the committee in July 2005. She continued, *"From the issue of equity or the issue of justice, there are advantages to being involved in research. We need to be aware that prisoners are motivated to be involved in research. They are motivated to give back, and that should be taken into account too."*

This message continues to be articulated today. This committee visited one prison and one prison medical facility to discuss experimentation with current prisoners and peer educators (see Appendix A). The prisoners actively expressed the desire to have access to research. They stated they would feel they had a choice as to whether to participate and that they know their rights when it comes to study participation. The prisoners and peer educators at those site visits also echoed the sentiment that prisoners possess sufficient autonomy to make informed decisions about whether to participate in a given study.[4]

This, combined with the myopic emphasis on informed consent, is why the current categorical regulatory approach should be abandoned in favor of a risk-benefit paradigm. The following recommendations strive to acknowledge that, in limited circumstances, the potential benefit of a research protocol can justify research involving prisoners. These limited circumstances cannot be captured by a rigid categorical approach but need to be

---

[4]Of course, this survey only represents the views of a limited sample of prisoners. Although many inmates might share these opinions, others might feel that their circumstances do not permit the exercise of autonomy. This emphasizes the need for setting specific collaboration, discussed in detail later.

> *Doris James, of the Bureau of Justice Statistics, added that some studies are very specific to the experiences and actions of prisoners. "Offenders are the only source of some of this data, data that are needed to provide programs, to produce policies to help meet their needs."*

rooted in a risk-benefit analysis that grapples with the balance between a need for protection and access to potentially beneficial research protocols.

Recommendation 5.1 *Apply a risk-benefit framework to research review.* The U.S. Department of Health and Human Services should revise regulations regarding research with prisoners from a model based on categories to a system based on weighing of risks and benefits for the individual human subject, similar to the approach currently used in Subpart D.[5]

The risks and benefits of human subjects research are the ethically relevant issues, not the category of the research. The current categorical approach is dependent on stipulated research categories that are subject to various interpretations. This approach does not provide sufficient or reliable protection for the human subject. In addition, the present structure does not address the actual conditions of confinement or the restrictions on liberty that attach to any prisoner (whether incarcerated or subject to restraints on liberty in connection with community-based alternatives to incarceration) who may consider becoming a research subject and for whom the regulations are intended to provide protection. A risk-based approach is preferable because it requires institutional review boards (IRBs) and the Office for Human Research Protections (OHRP) to (1) focus on the potential benefits and harms of each suggested research protocol, and (2) identify the particular ethical issues that each protocol raises in the specific context of the correctional setting.

The general principle holds for all research: Ethically permissible research must offer benefits to prisoners that outweigh the risks. On the risk side of the equation, it will be important to analyze all potential risks, even something as seemingly innocuous as an interview. Certain questions can trigger harmful emotional or psychological responses; these questions cannot be allowed among prisoners unless there is an associated benefit.

On the benefit side, there may be research protocols, most likely epidemiological or social/behavioral, that carry very low risks for the prisoner-

---

[5]Details of Subpart D in IOM, 2004, pp. 100–103.

subjects but no personal benefit for the subjects. Instead, the potential benefits may be for prisoners as a class (e.g., studies to identify factors that predict recidivism). Application of a risk-benefit analysis may determine that, because the risks are very low and important knowledge or benefits may accrue for prisoners as a class, the research may be considered ethically acceptable. The same may hold true for epidemiological studies (as distinct from biomedical research) that require analysis of biomedical samples, such as tissue, blood, or urine, but are not designed to assess outcomes of an intervention.

The idea of benefit can be flexible enough to include minimal risk protocols where the benefit to prisoners is indirect and/or temporally distant. It will be up to IRBs to determine whether there is a convincing affirmative reason for conducting research in a prison setting. When reviewing minimal risk research that does not present a direct benefit to subjects or prisoners as a class, IRBs should consider whether the research has the potential to yield important scientific information and the extent to which that information can only be obtained in a prison setting. For example, it would be appropriate to allow a prisoners' continued participation in a minimal risk longitudinal study (i.e., epidemiological study) that they began before being incarcerated. Such studies may not benefit either the individual prisoner or prisoners as a class, but may generate important information about the community to which the participant belonged before incarceration. This would be permissible because the subject was selected for reasons other than incarceration, and the subject's decision to participate is unlikely to have been influenced by the pressures of prison life. However, it should be noted that the flexible notion of benefit has distinct limits. In the absence of benefit, either to the prisoner-subject or to prisoners as a class, the research should be conducted in other settings

This balancing framework represents a departure from the way that decisions are currently made for approving research protocols. The present system utilizes the idea of "minimal risk" to evaluate the dangers associated with a protocol; studies are often characterized as presenting either minimal risk or more than minimal risk. The committee believes that this categorical approach is problematic and needs to be balanced with a consideration of benefit. Under a new risk-benefit framework, studies should be evaluated through a dynamic process of balancing risks and benefits, thus removing the need to rely on static definitions and categories. Nonetheless, as discussed in Chapter 6, the idea of minimal risk can be a useful tool for evaluating the risk side of a risk-benefit analysis. IRBs are accustomed to this starting point in their analyses, but should also move beyond strict reliance on this specific term in favor of a consideration of the balance between risks and benefits. Moreover, given the particularities of being a prisoner, the committee believes that the definition of "minimal risk" presently in Subpart C should be replaced by a slightly modified version of the definition, as follows:

> The probability and magnitude of physical or psychological harm that is normally encountered in the daily lives, or in the routine medical, dental, or psychological examination of healthy persons *living outside the correctional setting*.

This definition reflects the fact that prisoners are faced with a high baseline level of daily risk, thus making prison life an inappropriate reference point for determining whether a research protocol presents more than minimal risk.

Guidance on biomedical research The following guidance suggests how the risk-benefit framework should be applied to biomedical research. Specific direction is being supplied for this area because of the history and controversy surrounding medical and pharmacological studies in prisons. For other types of research (i.e., epidemiological, behavioral, and so on), these very specific limitations are not relevant.

There are two narrow circumstances in which biomedical research might be ethically acceptable:

1. In normal circumstances, a biomedical research study may be ethically acceptable if:

- for research on new therapies or preventive measures, there is already some evidence of safety and efficacy, as in phase 3 testing for new drugs, as defined by the Food and Drug Administration (FDA); and
- the ratio of prisoner to nonprisoner-subjects does not exceed 50 percent.

2. In exceptional circumstances, a biomedical research study may be ethically acceptable even if the benefit of an intervention has not been completely established, or if the research population is disproportionately composed of prisoners. This requires a federal-level review, for example, if the research addresses a condition that is solely or almost solely found in incarcerated populations. For studies of this nature to proceed, the protocol must be submitted to a national, specially convened panel of experts, who, in a public process, consider the ethical acceptability of the protocol (as is the process for Subpart D [45 C.F.R. § 46.407]), and make recommendations to the responsible government authority (the OHRP) regarding the special circumstances that do or do not provide a basis for research and the safeguards that must apply.

Rationale This approach starts with the presumption that biomedical research should be severely restricted and is allowable only in limited circumstances. Biomedical research involving prisoners as subjects is only permitted when the potential benefit to the prisoner-participants outweighs the risk to which the subjects are exposed. Under this framework, studies that offer no benefit to potential subjects would be precluded (e.g., testing of cosmetic products). The goal of the risk-benefit analysis is to prevent prisoners from being burdened by more than their fair share of risk, while allowing access to research that has potential benefits. This is especially relevant in circumstances in which effective treatments have not been developed to address a life-threatening or life-altering condition.

The guidelines articulated above illustrate how these principles would be applied in practice. The first allowable situation involves a treatment that appears to be safe and effective based on small-scale trials. The potential benefit of an experimental intervention must be established before engaging in a risk-benefit analysis. As such, phase 1 and phase 2 studies, as defined by the FDA to determine safety and toxicity levels, would not be allowable. Since these trials are principally designed to study a drug's safety and efficacy, potential benefits are not yet clear. In these cases, risks to the prisoner might well overshadow the uncertainty of unproven benefits. Only phase 3 studies would be allowed, since basic efficacy would already have been demonstrated.

This approach reflects the growing view that research presents not only burdens but can also present benefits that should be fairly distributed to prisoners. However, the distribution of burdens must still be considered—thus the requirement that the ratio of prisoner to nonprisoner-subjects does not exceed 50 percent. Biomedical research should involve prisoners only to provide a benefit to *individual prisoner participants*, not because they are a convenient source of subjects. This 50 percent limit represents the committee's strongly held view that prisoners should not compose the majority of a biomedical study's enrollment when nonincarcerated subjects are available. The just distribution of risks and the potential for abuse require that researchers not be permitted to unnecessarily rely on prisoners as subjects.

It should be noted that the 50 percent limit is a ceiling that should only be approached when extensive use of prisoners as subjects can be justified by potential benefit. If a disease is less common in prisons, ethical guidelines would suggest a lower proportion of prisoner-subjects. Inmates should only be part of the subject pool to the extent that the disease affects the prisoner population. A study that extensively enrolls prisoners when nonprisoner-subjects are available should be examined closely to ensure that benefit to the prisoner population, and not convenience, is the true justification.

Under guideline 2, the 50 percent ceiling can be exceeded in exceptional circumstances, such as for conditions that solely or almost exclusively affect prisoners (for example, repetitive sexual assault; see Example 7, Chapter 6, page 167). Due to the inherent risks associated with research involving prisoners, increased oversight is needed when a biomedical study enrolls a high proportion of prisoners or when the potential benefits are expected but not yet established. Thus, the second exception requires more stringent safeguards. In this instance, the protocol would need to be submitted to an expert panel of medical and ethical scholars, whose opinions would be collected by the supervising agency and published on the agency's Web site. The agency would then need to publicly post an opinion regarding its acceptance or rejection of the expert testimony and the reasons for either. This process is analogous to the process used under Subpart D § 407 (IOM, 204).

The preceding discussion should not be construed as an abandonment of the commission's "primarily protective framework." The goal of a risk-benefit framework is to maximize the safety and well-being of prisoners. As the commission emphasized, respect for persons requires that the risk of coercive practices and research abuses be negated (or at least minimized) by the use of protective measures. The commission's approach emphasized the prevention of deleterious research protocols, but it did not properly account for potential that research can offer positive benefits to prisoner-subjects. A risk-benefit framework is still primarily concerned with preventing harm, but does so in a manner that allows for participation in research when the potential for benefit to prisoners greatly outweighs potential risks.

Risk-benefit analyses of the type illustrated here provide the bases for the kinds of specific safeguards discussed and described in greater detail in Chapter 6.

Justice

In this section, the committee lays out its expansion of the principle of justice in two ways: To include: (1) collaborative responsibility for research proposals and setting a research agenda, and (2) enhancing the welfare of the prisoner population.

Collaborative Responsibility

The conceptualization of justice has expanded since the original commission's work. They primarily thought of justice in terms of the distribution of risks and benefits. Although this is still a legitimate concern, some recent scholarship suggests elevating collaborative responsibility under the rubric of justice.

> "We need to emphasize and reemphasize the voluntary nature of research in our collaborations with community-based agencies, with the Department of Corrections, and with the prisoners themselves. We need to be sure we are getting input from the incarcerated community," said Olga Grinstead, Ph.D., University of California, San Francisco Center for AIDS Prevention Studies, at its July 2005 meeting. Dr. Grinstead has been developing and evaluating human immunodeficiency virus, (HIV), sexually transmitted diseases (STD), and hepatitis prevention programs for incarcerated men and their female partners since 1993.

Specifically, Eckenwiler (2001) develops a proposal for incorporating particularity into the research review process that reflects the interest in subjectivities and participatory justice in contemporary feminist scholarship. She notes that analyses of potential harms and benefits, and trade-offs between them, can vary considerably depending on personal characteristics and on the social, economic, and institutional contexts. A determination to be impartial or to put oneself in the shoes of a particular kind of research subject will be inadequate in many circumstances: "When differences between the social positions of the deliberators and the targeted beneficiaries involve relations of privilege and oppression attempts to ignore one's own situation or imagine the perspectives of others are especially unlikely to be successful. Furthermore, as most IRB members are health-care providers and scientists, they are less disposed to question features of research that collude in perpetuating inequalities ... [and may also be] acutely aware of the financial environment in which they operate and of the importance of clinical research in their institutions' economic viability" (Eckenwiler, 2001). Eckenwiler recommends that, among other things, efforts be undertaken to enhance the participation of affected or interested groups. This involves acknowledging that groups are not monolithic and are themselves subject to a range of problems that should be addressed in the consultation process. This recommendation has two aspects: (1) including more laypeople who match the local population and common subject groups in key respects; and (2) shaping IRBs so they are hospitable places for lay members.

This committee agrees with this perspective. Thus, a new risk-benefit approach needs to be accompanied by an emphasis on collaboration. The ethical problems associated with research involving prisoners will manifest themselves differently in each correctional setting. The one-size-fits-all approach characterized by a focus on informed consent cannot adequately address the unique concerns presented by each setting. Thus, all relevant parties should be involved (prisoners, correctional officers, medi-

> "I would like to know more about how we could have a liaison between the inmates and the researchers. I really think that that is an important issue," stated Debra Breuklander at the committee's October 2005 meeting. Ms. Breuklander is a former prisoner who is now a nurse consultant at MECCA, a residential inpatient substance abuse treatment program in Des Moines, Iowa, and a member of the committee's prisoner liaison panel.

cal staff, administrators) when creating and implementing a research protocol. This effort, combined with a more specific focus on risks and benefits, can lead to research practices that better incorporate justice and respect for persons.

Recommendation 5.2 *Use a collaborative research approach.* Under an ethic of collaborative responsibility, investigators should find ways to obtain input from prisoners and other stakeholders on the design and conduct of any research protocol involving prisoners.

To satisfy the spirit of the Belmont Report principles in modern correctional settings requires recognition of an additional ethical imperative. Collaborative responsibility is a necessary ethical underpinning for research in correctional settings. Collaborative responsibility is a phrase intended to convey the idea that, to the extent feasible, all aspects of research (design, planning, and implementation) should include the active participation of relevant institutional stakeholders (prisoners, correctional officers, medical staff, administrators). Efforts should be made to consult with major stakeholders within the local institution, particularly prisoners as well as former prisoners and prison staff, to particularize the protocol to local conditions. A focus on collaboration would help cope with the reality that each institution has its own unique conditions and also may facilitate openness of the research environment. With collaborative input, research design and implementation could be tailored to the issues, needs, and capacities of a given setting. Prisoners have an interest in being consulted as part of the collaborative process. The responsibility for collaboration lies with investigators, who need to make the effort to engage prison administration and prisoners themselves for their input, and with the human research participant protection program, which must determine that the effort was made.

A valuable model can be found in *Responsible Research: A Systems Approach to Protecting Research Participants* (IOM, 2003), which sets forth the phases of human research (see Figure 5-1). Most of these phases provide an opportunity for collaboration that can facilitate the conduct of research in accordance with the principles of justice and respect for persons.

At the outset, a researcher must construct a research question. Collaboration with prisoners and prison staff at this stage can be a productive means of addressing topics that will have the most benefit for the prison population. Representatives from within the prison system can encourage study of the most pressing problems or discourage protocols that address insignificant issues. It is at this first stage that prisoners in particular can voice their thoughts on whether a given research question provides benefits that outweigh the risks.

Collaboration during protocol development is important because each correctional setting presents unique strengths and weaknesses. This is an opportunity to assess a specific prison's infrastructure (e.g., to determine what is feasible). In particular, collaboration during protocol development can reveal setting-specific characteristics that will make it significantly more difficult to conduct ethical research (i.e., presence of gangs, mistrust of outsiders, inadequate medical infrastructure). When such barriers exist, the researcher, in collaboration with prisoners, correctional officers, medical staff, and administrators, must consider whether it is even appropriate to perform human subject research in that setting, and if so, to design safeguards that protect subjects and overcome impediments.

Recruitment and enrollment make up a third area of potential collaboration. Involving prisoners in the recruitment process can go a long way toward minimizing potential coercion or undue inducement. If prisoners have a voice in how subjects are enrolled, they can help protect themselves from inappropriate recruitment practices that infringe on their autonomy (respect for persons) or unfairly distribute risks and benefits within the prison population (justice).

This model and discussion are not meant to provide a comprehensive list but merely to illustrate that collaboration can and should occur at every level of the research process. There is no objective way to say collaboration occurred. However, the human research participants protection program (HRPPP) can ask if all relevant people were consulted and determine that the process was transparent and fair. As long as all parties are consulted fully and fairly, given an opportunity to be heard, the goal is met.

The committee acknowledges that this will generally be a new model to many researchers and within most correctional settings, and, thus will require a significant commitment to implement.

Welfare of the Prisoner Population

Recent decades have seen an explosion in writing on justice, specifically in the context of research. As discussed previously, this has involved a

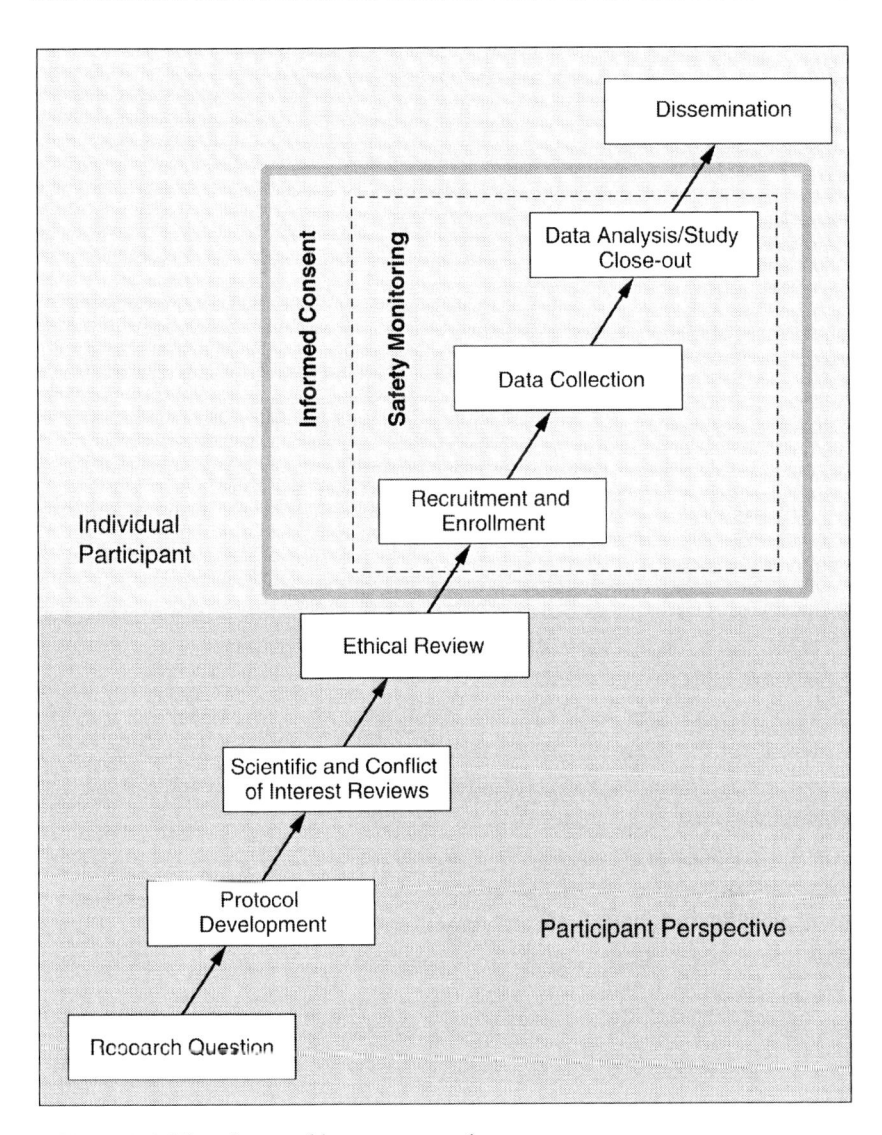

FIGURE 5-1 The phases of human research.
SOURCE: IOM (2003).

change in the way we view distributive justice. The commission thought of distributive justice as requiring the fair distribution of research risks and burdens. However, much of the recent philosophical work argues that although justice requires the protection of vulnerable subjects from exploitative research, sometimes it also mandates that research be done to improve the welfare of these populations. This perspective focuses on the idea that justice requires the fair distribution not only of risks but also of benefits.

In this area, the volume *Beyond Consent: Seeking Justice in Research* has synthesized and extended prior work on justice. In the chapter "Race, Justice, and Research," King (1998) argues that justice should take us beyond purely distributive concerns to the evaluation and modification of "institutional arrangements" and structures of "decision making and other procedural aspects of research." Another chapter, "Convenient and Captive Populations," provides a history of the regulation of research with prisoners, institutionalized persons, military personnel, and students in the United States. It concludes by endorsing a protectionist stance toward these populations, based on histories of abuse, while noting that "there are circumstances in which justice may permit, or even require, access to research" for these populations, such as "the prevalence of a disease that poses a particular threat" to its members and "cannot be studied as effectively with other subjects" (Moreno, 1998).

Similarly, two other philosophers have also thought about the idea that justice requires more than the protection of subjects from exploitation; to be truly ethical, research must actively consider what is best for a population. London, in his work on international research, argues that the permissibility of clinical research should rest in part on its contribution to "filling the gaps between the most important health needs in a community and the capacity of its social structures to meet them" (London, 2005). Even if a particular research project is not, strictly speaking, exploitative, it may still be ethically problematic if it is not the project that has the greatest potential to address the health problems and concerns of the community. Powers (1998) argues that "freedom of choice is important, but the availability of choice-worthy options also is important." He calls for a complex, comprehensive concept of justice in research that not only synthesizes elements of the various norms (e.g., adopting a dual focus on individuals and groups, benefits and burdens, and upstream and downstream) but also considers the connections between research and other realms of health (or, for that matter, social) policy.

The committee believes that this expanded concept of justice is an important ethical development. Justice requires more than the protection of prisoners from harm caused by the research itself. Ethical research carries with it a responsibility to grapple with the fact that potential harm is ubiquitous in everyday prison life, creating an environment for research in which the choice to participate in a study can be inherently coercive and potentially dangerous. Thus, in order for research to be ethical, justice requires that it must be done in a setting in which there is an adequate standard of health care in place.

How to assess the adequacy of a correctional health-care system? The committee acknowledges that the vast majority of researchers and IRBs do not have the expertise to directly measure health-care quality in correctional settings. Certain indirect measures, however, may help with this determination. For example, has the specific correctional system's health-care services been found to be unconstitutional by a court? Is it under a consent decree, settlement agreement, or a similar process relevant to the adequacy of the health-care services? Such situations create a presumption that the system was inadequate at that time. Research in a correctional facility that involves subject matter addressed under a court order/settlement/consent decree should be presumptively disapproved. (The concern is primarily biomedical research, but behavioral research could be implicated under the standards proposed here if the underlying mental health support is seriously lacking in the institution and if the proposed research project has mental health as an integral component of the behavioral research.)

To allow biomedical research under such circumstances, the IRB must apply the risk-benefit analysis the committee proposes in a heightened form and find that the research proposed is permissible only after reviewing the specific components of the research and its interaction with the specific components of the system presumed to be deficient. This risk-benefit application should address the theoretical aspects of the proposed research, as well as its administration and monitoring, including the informed consent. The IRB must assure itself that no prisoner is choosing to be a research subject in order to bypass the presumptively deficient system.

Other factors, which would be useful though not definitive, include:

- Is the system accredited by a third party, such as National Commission on Correctional Health Care (NCCHC), American Correctional Association (ACA), or Joint Commission on Accreditation of Healthcare Organizations (JCAHO)?
- Have any recent internal or external assessments been made of the health-care system?
- Do relevant quality improvement studies exist?
- Do other relevant assessments exist?

Recommendation 5.3 *Ensure adequate standards of care.* Human research participant protection programs,[6] together with the prison administration and prison health-care professionals, are responsible for

---

[6]The term *human research participant protection program* (HRPPP) is used throughout this report to mean the network of entities with direct responsibility for the safety of those enrolled in the studies carried out under its purview. The HRPPP most often includes the research organization, the study sponsor, investigator, IRB, and, when relevant, the data safety monitoring board (IOM, 2003). In the contexts described in this report, prison research subject advocates would be an important part of this network as well.

ensuring that research with prisoners occurs in an environment that is appropriate to the health and well-being of prisoners, including access to existing medical and mental health care that is adequate, protection from inmate attempts to coerce or manipulate participation or non-participation in research, and prompt access to decent health-care services in case the research causes physical or mental harm.

Ethical research requires an environment that is humane and provides reasonable access to supportive care, particularly when human subjects are exposed to physical or psychological risks. Without adequate medical or psychological care, subjects may be vulnerable to undue inducements to participate in research such that they would consent in order to gain access to medical care or other benefits they would not normally have. Finally, researchers have an ethical obligation, if they expose subjects to risk, to rapidly and professionally remedy any harms caused by the research.

HRPPPs can meet their obligations under Recommendation 5.3 by engaging in due diligence and going through a careful process to discover whether adequate heath care exists within the correctional setting, including analysis of the factors described above and any others that might reflect on the quality of the correctional setting. Obtaining answers to these questions would likely require visiting the setting, speaking to health-care staff, and reviewing relevant court cases.

Lastly, if research is to be done in prisons, there is an ethical responsibility to devote much of this research effort to determine how best to achieve all of the legitimate purposes of the criminal justice system.

> Recommendation 5.4 *Support critical areas of correctional research.* Government agencies should fund and researchers should conduct research to identify needed supports to facilitate prisoners' successful reentry into society, reduce recidivism, and inform policy makers about the most humane and effective strategies for the operation of correctional systems.

Society creates a correctional system for clear purposes, such as deterrence to future crime and rehabilitation of those who are convicted of committing offenses. It is of utmost social importance to better understand how best to achieve the purposes of incarceration, including reduction of recidivism and successful introduction back into the community. Perhaps unavoidably, the criminal justice system inflicts some harm on those it punishes. As ethical people, we constantly strive to develop and use corrective measures that are effective and humane, without causing unnecessary physical or mental harm to prisoners. However, prisoners are a vulnerable population subject to abuse and exploitation. Indeed, several subclasses of prisoners make up some of society's most vulnerable populations, such as young people, persons with mental disabilities, racial minorities, women, and people with diseases (addiction, hepatitis, HIV, hypertension, diabetes) that may or may not be treated during imprisonment. It is, therefore, especially important to better understand how to protect and promote the welfare and well-being of this large and growing segment of our society. Scientific knowledge and information about "best practices" gained from high-quality research is critically important to understanding how best to achieve all of the legitimate purposes of the criminal justice system.

REFERENCES

Agrawal M, Emanuel E. 2003. Ethics of phase 1 oncology studies: Reexamining the arguments and data. *Journal of the American Medical Association* 290:1075–1082.

Beauchamp TL, Childress JF. 2001. *Principles of Biomedical Research Ethics*. 4th ed. New York: Oxford University Press.

Dubler NN, Sidel VW. 1989. On research on HIV infection and AIDS in correctional institutions. *Milbank Quarterly* 67(2):171–207.

Eckenwiler L. 2001. Moral reasoning and the review of research involving human subjects. *Kennedy Institute of Ethics Journal* 11(1):37–69.

Emanuel EJ, Wendler D, Grady C. 2000. What makes clinical research ethical? *Journal of the American Medical Association* 283:2701–2711.

Hoffman S. 2000. Beneficial and unusual punishment: An argument in support of prisoner participation in clinical trials. *Indiana Law Review* 33:475.

Hornblum AM. 1997. They were cheap and available: Prisoners as research subjects in twentieth century America. *British Medical Journal* 315:1437–1441.

Hornblum AM. 1998. *Acres of Skin: Human Experiments at Holmesburg Prison*. New York: Routledge.

IOM (Institute of Medicine). 2003. *Responsible Research: A Systems Approach to Protecting Research Participants*. Washington, DC: The National Academies Press.

IOM. 2004. *The Ethical Conduct of Clinical Research Involving Children*. Washington, DC: The National Academies Press.

Kahn JP, Mastroianni AC, Sugarman J, eds. 1998. *Beyond Consent: Seeking Justice in Research*. New York: Oxford University Press.

King PA. 1998. Race, justice, and research. In: Kahn JP, Mastroianni AC, Sugarman J, eds. *Beyond Consent: Seeking Justice in Research*. New York: Oxford University Press. Pp. 88–110.

Lazzarini Z, Altice FL. 2000. A review of the legal and ethical issues for the conduct of HIV-related research in prisons. *AIDS & Public Policy Journal* 15(3/4):105–135.

London AJ. 2005. Justice and human development approach to international research. *Hastings Center Report* 35(1):24–37.

6

Systems of Oversight, Safeguards, and Protections

Participation in human subjects research has often been thought of as a burden, which suggests that the barriers to participation were significant. Although it is important to be vigilant to avoid unwarranted burdens, there is also an increasing awareness that research participation can sometimes afford benefits. Thus, when thinking about research involving prisoners, potential benefits and risks must be carefully considered. This chapter focuses on the systems of oversight, safeguards, and protections that would enable human research participant protections programs to weigh the potential benefits and risks and then apply important safeguards and monitoring processes, based on level of risk, to approved research. It includes a discussion of how prisoner research should be defined and how it should be reviewed (when, what, and by whom). Recommendations regarding the use of a prison research subject advocate (PRSA) and stronger national oversight of prisoner research are also discussed. The chapter ends with the committee's suggestions to modify the risk-benefit approach used in Subpart D of 45 C.F.R. Part 46 for application to apply it to research involving prisoners. Relevant examples are provided.

OVERARCHING PRINCIPLE

In considering a system of oversight, safeguards, and protections under the broader proposed definition of the term *prisoner*, the committee weighed the current system in view of the locus of specific threats to ethical research with prisoners and perceived need for concrete responses to those specific threats. In doing so, the committee considered (1) alternative conceptual frameworks for defining and reviewing permissible research with prisoners; (2) the substantial variability in threats to ethical research (e.g., the potential and likelihood for coerced participation; the degree of openness to outside review, and remediation of emergent research-related problems) across the expanded array of research settings (i.e., community settings as well as traditional institutions); (3) differing types and magnitudes of potential risks posed by specific types of research (i.e., biomedical as distinct from social/behavioral); and (4) specific safeguards related to research design and implementation monitoring that might facilitate safe and ethical research across these diverse settings.

To correct the inadequacies and lack of complete coverage of current regulations, as described in Chapter 3, the systems recommended by the committee are meant to apply to all research with prisoners to ensure that the same protections are afforded to every prisoner-subject. Prisoner-subjects are currently being enrolled in a broad spectrum of research on various topics at many different institutions and by many different researchers. To achieve the objective of adequately protecting prisoner-subjects, the system of oversight must cover all research involving this vulnerable population regardless of the funding source, the federal-wide assurance (FWA) status of the institution conducting the research, the correctional setting in which the research will take place, or the type of research being conducted. Additionally, the oversight system should cover research involving individuals meeting the definition of *prisoner* set forth in Chapter 4, which includes persons at all custody levels, from those who reside in prisons or jails to those who are under supervision in detention centers or other types of community placements.

DEFINING AND REVIEWING PRISONER RESEARCH

For the tasks of defining and reviewing permissible research with prisoners, the committee considered the current framework of the U.S. Department of Health and Human Services (DHHS) regulations at 45 C.F.R. Part 46 Subpart C (Additional DHHS Protections Pertaining to Biomedical and Behavioral Research Involving Prisoners as Subjects).[1] This regulation requires that a duly constituted institutional review board (IRB), with at least one prisoner representative as a voting member, review and approve the study, with consideration of the special circumstances inherent in conducting the research with prisoner-subjects. Subpart C defines permitted research using a combination of substantive research categories and risk levels and for certain

---

[1]Revised November 13, 2001.

types of research. All studies involving prisoners within this framework are subject to certification by the DHHS Office for Human Research Protections (OHRP), which verifies that (1) the IRB has appropriately reviewed the study, and (2) the study falls into one of the categories of permissible research (see Chapter 3 for details). This subpart also requires federal-level review (in consultation with a panel of experts) and published notice in the *Federal Register* for certain categories of research.

On close inspection and in light of the experiences of committee members who have served on IRBs, the Subpart C provisions appear problematic. The substantive categories are not mutually exclusive, and a study that might be permitted without secretarial review in one category (e.g., a study of drug addiction as a cause of criminal behavior) might require secretarial review in another (e.g., drug addiction as a condition particularly affecting prisoners). The classification and OHRP certification process for such studies can be lengthy and contentious, often resulting in (sometimes prolonged) delays, which may discourage investigators from conducting valuable research. The value added by the certification and review process, as it currently operates, is not clear. Further, the OHRP has reported receiving for review and certification studies that were designed to yield potentially important and useful information but could not be approved because they did not fall into one of the approvable substantive categories.

The committee considered whether a modified version of the framework provided under 45 C.F.R. Part 46 Subpart D might be preferable for the review of research involving prisoners. The Subpart D framework is structured primarily in terms of level of risk posed to the subject (minimal or greater than minimal) and whether the research presents the prospect of direct benefit to individual subjects (for a more detailed description, see IOM, 2004, pp. 100–103). With modifications that either (1) specify particular research categories that would be impermissible with prisoners, or (2) delineate specific kinds of design and monitoring safeguards necessary for IRB approval of permissible research, the committee judged that greater protections could be afforded prisoner-subjects by the use of a modified Subpart D framework (see page 160, "Applying Safeguards for Particular Kinds of Research").

What Is Reviewed

All research that involves prisoners must be reviewed by an independent body before it begins. Under 45 C.F.R. Part 46, the term *research* is defined as "a systematic investigation, including research, development, testing and evaluation, designed to develop or contribute to generalizable knowledge." This definition is subject to varying interpretations both inside and outside the prisoner research context. The main distinction between a research activity and a nonresearch activity is the primary intent of the activity: Research aims to test hypotheses and/or generate new knowledge, whereas nonresearch aims to control a disease or other condition or to improve a program or service. Clinical or epidemiological studies that are intended to reveal new information about a disease, behavior, or treatment are clearly research. In contrast, data collection efforts that are intended solely to aid in evaluating an internal system or in quality improvement (QI) initiatives may not be research.

There is little dispute that correctional health-care systems should have an ongoing system in place to monitor and evaluate health-care services from quality assurance and improvement perspectives. In general, measurable components of care include accessibility, appropriateness, continuity, effectiveness, efficacy, efficiency, patient perspective issues, safety of the care environment, and timeliness (Joint Commission on Accreditation of Healthcare Organizations, 1992). Such internal program assessments are central to policy makers and organization executives for management purposes, especially in the context of limited financial resources and increasing demand for services (Council of State Governments, 2002). These evaluation systems have a variety of different labels, including QI, comprehensive QI, total QI, and quality assurance (QA). In more mature systems, QA is an element of a more comprehensive QI process. Outcome QI studies examine whether expected outcomes of patient care were achieved. Process QI studies examine the effectiveness of the health-care delivery process.

Under the current federal regulations, only research activities that involve human subjects (or data from or about human subjects) require IRB review and approval. However, state-level departments of corrections (DOCs) have different rules and are not consistent in what they consider to be research and nonresearch (see Chapter 2). For example, (1) in some states internal evaluations are not considered research, whereas similar activities undertaken by outside researchers are, (2) in-house activities require fewer approvals or reviews than external activities, and (3) unless results are to be published, IRB review may not be required.

Because either type of activity (research or nonresearch, in-house or external) may involve the collection of private or sensitive information, there is a chance that prisoners who participate may be put at risk. Thus, to afford the greatest protection to prisoners, both activities may need outside scrutiny, especially in view of the heightened vulnerability of prisoners. If there is doubt about whether an activity requires review, it should be resolved in favor of providing additional protection to the human subjects through independent review and oversight. However, some activities (e.g., review of information from medical records to determine what therapies are most effective in a given correctional facility) are clearly designed to give clinicians and prison administrators information needed to provide quality care. Likewise, some activities are designed to improve the operations of the facility (i.e., QI processes) and are not intended to be disclosed outside that facility. These activities, as well as external surveys for accreditation purposes, would not require review by an IRB because they do not constitute research.

Who Reviews

Current regulations state that research involving prisoners must be reviewed by an independent review committee, such as an IRB, before any prisoner-subjects are contacted or any information about prisoner-subjects is accessed by the researcher. This independent committee should include members with diverse demographic (e.g., gender, race, ethnicity) and technical (e.g., scientific and nonscientific) backgrounds. In addition, the committee should include at least one prisoner representative who has experience with the prison setting, but is not an employee of the setting. This person should have particular knowledge of the correctional setting and should be able to represent the interests of the prisoners. The prisoner representative, who is a voting member on the committee, could be a person who works with prisoners (e.g., an attorney, a service provider, or a chaplain who is not an employee of the correctional institution or agency), a family member of an inmate, or an ex-offender. The committee should not include any individuals who have a conflict of interest in reviewing the study, such as the researchers themselves, representatives from a sponsor, or the prison staff. In the case of multisite studies, it may be necessary to obtain input from more than one prisoner representative, because local conditions are likely to vary from site to site.

Two implementation issues require specific discussion. First, it is vital that the prisoner representatives on the IRB have sufficient opportunity to be heard, independent from the people who work in prisons (correction officers, medical staff, and administrators). Prison staff can provide valuable input concerning the institutional needs and capacities. However, their institutional perspective may make it difficult for them to appreciate or articulate an accurate or sensitive assessment of the actual risk to prisoner subjects. As such, the prisoner representative must have the independence to freely express prisoner concerns, even when they may come in conflict with the institutional issues.

Second, it will be important to diligently seek out and train prisoner representatives. If a representative is an ex-offender or prisoner advocate from outside of the institution, he or she must be familiar enough with the characteristics of the particular setting in question to provide relevant comments. Representatives from inside or outside the correctional setting should be given access to the prisoners so that individual concerns can be expressed. To ensure sufficient understanding of the risks and potential benefits of a protocol, the prisoner representatives should receive adequate training on human subjects protections to understand the risks and potential benefits of protocols.

Currently, prisoner research that falls under 45 C.F.R. § 46 Subpart C must be reviewed by a properly constituted IRB that is registered with the OHRP and operates under an FWA. This IRB may be the same committee that reviews nonprisoner research, or it may be a distinct committee convened to review studies involving prisoner-subjects. Presently, research involving prisoners that is not governed by 45 C.F.R. § 46 Subpart C may or may not be reviewed by an IRB. Instead, it may be reviewed by another, independent prison review committee, such as a research committee that reviews research conducted at a specific prison. Although a prison review committee may review a study, theirs should not be the only review because of their close ties to the prison. According to the committee's survey of DOC representatives (Chapter 2), IRB review is not consistent, and DOC IRBs do not universally include prisoner representatives. Other DOC IRBs may include people designated as prisoner representatives who may lack sufficient detachment and objectivity to perform that function (e.g., healthcare professionals employed by the prison). Under the recommended oversight paradigm, review by an IRB (or other independent review committee) would be required for all research involving prisoners regardless of whether review by a prison review committee is also done. For studies conducted at more than one facility, reviews may be required by a local IRB or review committee for each facility.

It should be noted that the IRB is only one component of an institution's human research participants protection program (HRPPP).[2] The HRPPP is a broader organizational structure in which the responsibility for protecting research participants is shared among the sponsor, the larger research organization, the investigators, and the IRB (IOM, 2003). Components of the HRPPP, in addition to the IRB, may entail additional levels of review and monitoring for prisoner studies, depending on the type and the risk level of the research.

---

[2]The term *human research participant protection program* is used throughout this report to mean the network of entities with direct responsibility for the safety of those enrolled in the studies carried out under its purview. The HRPPP most often includes the research organization, the study sponsor, investigator, IRB, and, when relevant, the data safety monitoring board (IOM, 2003). In the contexts described in this report, prison subject research advocates would be an important part of this network as well.

How Reviews Are Conducted

The committee determined that the way in which IRB reviews of prisoner studies are conducted need not vary substantially from how these reviews are done currently, except for an increased emphasis on assessing risks and benefits. (Biomedical research, compared with other types of research, remains a critically important area of concern.) This accounts for the committee's recommendation to replace the current Subpart C framework, which requires categorization of the research study, with a modified Subpart D framework, which focuses on risks and individual benefits, to guide the IRB in reviewing research involving prisoners.

Prisoner studies should be reviewed by a fully convened (and properly constituted) IRB or other independent review committee, as is presently done and recommended by the OHRP. One or more prisoner representatives must be in attendance at this review. The committee reviews the study protocol and all associated study materials (e.g., letters, consent forms, questionnaires, experimental protocols, drug information, and monitoring procedures). Committee members discuss the procedures in detail, with particular emphasis on potential risks to the prisoner-subjects and whether proper protections are proposed to mitigate these risks. They also evaluate other issues that are unique to performing the research with prisoners in a correctional setting, such as the following:

- Is it necessary to involve prisoners in the study? This first question addresses the concerns expressed by several prisoner liaison panel members (Chapter 5). There are many more nonprisoners than prisoners in this country. Why are prisoners an appropriate source of subjects for the study?
- Will prisoners constitute a majority of the study subjects? The committee determined that, for most biomedical research, no more than 50 percent of the subjects may be prisoners.
- How will the prisoners be recruited for the study, and how will prison staff be involved in this process?
- How will informed consent be obtained from the prisoner subjects? Voluntary informed consent is difficult to ensure in prison settings because of the inherently coercive environment. Thus, this evaluation by the IRB will include a full review of the consent process. With regard to the consent form itself, are all elements of consent included and explained in lay language and translated into a language the prisoner can understand if he or she does not speak English? For prisoners with poor reading skills, is the informed consent process modified to accommodate their needs, perhaps including a test of comprehension? Just as critical is the IRB's review of the procedures that will be followed to obtain consent: Who will obtain con-

sent? How will the information be presented to the potential subject to ensure full comprehension? How will the prisoner's questions be answered?

- Will the prisoner be informed of any special implications related to participation in the research study in a given facility (e.g., in some facilities, testing positive for HIV may lead to transfer to a different facility, limitations on work opportunities and family visits, or specific medical treatments)? The consent must address the policies and practices of the correctional setting in which the study is conducted; it is the investigator's responsibility to become informed about these issues before presenting the study procedures to the IRB.
- Will the prisoner-subject be paid for participation in the study? If so, how will this payment be made (e.g., into a spending account, as a noncash item)? What assurances have been given that such payments are both allowed by the facility and appropriate?
- Will the prisoner-subject feel that participation is truly voluntary and feel free from coercion (either to participate or not)? Is it possible to hold in confidence the prisoner's decision whether or not to participate? The IRB must also be assured, and the prisoner-subject informed, that neither parole nor the confinement situation will be affected by the decision to participate or not in the research.
- How will privacy be maximized? The interview setting is of particular concern, including the physical location of the room and the location of officers while the interview is underway. Officers need to be out of earshot, but it may also be important to make provisions to conduct the interview out of sight or with the prisoner facing away from officers and passersby. Computerized data collection methods (e.g., audio-assisted self-interviewing in which the respondent hears the questions through earphones and then types responses into the computer) can provide extra privacy protection for especially sensitive interview topics. Clinical studies under the purview of the Food and Drug Administration (FDA) require that a copy of the written informed consent, which contains details on the protocol, be placed in the participant's medical record. However, for other studies, such as those of a social or behavioral nature, unless the correctional setting has a policy that requires the same, a copy of the consent form need not be entered into the file, and perhaps need not be left with the prisoner-subject. (There are circumstances under which possession of the consent form itself could compromise privacy.) The IRB could waive that requirement, while ensuring informed consent occurs. The IRB could also assign a unique study number to a research protocol (e.g., USF#12.344). Because IRBs (and correctional agencies) may both require evidence that the prisoner gave written informed consent, it could be arranged that the final/signature page of the consent form include only the following language, plus signature blocks: "I have had an opportunity to read and discuss the consent form

> *"You have to know what the perception is going to be, not just the exact design, but how it is going to be perceived in the populace and by staff. Does involvement say the participant is a snitch? Will it reveal HIV status or sexual preference? That is a precursor to doing the risk-benefit analysis,"* said Jack Beck, director of the Prison Visiting Project at the Correctional Association of New York, and a member of the committee's prisoner liaison panel, at the committee's October 2005 meeting.

that explains research study Number USF12.344. I have had ample time to discuss this study with a member of the research staff and have received satisfactory information to allow me to decide about taking part in the study. By my signature below, I do voluntarily consent to participate in this study." The prisoner could keep a copy of this consent form which, if discovered by corrections staff or other prisoners, would not disclose anything substantive about the nature of the research; similarly, if the corrections agency required evidence that the prisoner consented to and/or participated in the study, a copy of this in the file also would not violate confidentiality concerns beyond the fact of participation (which the agency almost inevitably and unavoidably knows because of movement control).

- Will a prisoner's status as a research subject have social or other consequences (either positive or negative) for the prisoner?
- What arrangements will be made for prisoners to voice complaints about the study or concerns about their rights as subjects, and how will these communications be facilitated in the correctional setting? (Access to telephones is commonly restricted in correctional facilities, so this too must be considered.)
- How will the confidentiality of the study data be maintained? The IRB will assess whether adequate plans are in place to prevent breaches of confidentiality, including how hard copy forms are handled by the study staff within the correctional setting and how electronic data are protected. Unless names of prisoners are critical to the study (i.e., the study involves continuing treatment, future follow-up, or linkage to other records), the link between names and study data should be destroyed at the earliest possible time. Different types of confidentiality provisions will be required for different types of data (e.g., How are HIV results or other lab results protected? What happens when a prisoner reports an illegal behavior or a parole violation? Who is informed when a prisoner-subject requires follow-up care?). The limits of confidentiality that can be ensured may also vary by

> "The research on women in the prison is very touchy for me," explained Jean Scott, deputy regional director of New York City Correctional Treatment Programs, Phoenix House, and a prisoner liaison panel member. "I see a lot of researchers going in to [get the women to] 'tell your story.' This woman bears her soul, and that's it, she goes down as another number. She's left feeling bad, somebody else now knows her story. Now what do we do? They send these research teams in to start opening up all these wounds with these women, and it is not a good thing. [We need] to have a program that is going to spend the time that is needed for the women."

location (i.e., related to individual state laws or facility rules), and prospective prisoner-subjects must be informed of these limits during the consent process (e.g., some jurisdictions require reporting of child abuse or threats to harm oneself or others).

- How will the research subjects access adequate health care if participation in the research leads to the need for medical or psychological services?
- How will follow-up care be provided to prisoners who may need it? Will it be possible for prison health-care providers to be informed of a person's participation without informing other prison authorities?
- How will study procedures be adapted to fit different settings in multisite studies? The researcher must present information about each research site to assure the committee that local conditions have been considered in the fashioning of responsive and appropriate study procedures. Gathering this facility-specific information and customizing the study procedures are likely to require substantial effort by the investigator, depending on the number of participating study sites, as well as approval by a local IRB that had the benefit of participation by a prisoner advocate familiar with the particular facility.

The IRB needs as much insight into the correctional setting as possible. To optimize a collaborative research relationship between correctional agencies, investigators, and prisoners to answer the questions listed above, some institutional initiative will be required. In addition to including a prisoner representative on the IRB and consulting with prison staff at each study site, it may be desirable for researchers to convene a prison advisory group to assist them in developing appropriate and feasible procedures for each study site. This group should be composed of current prisoners who can inform the researchers about unique factors to consider at their particular institution. For example, they could provide suggestions about how to publicize the study, the best times and locations for recruitment, and how to minimize outside influences on a prisoner's participation decision. This information will also be critical to the IRB as it decides whether adequate protections are in place to allow the study to go forward. It may also be advisable for an individual who is monitoring related or other studies within the same setting (the PRSA) and/or prison staff to attend IRB meetings relevant to research within their institutions. Investigators could consider scheduling periodic (e.g., annual or semiannual) meetings with correctional agencies. With such exchange, investigators may be able to broaden their research protocols to address issues of concern in the correctional setting that would "host" their study, even if the original or primary focus of the investigation is derived from the investigators' own research program. Similarly, corrections staff may get a preview of the kinds of issues and proposals that the investigators intend to pursue and be able to contribute at the early (and later) stages of study design and implementation.

During the deliberation phase of the review, the IRB will decide whether prisoners can be involved in the research study at all in view of the risks and benefits affecting this special population. The IRB may vote to approve the study, approve with modifications, defer, disapprove the study, or it may determine that the study requires a federal-level review.

Two elements of research discussed previously—informed consent and privacy—are so integral to high-quality, ethical research that they require special attention. As such, the committee formulated recommendations regarding both issues.

> **Recommendation 6.1** *Ensure voluntary informed consent.* Human research participant protection programs should ensure voluntary informed consent is obtained from subjects in all research involving prisoners.

Informed consent is vital to autonomous decision making and respect for persons and is considered a bedrock of ethical research—whether it involves prisoners or nonprisoners. Informed consent is an interactive and ongoing process to ensure that participants are voluntarily participating in research and that they understand the level and nature of the risks and the uncertainty of potential benefits. The written consent form—one part of the process—is the mechanism for documenting that communication with the participant regarding relevant considerations to enrollment in a protocol has taken place. The informed consent process must help the prisoner to exercise autonomous decision making. The process poses special challenges in the correctional setting, where autonomy may be inconsistent with institutional order and judicially imposed limitations on liberty. In a correctional setting, a prisoner's capacity to exercise independent judgment may have atrophied. The consent process and discussion must include a focus on the risks and benefits of the research in the context of confinement or the manner in which liberty has been restricted. This would include the effect of any research data on a prisoner (e.g., how would testing positive for a communicable disease effect housing, work opportunities, medical treatment, family visiting). There is no question that, within correctional settings, it is more difficult to provide integrity to the process of informed consent, but this does not remove the obligation. If it is determined that voluntary informed consent is not obtainable, then a research proposal should not go forward.

Some researchers would argue that obtaining informed consent may impede some types of research, for example, studies of social phenomena via participant observation. Informing the subjects that they are being watched would undermine the research. For nonprisoner research, studies may not require informed consent under two sections of the Common Rule:

> (1) Some research can be deemed exempt from IRB review, including: "Research involving the use of educational tests (cognitive, diagnostic, aptitude, achievement), survey procedures, interview procedures or observation of public behavior, unless: (i) information obtained is recorded in such a manner that human subjects can be identified, directly or through identifiers linked to the subjects; and (ii) any disclosure of the human subjects' responses outside the research could reasonably place the subjects at risk of criminal or civil liability or be damaging to the subjects' financial standing, employability, or reputation."[3]

> (2) An IRB could also waive the requirement for informed consent under 46.116: "An IRB may approve a consent procedure that does not include, or that alters, some or all of the elements of informed consent set forth in this section, or waive the requirements to obtain informed consent provided the IRB finds and documents that: (i) The research involves no more than minimal risk to the subjects; (ii) The waiver or alteration will not adversely affect the rights and welfare of the subjects; (iii) The research could not practicably be carried out without the waiver or alteration; and (iv) Whenever appropriate, the subjects will be provided with additional pertinent information after participation."

However, the committee believes that neither of these justifications apply to prisoner subjects. Questions of autonomy and liberty are so different in correctional settings that the IRB should always be required to exam-

---

[3] 45 C.F.R. § 46.101(b)(2).

ine the ethical implications and require voluntary informed consent. In the first case, the committee feels that no research involving prisoner-subjects should be deemed exempt from IRB review because the second condition ((ii) above) cannot be met. It is conceivable that even just observation of a prisoner's behavior, if that is disclosed to prison officials, could put the prisoner at risk. In the second case, it is not possible to say with certainty that the conditions (1) and (2) above will be met for prisoner subjects, regardless of the stated objective of the study. Even a seemingly benign study could pose more than minimal risk to the prisoner subjects. For example, prisoners might be observed selling drugs in the yard in a study whose purpose was simply to observe how different racial or ethnic groups interacted with each other in the yard. If so, a waiver of informed consent could adversely affect their rights and welfare (if the prison officials learned of this observation and took action against the prisoner). The prisoner would need to be informed of these risks before the study began.

Recommendation 6.2 *Protect the privacy of prisoners engaged in research.* **Human research participant protections programs should collaborate with prison officials, probation officers, and other staff relevant to the correctional setting to protect the privacy of subjects in prisoner research.**

Privacy is considered one of the necessary prerequisites for ethical research. In most circumstances, this means nondisclosure of the identity of the research subject and ensuring confidentiality of the specific data collected. Privacy is exceedingly difficult to attain in prison settings, however, because of the inherently coercive and institutionalized contexts and the controlled and public nature of physical movement. Maximizing privacy within a correctional setting will require collaborative planning efforts that involve potential subjects and staff from the correctional setting to consider the impact of participation on privacy issues.

Given that it may not be possible to guarantee absolute privacy in some situations, researchers, IRBs, and other HRPPPs should consider the extent to which core privacy issues can be protected from disclosure through realistic and practical approaches. For instance, it may be clear to prisoners and staff that research is being conducted, but the specific nature of the study or the characteristics common to human subjects need not be generally known or discernible. These measures, and their limits, should be discussed in detail with prospective participants in the context of the consent process.

In determining whether to approve or to continue research, HRPPPs should balance the effectiveness of measures designed to protect participant privacy, the extent of confidence that human subjects understand and willingly accept the risks in view of possible benefits, and the anticipated value of the research.

> *Allen Hornblum, a member of the committee's prisoner liaison group, recalled the lack of prison privacy he witnessed as a member of the board of trustees of an 8,000-person prison system. "I would go through the rolodexes of the inmates. There were inmates who had on their cards that they were HIV positive, which absolutely was not supposed to be known to anybody in the institution except the doctor and the inmate. But on every cell block I could find it. And if the guards know it, the inmates know it."*

The committee investigated whether the Health Insurance Portability and Accountability Act (HIPAA) of 1996[4] afforded any special privacy protections to prisoners involved in research and found that it does not. This law protects medical information for all research participants, not just prisoner participants. In addition, not all medical information is covered; only protected health information falls under HIPAA. Protected health information includes any medical data that contain uniquely identifiable information, such as a Social Security number, address, or fingerprint and that is held by a health-care provider (or other "covered entity").[5] Thus, HIPAA applies only to information collected in the course of medical service provision. Researchers could not obtain and analyze this protected health information unless they comply with specific privacy protections that are provided under the HIPAA research provisions.[6] However, researchers, assuming they are not themselves a covered entity, could collect their own data directly from prisoner research subjects without concern for these regulations.

When Reviews Are Done

As is the case for research that involves persons in the community (i.e., the free world), the review by an IRB or other ethics review committee for research involving prisoners should be conducted at the following times:

- Initial review: This occurs before any subjects are contacted or any

---

[4]Pub. L. No. 104-191.
[5]45 C.F.R. § 160.103, 2003.
[6]Otherwise protected data may be used and disclosed for research if (1) it has been deidentified; (2) the individual has given written authorization; (3) without authorization, in limited circumstances such as for activities involved in preparing for research or for research on decedents; or (4) without authorization, if a waiver has been obtained.

information about them is accessed. The elements of this review and the types of issues to be discussed during this review were detailed previously.
- Amendment review: This occurs any time the researcher wants to change a procedure, consent process, or data collection form.
- Adverse events or unexpected problems: A review should be done at the time any such events or problems occur.
- Continuing review: Such a review is done at an interval specified by the IRB at initial review and is dependent on the risk level for the study (e.g., monthly or quarterly, but no less often than once per year).

Depending on the nature of an amendment or adverse event, and at the discretion of the IRB, it may be acceptable to use an expedited IRB review procedure for these types of reviews. Expedited reviews can be done by an IRB chair or experienced IRB member (rather than by the full committee), but they must include consultation with the prisoner representative. No research involving prisoner-subjects should be deemed exempt from IRB review. Even a low-risk questionnaire involving prisoner-subjects requires an IRB review.

There are other situations for which IRB review is required. A preliminary review can be conducted before funding has been obtained for the study. During this review, the IRB can assess at the most fundamental level whether prisoners can be ethically involved in the proposed research. If so, the adequacy of the protections are assessed and suggestions offered to the researcher about how to strengthen the protections. However, the preliminary review does not substitute for the initial review. No subjects can be contacted and no information can be accessed based on a preliminary IRB review. An IRB review is also needed when an investigator wants to use data for research purposes that was collected during an activity initially classified as treatment or QI (i.e., not research).

SYSTEMATIC OVERSIGHT OF RESEARCH WITH PRISONERS

Although approval of research by the IRB or other independent review committee is a critical first step in protecting research subjects, it is not sufficient. Research involving prisoners, like other types of research, must be monitored throughout the course of the study to verify that study procedures are being conducted as approved and to detect adverse events or unexpected problems in a timely manner. Ongoing monitoring, then, is another key issue that must be considered in the new oversight requirements. The monitoring process may need to differ depending on the setting or type of study. For example, studies that take place in closed institutions that restrict subjects' access to investigators or advocates may require more proactive (inside the institution) monitoring than those that take place in the community, where subjects are more at liberty to pick up the phone and call someone. Similarly, higher-risk or more intrusive studies (e.g., research that involves medical, pharmaceutical, or biological agents or interventions) probably require more intrusive monitoring, whereas social/behavioral studies (e.g., involving questionnaires) and program evaluations may require less stringent monitoring.

Highly coercive environments, such as higher-security jails and prisons, pose well-documented challenges to conducting ethical research with prisoners. Specific threats to principles of individual autonomy (e.g., voluntary consent) and justice (e.g., not bearing disproportionate weight of research risks) are more likely to occur in such closed environments, and it is these environments to which the national commission's recommendations and the current Subpart C regulations were most responsive.

The committee has proposed broadening the definition of the term *prisoner* to apply to a much larger number of individuals in a broader array of environments (see Chapter 4). This expanded definition of prisoner was developed in view of the committee's awareness that the types of threats (i.e., coercion, undue inducement, lack of access to the outside) observed in these traditional institutional settings exist to some degree in other, less traditional settings as well. However, there are also quantitative differences in the extent to which these threats exist and in the likelihood that they will arise in less restrictive prisoner settings. There continues to be a power differential between criminal justice-involved individuals and agents of the justice system (e.g., parole or probation officers or staff in community agencies, such as residential treatment programs and halfway/transition houses where prisoners reside or receive services). Of course, the level of day-to-day control and scrutiny is likely reduced in these community settings, and there is likely a greater degree of openness in such settings. As the level of restrictiveness and external control decreases (e.g., from closed residential facility to probation or house arrest), individuals are likely to have greater opportunities for unmonitored communications with others, including telephone or visitation access to friends, family, or other third parties who may have the prisoner's interests at heart. Depending on individual resources, increased access and individual choice in health-care services are also likely.

As a consequence of the broader proposed definition of *prisoner* and the expanded array of settings in which regulations governing research with prisoners as subjects may apply, it follows that IRBs responsible for reviewing and approving research with prisoners must consider the variety of settings and associated features of those settings in relation to the level of scrutiny and control, openness, and, particularly in the case of medical research protocols, quality of agency health-care services and prisoner-subjects' access to alternatives. In this expanded definition of prisoner and the broader landscape of settings in which research with prisoners may be conducted, research protections must be tailored to some degree to particular types of research (e.g., social and behavioral as compared with biomedical [broadly conceived] and the features of the particular setting).

In the context of this greater need for local identification and scrutiny of the nuances of research settings in relation to the potential for control and coercion, openness, and access, the committee considered an array of specific research design controls and research monitoring practices that IRBs should consider imposing as a function of the research setting. These controls and practices were derived from the ethical analysis described in Chapter 5. It was the committee's view that, in most instances, such judgments and determinations could not likely be made easily or effectively by a remote, centralized review entity that had little firsthand knowledge of local circumstances. Thus, the safeguards proposed in the following section provide for federal-level administrative oversight of particular research protocols in only limited circumstances. Instead, federal-level oversight would focus on making determinations about sensitive research proposals that require federal-level review; enforcing compliance with regulations, investigating problems, intervening to curtail abuses, and applying sanctions for noncompliance; serving as a national resource for HRPPPs; and maintaining a national registry of all research involving prisoners (see later discussion). Various options for monitoring, including the use of a PRSA, the IRB itself, and a national oversight group, are discussed next.

Prison Research Subject Advocate

A PRSA would be assigned to monitor prisoner research of certain risk levels. The scope and intensity of monitoring would be determined by the IRB with input from the investigator and correctional setting staff. The PRSA concept is, in part, modeled on the research subject advocate position now in place in clinical research centers at medical research institutions around the country. However, the PRSA is distinct from a clinical research associate, who is employed by a research sponsor or contract research organization in clinical trials strictly to monitor regulatory compliance at sites participating in clinical trials. Another model for the PRSA concept comes from the European Convention for the Prevention of Torture and Inhuman or Degrading Treatment or Punishment (Council of Europe, 1987). The intent of the convention is to strengthen the protection of persons deprived of liberty. The convention establishes a committee that visits places where persons are deprived of their liberty, including prisons and hospitals where patients are subject to detention, and writes a report of findings to the government with recommendations. The report and recommendations may be made public only at the government's request.

Recommendation 6.3 *Strengthen monitoring of research involving prisoners.* Institutional review boards that review and approve research involving prisoners should establish an onsite, ongoing monitoring function through a prison research subject advocate.

A PRSA helps provide assurance, via ongoing onsite monitoring, such that research subjects within a specific facility or program are protected. The PRSA must be local to the correctional facility in which the research is being conducted to enable frequent visits to the facility, to establish trust among the prisoners, and to respond quickly to any adverse events. The IRB should have free access to the PRSA and be able to meet with the PRSA separate from the investigator and correctional setting staff. The extent of monitoring should be calibrated to the level of restrictions imposed on prisoners in the particular correctional setting and the degree of risk involved in participation, regardless of whether this research is biomedical or social/behavioral in nature.

The PRSA's responsibilities would include the following:

- Monitor compliance with the protocol and full implementation of any IRB-approved research.
- Monitor adverse events, including how these events are tracked, the submission of timely adverse event reports to the IRB and appropriate federal agencies, and IRB review of these reports.
- Monitor compliance with all relevant regulatory requirements.
- Determine that research is conducted only on current, approved protocols and with current, valid informed consent.
- Monitor the consent process by investigators and study coordinators to verify that the prisoners are able to make informed—and uncoerced—decisions about participation.
- Provide a mechanism for receiving and responding to any participant or staff-generated questions regarding participation of human subjects in the research. The PRSA should be able to receive complaints and questions from individual prisoner-subjects, so there must be mechanisms in place to ensure that prisoner-subjects have timely access to the PRSA.
- Assess the implementation of arrangements to protect the privacy and confidentiality of research participants, particularly in connection with personal health information.

The PRSA should be an individual who has formal training in the human research participant protections system and human research ethics. Study sponsors may be required to provide all or a reasonable portion of the PRSA's salary as an overhead expense of the study. Among various candidates for the PRSA position discussed by the committee, the following were considered viable and adequate:

- An ombudsman
- A person employed by the IRB
- A person affiliated with a national entity, an independent contractor hired by the study (if this is the only way to pay the PRSA using grant funding)
- A QI director if the QI program at the facility is adequate

To help ensure the PRSA's independence and credibility with prisoner-subjects, the PRSA should not be an employee of the correctional facility.

> *"I don't think that a person who worked for the department of corrections would be the ideal person to go in and monitor. I think it would have to be somebody that has no vested interest,"* said Jean Scott, at the committee's October 2005 meeting. Ms. Scott is deputy regional director of New York City Correctional Treatment Programs, Phoenix House, and a member of the committee's prisoner liaison panel.

The QI option proposed above is considered secondary to the other options because of concern that an individual who is an employee of the correctional setting would not be able to provide the kind of impartial monitoring that would be required to keep prisoner-subjects as the top priority. If every effort is made to identify a PRSA from outside the correctional facility and none can be found, the PRSA functions could be performed by a QI director already in place at the facility, under the following four conditions:

1. The IRB approves the procedures that will be used by the QI director for monitoring the study.
2. The QI process has written protocols for auditing/reviewing the responsibilities previously listed for the PRSA.
3. The IRB receives and reviews the reports generated by the QI director relevant to the pertinent research activities and has the right to have the QI director revise/redo audits if they are not adequate for monitoring purposes.
4. The QI director reports directly to the IRB.

The activities of the PRSA go beyond the routine annual reviews that IRBs currently conduct. The PRSA's activities are study specific (although a single person could be a PRSA for more than one study) and are "on the ground" activities, involving varying degrees (depending on the type and risk level of the research) of direct observation of specific research activities. The requirement of PRSA monitoring does create an additional expense, which should be borne by the institution conducting the research as an inherent cost of ethical research.

IRB Postapproval Monitoring

Most IRBs have some mechanism for monitoring studies after they are initially approved. These vary by IRB and type of study but may include audits of study records, contact with subjects, and sometimes even direct observation of interviews. For studies involving prisoners, the type of monitoring required depends on the nature of the correctional setting, the extent of restrictions imposed on prisoners in that setting, and the degree to which the proposed research poses a risk to the health or well-being of the prisoner-subjects. At minimum, there should be some mechanism whereby prisoner-subjects can contact the IRB to report problems or ask questions. Guidance and support should be provided to IRBs to allow them to be more proactive in their approach to monitoring of research involving prisoners.

> **Recommendation 6.4** *Modify institutional review board considerations for independent ethical review of research protocols.* Institutional review boards should focus on the particular ethical issues that each protocol raises in the specific context of the correctional setting. Institutional review boards would no longer be required to forward research proposals to the Office for Human Research Protections for certification, except for those rare proposals that require federal-level review.

IRBs should:

- review studies at the local level, make the initial assessments of risk and potential benefits, and approve or reject individual studies based on detailed information about the protocol and correctional setting;
- determine if a study requires federal-level review;
- evaluate investigator efforts to obtain input from prisoners and other stakeholders on the design and conduct of the protocol;
- evaluate the proposed research environment in terms of adequacy of existing health services;

- calibrate the extent of safeguards and monitoring to the level of restrictions imposed upon prisoners in the particular correctional setting and the degree of risk involved in study participation; and
- receive monitoring reports directly from PRSAs and researchers, at a scope and frequency determined during study review.

National Oversight

Monitoring by IRBs is not sufficient to provide the level of protection needed for research involving prisoners. It may be difficult for IRBs to engage in the kind of self-reflection necessary to rethink how a protocol, which they themselves approved, might go awry. The committee recommends that, although IRBs should retain the bulk of the approval and monitoring functions to keep these at a local level, a national independent body is also needed as an additional safeguard (see following discussion). Recommendation 6.5 first deals with enhancing the capacities of the oversight system under DHHS jurisdiction. A further expansion to cover all research involving prisoners follows later in this chapter.

Recommendation 6.5 *Enhance the Office for Human Research Protections' capacity to provide systematic oversight of research involving prisoners.* **The Department of Health and Human Services should strengthen the capacity of the Office for Human Research Protections to provide systematic oversight of research involving prisoners that is within its purview.**

Four necessary functions are currently lacking in whole or in part in oversight of research involving prisoners:

1. Maintain a national registry of all prisoner research that is conducted.
2. Make determinations about studies that require federal-level review.
3. Enforce compliance with the regulations, investigate reports of possible problems, intervene to curtail abuses, and impose sanctions for noncompliance.
4. Serve as a national resource for HRPPPs to promote a uniform understanding and consistent application of the regulations.

For research under DHHS jurisdiction, the OHRP is currently designed to perform three of the four functions listed in Recommendation 6.5. However, the OHRP does not have the funding or personnel to adequately carry out the tasks. The universe of research involving prisoners is larger than that covered by the current regulations. Furthermore, there are vast inconsistencies in how research is defined, who reviews it, and how it is monitored. The OHRP needs to be revitalized and refocused to carry out the three functions already within its purview. As a fourth, new function, the national registry should be housed within the OHRP as well.

IRBs or other independent review committees would still review studies at the local level, making the initial assessments of risk and approving or rejecting individual studies based on detailed information about the study. A revitalized OHRP would be more involved in investigating and intervening when problems occur and promoting consistency on a nationwide basis, thus filling critical voids in the current oversight system. To ensure that research involving prisoners is conducted in an ethically responsible way, the OHRP needs greater resources and broader powers than presently exist. The enforcement division of the OHRP, for example, presently consists of fewer than four full-time positions, and its responsibilities encompass all research (not just prisoner research) conducted under existing regulations.

Because there is no central repository for the collection of data regarding research involving prisoners, it is difficult or impossible to quantify the number of such studies underway at any given time, the number of prisoners involved, the types of studies being conducted, the subject of inquiry in this research, the incidence of protocol deviations, or the occurrence of adverse outcomes (see Chapter 2). A national registry would help the OHRP provide technical assistance and training as well. With this registry, the OHRP and others would have access to valuable information about the kinds of research being conducted, problems and adverse events that have been identified, and the types of protections appropriate for different research projects in various correctional settings. Additionally, as the national body charged with the enforcement of the governing regulations, the OHRP could provide authoritative interpretations of the regulations and their application in various circumstances. In its charge to enforce governing regulations, when less formal procedures prove inadequate, the OHRP must have the authority to initiate legal action to compel compliance, including discovery and subpoena power to uncover abuses and enforce regulations. Anyone should be able to report alleged violations of prisoner-subject rights to the OHRP without fear of retaliation (the OHRP would have to be able to invoke whistle-blower protection for people who disclose problems), substantially improving the safeguards to prisoners who agree to participate in research.

Revitalizing the OHRP to take on these four oversight functions would, however, leave a gaping hole in the national oversight structure that must be acknowledged and remedied. The OHRP's jurisdiction regarding research involving prisoners is limited to studies funded by the DHHS, Social Security Administration (SSA), and Central Intelligence Agency (CIA). The remaining federal agencies and nonfederal and private entities are not required to submit to OHRP oversight. According to the committee's review of current research involving prisoners (see Chapter 2), only 11 percent of all of the studies reviewed were funded by the DHHS, indicating that the vast majority of research involving prisoners does not fall within the OHRP's overview jurisdiction. Therefore, to ensure the ethical conduct of all research involving prisoners, the enhanced OHRP oversight model must be replicated for all research involving prisoners, regardless of funding source, so that research supported by any federal agency, all nonfederal agencies, and the private sector is subjected to the same systematic oversight.

> **Recommendation 6.6** *Establish systematic oversight of all research involving prisoners.* To expand prisoner protections beyond the narrow jurisdiction of the Department of Health and Human Services, Congress should establish a national system of oversight that is applied uniformly to all research involving prisoners, performing all of the functions listed in Recommendation 6.5. The vast majority of research involving prisoners does not fall within the Office for Human Research Protections' overview jurisdiction. Strengthening the safeguards provided for all prisoners involved in research, regardless of funding source, will facilitate safe and ethical research across the full range of prisoner-involved research.

These functions could be performed by the revitalized and properly funded OHRP if its jurisdiction were extended to the entire range of research involving prisoners regardless of funding source—federal or nonfederal, public or private. An alternative is to compose a national entity to perform the necessary oversight functions. Placing the functions within the OHRP may be more feasible and less disruptive, but it must be done with serious attention to the extra support needed within the OHRP to undertake those tasks fully and much more broadly than its current limits to Common Rule agencies. The committee is calling for substantial improvements to the existing system of oversight; if a new entity is necessary to make it happen, then it should be created.

Finally, for reasons similar to those underlying the committee's recommendation for establishing systematic oversight, the research process needs to be characterized by transparency and accountability.

> **Recommendation 6.7** *Ensure transparency and accountability in the research enterprise.* Human research participant protections programs and prison administrations conducting human subject research should be open, transparent, and accountable.

A sound, ethical protection program involves an open, transparent research process. It requires that the mechanisms used to protect participants from undue harm and to respect their rights and welfare must be apparent to everyone involved. This transparency requires open communication and interaction with the local community, research participants, investigators, and other stakeholders in the research enterprise. Accountability entails maintaining fidelity to the methodology stipulated in the protocol as well as accountability to ensure the quality and performance of the protection program itself.

APPLYING SAFEGUARDS FOR PARTICULAR KINDS OF RESEARCH

As noted earlier, the committee recommends that the current Subpart D framework, with modifications for application with prisoner-subjects, be utilized to define permissible research. The modifications necessary for such research to be approvable include (1) a risk-benefit analysis to ascertain whether participation carries potential benefits that outweigh risks, and (2) the utilization of special design and monitoring safeguards,[7] which would vary as a function of the type of research, the risks it poses, and the nature of the research setting. The greater the restrictions upon liberty in a particular correctional setting, the greater the need for safeguards and protections of prisoner-subjects.

The guidance and examples in this section are intended to be illustrative of the ethical framework presented in Chapter 5. Specifically, it demonstrates the importance and application of the risk-benefit approach with appropriate safeguards and monitoring based on the level of risk and the restrictions of the correctional setting. The framework respects the principle of justice and provides adequate protection and potential benefit for prisoners involved in research.

As stated in Chapter 5, a risk-benefit analysis would normally prohibit the following types of biomedical research involving prisoners because potential risks outweigh potential benefits:

- phase 1 and phase 2 studies of experimental treatments, as defined by the FDA, because of insufficient evidence of prospect of direct benefit at this early stage of testing (Example 7 provides a rare, specific circumstance in which phase 1 and phase 2 studies might be permissible, and in which case, federal-level review and high-level safeguards and monitoring would be required);

---

[7]Special safeguards mean those safeguards above and beyond the usual safeguards routinely considered necessary for the approval of research protocols.

- studies that involve exposing subjects to potentially noxious biological or chemical agents merely for the purpose of determining and/or evaluating human reactions to such agents; and
- biomedical studies that would enroll more prisoners than nonprisoners, unless a federal-level review authorizes the study.

Once the IRB determines that a study involving prisoners offers more potential benefits than risks and does not fall within one of the categories of impermissible research noted above, it must determine the appropriate safeguards and monitoring. The types and levels of safeguards and monitoring required depend on the nature of the correctional setting, the extent of restrictions imposed on prisoners in that setting, and the degree to which the proposed research poses risk to the health or well-being of the prisoner-subjects.

Box 6-1 presents the kinds of special design and implementation safeguards and special monitoring safeguards that an IRB might mandate for particular research protocols. In the examples that follow, research involving low risk and conducted in less-restrictive settings may be approvable without the IRB imposing any special safeguards; however, additional special safeguards from Box 6-1 may be necessary for prisoner research that involves greater risk and is planned for more restrictive settings. Stronger safeguards would also be needed in those extremely limited circumstances when it would be ethically permissible to utilize a greater proportion of prisoners than nonprisoners.

The safeguards in Box 6-1 are designed to be responsive to specific ethical (and in some instances, practical) considerations in research with prisoners. The obvious general principle is that as the level of research risk increases and as greater restrictions on liberty appear in a particular correctional setting, additional safeguards should be used. With respect to design safeguards, D1 (federal certificates of confidentiality) is responsive to the concern that correctional settings may pose greater challenges to privacy and confidentiality. D2 (50 percent ceiling) is designed to prevent investigators from capitalizing on prisoners as a captive population and to ensure that prisoners do not bear an undue share of the burdens of research in higher risk studies. D3 (prohibiting incentives for recruitment quotas), D4 (availability of control-arm standard-of-care medications and treatments to nonresearch participants), and D6 (adequate prison health services) are viewed as protections against potentially coercive conditions. D5 (openness of the research setting) is responsive to the concern that, compared with nonprisoner research subjects, prisoners may generally be at greater risk of experiencing harmful effects of research because of limited access to researchers. D7 (30-day review presentation to IRB) provides an extra safeguard to evaluate high-risk studies once they have begun.

> **BOX 6-1**
> **Special Study Design and PRSA Monitoring Safeguards**
>
> *Special Study Design Safeguards (D1–D7)*
>   D1. Investigator should obtain a federal certificate of confidentiality to protect against the disclosure of prejudicial, confidential, or personal information.
>   D2. The proportion of prisoner-subjects to nonprisoner-subjects may not exceed 50 percent.
>   D3. Neither the PI nor any member of the research team or staff member of the institution/agency at which the study is conducted may receive financial or other incentives for meeting recruitment quotas.
>   D4. In clinical trials of medications in which some study arms provide for the administration of standard-of-care treatment, those same medications must be available to prisoners diagnosed with the same disease who are not recruited for, or if recruited decline to participate in, the clinical trial.
>   D5. The PI must demonstrate to the satisfaction of the IRB that the research setting is sufficiently open to permit regular, prompt, and proactive monitoring of prisoner-subjects' clinical status by research staff or PRSA staff required by the research protocol.
>   D6. The PI must demonstrate, to the satisfaction of the IRB, that the quality of physical/mental health services in the particular correctional setting is adequate to respond in a timely and professionally responsible manner to complaints, problems, and side effects that may emerge from prisoners' participation in a research study.[a]
>   D7. The researcher must present to the IRB how the research is proceeding after the first 30 days that subjects are enrolled.

Monitoring safeguards generally permit IRBs to obtain information about recruitment and protocol administration that is independent of the investigator or correctional setting. These safeguards are justified on the principle that research activities should be open and that investigators should be accountable for the proper administration of their protocols. M1, M2, and M3 provide independent checks on the validity of the informed consent process, which may face various threats because of the potentially coercive nature of correctional settings. M4 provides for an independent check of the protocol implementation that protects against protocol deviations that have not been approved by the IRB. M5 and M6 provide for an independent assessment of subjects' reactions to protocol stimuli and the appropriateness and timeliness of investigators' intervention to remedy or ameliorate untoward adverse reactions.

Special PRSA Monitoring Safeguards (M1–M6)

M1. Periodic observation (spot-checking) of informed consent dialogues at recruitment.

M2. Soon after enrollment, test randomly selected subjects for comprehension of the consent disclosure.[b]

M3. Periodically debrief subjects to determine whether they experienced any pressure or coercive actions by investigators or correctional personnel regarding the prisoner-subject's participation.

M4. Periodically observe (spot-check) protocol administrations to ensure fidelity to and compliance with the approved protocol.

M5. Periodically debrief subjects regarding personal reactions to research stimuli (e.g., interviews, questionnaires, medications, or devices).

M6. Periodically debrief subjects regarding timeliness and adequacy of investigator responses to any problems or complaints that the subjects associate with study participation (e.g., side effects or adverse reactions to medications or devices; adverse psychological reactions).

NOTE: PI, principal investigator.

[a] See Chapter 5, page 154 for indirect measures for assessing adequacy of health-care services.

[b] The PRSA needs to determine that the person understands, or has access to information that enables them to understand, the basic study parameters. This should not be a "memory test" of the consent disclosure. Subjects could display comprehension of the basic study parameters by retrieving their copy of the consent disclosure and "explaining" to the PRSA the information therein. A problem would exist, however, if a subject did not appear to understand the study parameters even with access to and opportunity to review the disclosure.

Sample Situations

The following vignettes are provided as exemplars of the kinds of considerations that might arise in IRB deliberations about particular types of studies. The vignettes are clearly not exhaustive, nor are the particular hypothetical "solutions" embedded in them intended to be prescriptive. IRBs encounter a wide variety of prisoner research proposals that vary in the intrusiveness of the experimental stimuli, the restrictiveness of the correctional setting, the level and extent of risks and benefits to prisoner participants as individuals or as a class, and in other study parameters. The current Subpart D framework, with modifications for application to research with prisoners, provides a better conceptual scheme for evaluating such proposals. However, IRBs should impose special study safeguards, such as those indicated in Box 6-1, when levels of restrictiveness and/or risk require them. At the highest level of risk, federal-level review becomes an added requirement, as in Subpart D of 45 C.F.R.§ 46.407).

It is beyond the scope of this committee's charge to prescribe extensive and highly detailed requirements that would accommodate any foreseeable study design; the judgment of the IRB will be required to implement special safeguards in any given case. However, this discussion of IRBs imposing special safeguards should not be read as a mere suggestion; the committee is unanimous in asserting the need for regulations that expressly require IRBs to proactively impose special safeguards when needed to adequately protect prisoner-subjects. Moreover, it is anticipated that regulations based on the committee's deliberations will ensure adequate protection for prisoner-subjects in all research settings.

Example 1: A psychologist administers a measure of general personality traits, such as impulsivity, extraversion, and anxiety sensitivity, to prisoners as they prepare for discharge from prison to a community halfway house. This is a noninterventional study that does not elicit any sensitive or prejudicial information;[8] the questions on these measures are of the type usually encountered in routine psychological evaluations and thus meet the conventional and historical definitions of "minimal risk." The investigator obtains a report of disciplinary infractions for each inmate in the study. Correlational analyses are conducted to determine the extent to which these general personality traits predict the subsequent disciplinary problems. Based on these analyses, suggestions are made to the prison staff responsible for discharge planning about the potential utility of these kinds of measures for identifying prisoners more or less likely to adjust successfully in this particular type of placement. The study has the potential to benefit prisoners as a class by informing the placement decisions that DOC officials make when prisoners are transitioned to the community, potentially increasing the likelihood of a successful return to the community. Thus the study is considered low enough risk that the IRB might opt not to impose any special safeguards. Informed consent can be obtained in the usual way without requiring PRSA monitoring or spot-checking, and there is no apparent

---

[8]Prejudicial information includes the personal information that, if disclosed to or discovered by certain third parties, might result in formal consequences for the individual. Examples include self-reporting of (1) having previously abused children or the elderly (potentially subject to state mandatory reporting laws), (2) medical conditions or vulnerabilities that might be stigmatizing or adversely affect ability to obtain or retain medical insurance, (3) prior criminal activity (only if described in sufficient detail to render the subject a suspect in a particular crime), or (4) conduct that violates institutional or program rules or conditions of probation or parole, the revelation of which could result in the imposition of punitive or disciplinary measures (e.g., drug use). Sensitive information is that which might be potentially embarrassing if revealed to third parties (e.g., sexual habits) even if such disclosure might not put the person at risk for formal sanctions.

reason to require the investigator to seek a certificate of confidentiality. At minimum, there should be some mechanism whereby prisoner-subjects can contact the IRB to report problems or ask questions.

Example 2: An investigator is interested in the personality correlates of risky behavior. With the cooperation of a probation services office, she recruits voluntary participants from individuals living in the community who come in for monthly probation supervision. Her protocol includes self-report questionnaires that assess general personality features; she also conducts a semistructured interview that queries the individual about risky behaviors, such as participating in unprotected sex, illicit drug use, reckless or fast driving, and other kinds of risky behaviors. Although the protocol may meet traditional and historical criteria for "minimal risk," the dependent measure (risky behavior questionnaire) solicits information (e.g., contemporary drug use or law violations) that, if revealed to the probation officer, could result in violation of probation; the questionnaire also solicits information (e.g., sexual activity) that might be potentially embarrassing under some circumstances. The study does have the potential to benefit prisoners as a class by identifying personality features that may lead to a risky lifestyle, and this information could potentially form the basis for interventions that target the reduction of such behaviors in other prisoners in the future.

When a protocol will solicit sensitive or prejudicial information, the IRB should consider requiring safeguards and monitoring procedures of the type indicated in Box 6-1. For research in a relatively lower security setting (e.g., a probational services office), the investigator might be required to obtain a federal certificate of confidentiality; a PRSA might also be assigned to periodically debrief randomly selected subjects to determine whether they had experienced any untoward actions by investigators or their probation officers, such as coercion. In higher-security settings (e.g., a jail or prison), additional and stronger safeguards and monitoring might be deemed necessary. For example, the PRSA might be assigned to spot-check protocol administration to ensure that the protocol was administered within the institution in a way that protected the prisoner's privacy. And of course, in any study that elicits sensitive or prejudicial information, the potential prisoner-subject must be advised in clear terms of the risks associated with disclosure of such information. The potential participant must also be advised that he or she may refuse to answer any questions, and that he or she may discontinue his participation in the study at any time without adverse consequence to his personal circumstances or the conditions of his confinement.

Example 3: A phase 3 study plans to enroll more prisoners than non-prisoners comparing an experimental treatment for hepatitis C with an existing therapy. This research involves greater than minimal risk, but presents the prospect of direct benefit to the individual participants (currently § 46.405 Subpart D). The study is not approvable, however, unless it reduces the percentage of prisoner-subjects to no more than 50 percent. If prisoner enrollment is reduced, safeguards and monitoring should still be extensive. They might include all of the safeguards listed in Box 6-1, plus M3-6 of the PRSA monitoring safeguards.

Example 4: A phase 3 study is planned to compare an experimental treatment to placebo for a condition for which no standard therapy exists. Placebo-controlled studies are not allowable if there is a standard therapy for the condition. Current standard therapy would have to be the comparator to the experimental therapy in order for the study to provide potential benefits to the individual prisoner-subjects. If there is no standard therapy and placebo control is proposed, concerns regarding use of placebo are sufficient for the committee to determine that federal-level review would be necessary. Exceptional safeguards would need to be put in place as well. The PRSA should attend informed consent dialogues to ensure prisoners understand that they may be receiving a placebo. Also appropriate are M5 and M6 from Box 6-1, which provide for reactions to study medications and subjects' experiences with the responsiveness of the prison staff and investigators to adverse events that they may have experienced. In addition, M7 should be used, requiring researchers to present the study's status to the IRB after the first 30 days the subjects are enrolled.

Example 5: In a study of post-traumatic stress disorder, participants will be queried in depth about prior traumas and associated reactions, but the study does not involve investigation of treatments for such conditions. In-depth explorations of traumatic events and the deliberate uncovering of associated feelings and emotions might result in a degree of psychological discomfort that increases potential risk to some participants. In addition, this study provides no potential benefit for the individual, but may benefit prisoners as a class if the investigation aims to understand the impact of trauma on crime or recidivism after release from prison, or serves as a potential basis for developing therapeutic interventions.

The research may be approvable if benefits to prisoners as a class can be ascertained. However, level of risk is greater than minimal; therefore, the IRB may deem necessary a type of PRSA monitoring that has a higher frequency and a greater extent (as described in Box 6-1) than would be needed for a study that delved only superficially into past traumatic experiences (e.g., some research questionnaires include only one or two cursory questions about whether the respondent believes that he or she has ever been abused or experienced trauma, without exploring any details of such experiences). For example, M4 (PRSA monitoring, spot-checking administration of the protocol) might reveal the extent to which the investigator evaluated the immediate impact of the protocol on the subject and took appropriate action (e.g., crisis intervention, referral to services) when subjects became upset as a consequence of participation.

Example 6: A study will utilize functional magnetic resonance imaging to study brain activity during subjects' responses to visual or verbal stimuli that invoke feelings of anger and aggression. This study is an example of a behavioral study in that the outcomes involve monitoring of brain activity (behavior). It does not provide direct benefit to prisoner-subjects, but it might benefit prisoners as a class if methods to reduce anger could be developed based on the magnetic resonance imaging (MRI) results. Because MRI is considered an invasive monitoring procedure, the study would involve somewhat greater than minimal risk. Safeguards and monitoring must be correspondingly more stringent. In addition, safeguards and monitoring would need to be more stringent if the study were taking place in a high-security correctional setting than if it were in a less-restrictive setting.

Example 7: A phase 1 study of a medication may reduce repetitive sexual assaults. Research that presents an opportunity to understand, prevent, or alleviate a serious problem that solely or almost exclusively affects the health or welfare of prisoners is a narrow category that the committee expects will be used in only rare cases. The committee recommends that proposals for this type of research be permissible only under the added scrutiny of federal-level review and approval. Such studies may not proceed until after the secretary has consulted with the appropriate experts, such as an ad hoc committee as used for Subpart D of § 46.407, and published notice in the *Federal Register* of the intent to approve such research. It includes studies seeking to develop medications for the treatment or management of certain behaviors that are unique to, or almost exclusively found in, prisoner populations. For example, repetitive violence or repetitive sexual assault are behaviors not widely distributed in the general population. Individuals who exhibit these behaviors are confined for long periods of time with little prospect for release unless methods are developed to manage their deviant behavior. Insofar as the committee has recommended against permitting prisoners to participate as research subjects in phase 1 and phase 2 clinical trials of medications, in the case of such conditions an exception is necessary as there are no alternative candidate research populations to draw from. Due to the potential risks (prisoners make up more than 50 percent of the study population and phase 1 testing is early testing with little data on benefit), this study would require the most stringent design safeguards and PRSA monitoring, some of which is described in the Box 6-1.

Example 8: Research will study segregation or other isolated settings and its effects. There would be significant problems gaining reliable voluntary consent from individuals within the isolated confines of segregation or who face the bleak future of death row. Approval of any studies within these settings would require a federal-level review process, including consultation with the appropriate experts, such as an ad hoc committee as used for Subpart D of § 46.407, and published notice in the *Federal Register* of the intent to approve such research. Studies proposed within these settings would have to establish a clear potential benefit to the prisoner-subjects and would likely be limited to studies designed to measure the adverse effects of segregation on mental or physical health or well-being. Extraordinary safeguards must be in place to minimize coercive forces and maximize the likelihood that prisoner participation is voluntary. Monitoring should be extensive as well, including PRSA attendance at every enrollment interview to ensure and reinforce disclosure that participating (or not) in the research does not affect how long the person may remain in his or her current special status or setting.

Example 9: A study is proposed to compare drug X with drug Y to treat impulse control disorders. Clinicians currently use drug Y to treat such disorders; however, it is not on the prison's formulary due to its cost. Available instead is the lower-cost generic form, which is more likely to cause gastric side effects than drug Y. The study would not be approvable because of standard-of-care and consent issues. Some prisoners may be willing to expose themselves to unknown risks of taking drug X in the hope of receiving drug Y, which is considered a useful drug for impulse control disorders, but is not available, except through this research project.

Example 10: A person sentenced to probation is released from jail and resumes living at home and makes monthly visits for probation supervision. This prisoner reads in the newspaper that the local university medical school is conducting a phase 2 study of a drug to treat adult attention deficit disorder (ADHD). Having previously been diagnosed with ADHD, he calls the university and makes an appointment to meet with the study coordinator and eventually enrolls in the study. This is an example of the situation described in Chapter 4, in which the prisoner is voluntarily participating in a study that has no necessary connection to his status as a prisoner; no criminal justice agent (e.g., his probation officer) is involved in the identification or recruitment process, and his status as a "prisoner" is of no interest or consequence to the investigators—they are simply interested in adults with ADHD. The proposed regulations and guidelines in this report pertaining to "prisoner research" would not apply to this individual because there is no criminal justice nexus to his study participation.

Example 11: A study compares the effectiveness of two in-prison education programs for prisoners with HIV. The study would assess prisoner actions after release from prison. Many DOCs have recently instituted "transitional case management programs" for prisoners with HIV, diabetes, tuberculosis, or mental health issues as a standard of care when prisoners are released from custody. Researchers are trying to better understand the impact of this new case management model and how to improve it and compare it with other models. This research would involve recruiting prisoners and starting the health education and/or behavioral intervention before their release, then following prisoners after their release to determine if they follow up with their treatment, for example, or if they are using condoms. The risks are low, and potential benefits exist for prisoners as individuals and as a class. Regarding important safeguards, the researchers would need to (1) obtain a federal certificate of confidentiality to protect the confidentiality of the information the prisoner provides for the study, (2) convince the IRB that financial or other incentives are not provided for meeting recruitment quotas, and (3) find that the setting is sufficiently open to conduct the research (D1, D3, and D5). Although risks are considered low, the IRB will still want to be convinced that participants know what they are getting into and that the researchers are adhering to the protocol. Periodic monitoring (spot-checking), as described in Box 6-1 should accomplish this goal. And of course, in any study that elicits sensitive or prejudicial information, the potential prisoner-subject must be advised in clear terms of the risks associated with disclosure of such information. The potential participant must also be advised that he may refuse to answer any questions, and that he may discontinue his participation in the study at any time without adverse consequence to his personal circumstances or the conditions of his parole.

Example 12: A study will compare the effect of standard diet plus a dietary supplement versus standard diet alone on violent behavior among prisoners.[9] Nonprisoner research has shown a correlation between high intake of omega 3 fatty acids (fish) and lower murder rates. A researcher proposes to enroll 231 volunteers in a prison. Half would receive omega-3 fatty acids and other supplements; half would receive a placebo. A placebo is used so that the study subjects and others do not know who is receiving the supple-

---

[9]Interesting note: This study was actually published in 2002 in the United Kingdom (Mihm, 2006). Antisocial behavior (assaults and other violations) dropped by a third (relative to previous records) in the group that received the supplements. There was no behavior change in the control group. The investigator is planning a larger study and similar trials are underway in Holland and Norway.

ment and who is not. Reports of antisocial behavior (assaults and other violations) would be measured before and during the intervention. Approval or disapproval of this study would depend on whether the IRB views it as behavioral or biomedical. The researchers are measuring behavior, but what is the supplement considered—a behavioral intervention or a biomedical intervention? No diagnosed condition is being "treated" and the supplement is not a drug controlled by the FDA. This may be a case in which fitting a study into a clear category is less helpful than doing a straightforward risk-benefit analysis. If viewed as biomedical, the study would be unapprovable because of the 50 percent rule. The placebo question is tricky as well. If a standard of care exists, it should be provided as the comparator arm. There is no standard of care in terms of dietary supplements, but both groups are getting the same standard diet. If considered a behavioral study, it would likely be approvable. What safeguards and monitoring would be necessary? If the study is approvable, as prisoners will be ingesting a substance, it is worth putting special safeguards in place, including D1, D3, D5, and D6. The PRSA should periodically attend informed consent dialogues to ensure prisoners understand that they may be receiving a placebo. Also appropriate are M5 and M6 from Box 6-1, which provide for reactions to study medications and subjects' experiences with the responsiveness of the prison staff and investigators to adverse events that participants may have experienced.

OTHER CATEGORIES AND TYPES OF RESEARCH INVOLVING PRISONERS PROHIBITED

Because of the history of abuse in prisoner research and the continuing existence of powerful incentives to exploit this vulnerable population, the committee encourages a conservative approach to the approval of any research involving prisoners. Those studies that are approved should incorporate safeguards necessary and appropriate to ensure the safety of prisoner-subjects in view of the correctional setting in which the study will be conducted. The committee unanimously recommends against the conduct of any research involving prisoners that is not specifically permitted under this report.

IMPACT OF COMMITTEE RECOMMENDATIONS ON STAKEHOLDER RESPONSIBILITIES

The recommendations offered in this report are intended to support the development of a uniform system that provides critically important protections for prisoners involved in research. Strengthening the systems of oversight and requiring collaboration at every level of the research process will

TABLE 6-1 Impact of Committee Recommendations on Stakeholder Responsibilities

Stakeholders	Current Duties	Proposed Duties Based on Committee Recommendations
Congress		1. Mandate uniform guidelines. 2. Adequately fund OHRP to strengthen its capacity to provide uniform oversight. 3. Establish national oversight entity (OHRP or other) to provide same OHRP oversight functions for the larger universe of research involving prisoners that is not within DHHS jurisdiction.
DHHS/OHRP	1. DHHS agencies follow Subpart C, OHRP also has oversite for research involving prisoners for two other agencies (CIA, SSA) that signed on to Subpart C. 2. For above mentioned studies involving prisoners, OHRP must certify that IRB has followed Subpart C. 3. If a protocol does not fit within one of five categories, regardless of risk benefit, it is not approved.	1. Expand definition of the term *prisoner*. 2. Support critical areas of correctional research. 3. Revise Subpart C regulations to reflect a risk-benefit approach to research review similar to Subpart D. 4. Establish a system of safeguards to be applied uniformly. 5. Revitalize OHRP to enhance its capacity to provide uniform oversight. 6. Maintain a national registry of all prisoner research. 7. OHRP no longer certifies all studies, although it still oversees process of "exceptional" study review. 8. OHRP focus shifts to national oversight, data collection, compliance, enforcement, and technical assistance role.
Other federal agencies	Only CIA and SSA follow Subpart C.	1. All federal agencies follow Subpart C. 2. Support critical areas of correctional research.
Nonfederal and private sponsors	Not required to follow Subpart C.	Must follow revised Subpart C.

continued

TABLE 6-1 Continued

Stakeholders	Current Duties	Proposed Duties Based on Committee Recommendations
Correctional settings	1. No clear, standard expectations for providing input in design or access for onsite monitoring. 2. May or may not require IRB review for research at their facility.	1. Be open to providing input to investigators regarding the design and conduct of research protocols involving prisoners. 2. Require that research be approved by an IRB before it is conducted at their facility. 3. Assist in protection of subject privacy. 4. Provide for timely and adequate medical response to adverse events experienced by the research subjects. 5. Ensure that PSRAs have open access to monitor research activities.
HRPPP/IRB	1. Protocol review is based on categories. 2. For DHHS-supported research involving prisoners, submit to OHRP for certification, and if necessary, federal-level review. 3. Wait for OHRP certification before study can be approved. 4. Ensure informed consent. 5. Protect subject privacy. 6. Include prisoner representative as voting member of IRB.	1. Review shifts from category-based to risk-benefit approach, with focus on the particular ethical issues that each protocol raises in the specific context of the correctional setting. 2. Only "exceptional" studies are submitted to OHRP for federal-level review. 3. Evaluate investigator efforts to obtain input from prisoners and other stakeholders on the design and conduct of research protocols involving prisoners. 4. Evaluate the proposed research environment in terms of adequacy of existing health services to ensure that prisoner participation is truly voluntary, and assess existing capacity to provide for timely and adequate medical response to adverse events experienced by the research subjects.

	5. Ensure informed consent. 6. Protect subject privacy. 7. Include prisoner representative as voting member of IRB. 8. Be open, transparent, and accountable.
Investigators	1. Present studies to IRB and await IRB approval and OHRP certification. 2. No standards for getting input or ensuring adequate medical response 3. Obtain informed consent.	1. Present study to IRB for approval. Only requires OHRP review for "exceptional" studies. 2. Demonstrate efforts to obtain input on study design and implementation from stakeholders, including prisoners. 3. Demonstrate to the IRB that the proposed research environment provides for timely and adequate medical response to adverse events experienced by the research subjects. 4. Obtain informed consent. 5. Be open, transparent, and accountable.
PRSAs	Do not exist.	1. Provide assurance, via ongoing, onsite monitoring, such that research subjects within a specific facility or program are protected. 2. Multisite studies would likely have more than one PRSA. 3. Duties expand as potential risks to participants increase.
Prisoners	1. Provide informed consent.	1. Provide informed consent. 2. Provide input, on request, on study design and implementation.

NOTE: OHRP, Office for Human Research Protections; DHHS, Department of Health and Human Services; CIA, Central Intelligence Agency; SSA, Social Security Administration; IRB, institutional review board; PRSA, prison research subject advocate.

require substantial commitments from every stakeholder (Table 6-1). The committee acknowledges, for example, that the collaboration model will be new within most correctional settings and among many researchers. However, if research is to be supported to improve the welfare of prisoner populations, it must be done with rigorous safeguards and under a comprehensive HRPPP.

REFERENCES

Council of Europe. 1987. *European Convention for the Prevention of Torture and Inhuman or Degrading Treatment or Punishment.* [Online]. Available: http://conventions.coe.int/Treaty/EN/Reports/HTML/126.htm [accessed December 26, 2005].

Council of State Governments. 2002. *Criminal Justice/Mental Health Consensus Project.* New York: Council of State Governments.

IOM (Institute of Medicine). 2003. *Responsible Research: A Systems Approach to Protecting Research Participants.* Washington, DC: The National Academies Press.

IOM. 2004. *The Ethical Conduct of Clinical Research Involving Children.* Washington, DC: The National Academies Press.

Joint Commission on Accreditation of Healthcare Organizations. 1992. *The Transition from QA to QI: Performance-Based Evaluation of Mental Health Organizations.* Oakbrook Terrace, IL: Joint Commission on Accreditation of Healthcare Organizations.

Mihm, S. 2006, April 16. Does eating salmon lower the murder rate? *New York Times Magazine.* [Online]. Available: http://www.nytimes.com/2006/04/16/magazine/16wwln_idealab.html?ex=1146110400&en=2528d21f31d15f30&e=5070 (accessed April 25, 2006).

A

Data Sources and Methods

To comprehensively address the committee's overarching task of reviewing ethical considerations for protection of prisoners involved in research, the committee cast a broad net for the collection and assessment of information. These sources included commissioned papers (Box A-1), open sessions and workshops, telephone interviews and e-mail surveys to the state departments of corrections (DOCs), a survey of recent literature (to assess basic characteristics of research with prisoners), and two site visits to the correctional facilities.

In addition, a liaison panel of former prisoners and prisoner advocates was assembled for the committee to consult with throughout the project (Box A-2). The committee organized two meetings with the liaison panel to receive their expert advice and guidance in framing the issues, identifying important sources of information, and ensuring a comprehensive analysis. A summary description of the committee's evidence gathering activities and results follows.

OPEN SESSIONS AND WORKSHOPS

Over the course of the study, the committee sought and received input from former prisoners, representatives of the prisoner advocacy community, bioethics researchers, health professionals, prison services researchers, and other organizations involved with research in prisons. To help accomplish this, the committee held three open meetings. The first was part of the first committee meeting on March 16, 2005. Staff from the Office for

> **BOX A-1**
> **Commissioned Papers**
>
> *Ethical Issues Regarding HIV/AIDS Research Among Prisoners*
> Theodore M. Hammett, Ph.D., Abt Associates, Inc.
>
> *10 Years of HIV/AIDS Research Behind Bars: Time for Change*
> Jason Farley, Ph.D.(c), MPH, CRNP, The Johns Hopkins University
>
> *Rethinking the Ethics of Research Involving Prisoners*
> Alex London, Ph.D., Carnegie Mellon University
>
> *Research with Prisoners: A Reexamination of Ethical Foundations*
> Mary Anderlik Majumder, J.D., Ph.D., Center for Medical Ethics and Health Policy
>
> *Current Status of the Process of Mental Health Research and Substance Abuse Research with Prisoners: Practical Burdens and Benefits of the Current System*
> Robert Trestman, Ph.D., M.D., University of Connecticut Health Center

> **BOX A-2**
> **Former Prisoners/Prisoner Advocates Liaison Group**
>
> **Edward Anthony**, Philadelphia, PA
> **Jack Beck, Esq.**, Correctional Association of New York
> **Debra Breuklander**, MECCA
> **James J. Dahl, Ph.D.**, Phoenix House
> **Allen Hornblum, M.A., M.P.A.**, Temple University
> **Daniel S. Murphy, Ph.D.**, Appalachian State University
> **Barry Nakell, Esq.**, North Carolina Prisoner Legal Services, Inc.
> **Osvaldo Rivera, LADC I**, Span, Inc.
> **Jeffrey Ian Ross, Ph.D.**, University of Baltimore
> **Jean Scott**, Phoenix House

Human Research Protections (OHRP) discussed the current federal regulations and their goals for this Institute of Medicine (IOM) project. Perspectives on the current federal regulation and needed changes were also provided by representatives of the prisoner advocacy community, bioethics researchers, prison services researcher, and a representative from the federal Bureau of Prisons (BOP). The second was a workshop in Washington, D.C., on May 4, 2005. This public workshop focused on the ethical, legal, regulatory frameworks that underlie research involving prisoners. The committee also heard from representatives of the corrections industry about the practicalities of conducting research in correctional settings. A panel of

> **BOX A-3**
> **Individuals and Organizations that Addressed the Committee**
>
> Elizabeth Alexander, J.D., National Prisoner Project of the American Civil Liberties Union (ACLU)
> Edward Anthony, Philadelphia, PA
> Larry Bench, Ph.D., Utah Department of Corrections
> Jessica Berg, J.D., Case Western Reserve University
> Joseph Bick, M.D., California Medical Facility
> Debra Breuklander, MECCA
> Alvin J. Bronstein, J.D., ABA Task Force on Legal Status of Prisoners, ACLU National Prison Project
> James Childress, Ph.D., University of Virginia
> Gwendolyn C. Chunn, M.A., American Correctional Association
> Hazel D. Dean, Sc.D., M.P.H., Centers for Disease Control and Prevention
> Nancy Dubler, LL.B., Montefiore Medical Center
> Bernice Elger, Ph.D., Timothy Harding University of Geneva, Switzerland
> Gerald Gaes, Ph.D., National Institute of Justice
> Julia Gorey, J.D., Office for Human Research Protections
> Olga Grinstead, Ph.D., M.P.H., University of California, San Francisco (UCSF)
> Alison Hardy, J.D., Prison Law Office
> Edward Harrison, CCHP, National Commission on Correctional Health Care
> Allen Hornblum, M.A., M.P.H., Temple University
> Doris J. James, M.A., Bureau of Justice Statistics
> Denise Johnston, M.D., Center for Children of Incarcerated Parents
> Patricia King, J.D., Georgetown University
> Peter Leone, Ph.D., University of Maryland at College Park
> Phillip Lyons, J.D., Ph.D., Sam Houston State University
> Philip Magaletta, Ph.D., Federal Bureau of Prisons
> Monika Markowitz, MSN, RN, M.A., Virginia Commonwealth University
> Mary Faith Marshall, Ph.D., University of Minnesota
> Nena Messina Ph.D., University of California, Los Angeles
> Daniel S. Murphy, Ph.D., Appalachian State University
> David Paar, M.D., University of Texas Medical Branch, Galveston
> Darrel A. Regier, M.D., M.P.H., American Psychiatric Association
> Bernard Schwetz, DVM, Ph.D., Department of Health and Human Services
> Vera Hassner Sharav, M.L.S., Alliance for Human Research Protection
> Christopher Slobogin, J.D., LL.M., University of Florida School of Law
> Susan Sniderman, M.D., IRB Chair, UCSF
> Irene Stith-Coloman, Office for Human Research Protections
> T. Howard Stone, J.D., LL.M., University of Louisville
> David Thomas, M.D., Nova Southeastern University College of Medicine
> Dan Wikler, Ph.D., Harvard University
> Gary Zajac, Ph.D., Pennsylvania Department of Corrections

former prisoners and prisoner advocates talked about needed protections for research involving prisoners. The third workshop was held in San Francisco on July 18, 2005. This workshop focused on topical research areas and methodological issues related to conducting research with correctional populations. Former prisoners and prisoner advocates also presented their views of needed protections. The organizations and individuals that addressed the committee in these open sessions are listed in Box A-3. In

> **BOX A-4**
> **Public Meeting Participants**
>
> **Sue Allison**, Federal Bureau of Prisons
> **Susan Bankowski**, Johns Hopkins School of Public Health
> **Jessica Baumann**, Bureau of National Affairs
> **Francis Beylotte**, American Psychological Association
> **Laura Bishop**, Kennedy Institute of Ethics
> **Kristina Borror**, Office for Human Research Protections
> **Bret Bucklen**, Pennsylvania Department of Corrections
> **Scott Camp**, Federal Bureau of Prisons
> **Michael Carome**, Office for Human Research Protections
> **Erika Check**, *Nature*
> **Michael D. Cohen**, New York State Office of Children and Family Services
> **Jennifer Couzin**, *Science*
> **Joyce Cutler**, Bureau of National Affairs
> **Pamela Diamond**, University of Texas School of Public Health
> **Erik Dietz**, Federal Bureau of Prisons
> **Glen Drew**, Office for Human Research Protections
> **Jessica Ebert**, *Nature*
> **David Egilman**, Brown University
> **Bernice Elger**, University of Geneva and National Institutes of Health (NIH)
> **Patricia El-Hinnawy**, Office for Human Research Protections
> **Julie Falk**, CorrectHELP
> **Christine Fornwalt**, Johns Hopkins Bloomberg School of Public Health
> **Gerald Gaes**, National Institute of Justice
> **Doreen Geiger**, Washington State Department of Corrections
> **Harold Goldstein**, American Psychiatric Institute for Research and Education
>   Te Guerra
> **Erica Hall**, KPFT Pacifica Radio, *Houston News*
> **Shirley Hicks**, Office for Human Research Protections

addition, many other individuals attended and participated in the three public meetings (Box A-4).

LITERATURE SURVEY TO ASSESS GENERAL CHARACTERISTICS OF RESEARCH WITH PRISONERS

To help characterize the landscape of published research with prisoners (i.e., who is doing what type of research in what type of prisoner settings), the committee conducted an assessment of prisoner research published in peer-reviewed journals. The preliminary search consisted of English language articles published since 1990, using the following databases: MedLine, PsychLit, Sociological Abstracts, Cumulative Index to Nursing & Allied Health Literature, Criminal Justice Abstracts, Education Resources

APPENDIX A

Terry Hill, Lumetra
Sally Hillsman, American Sociological Association
Bill Holman, Gilead Sciences, Inc.
Craig Hutchinson, UCSF Center for AIDS Prevention Studies
Victoria Joseph, Bureau of Prisons
Julie Kaneshiro, Office for Human Research Protections
Alexa Kasdan, San Francisco AIDS Foundation
Steven Krosnick, NIH/Center for Scientific Review
Dan Landrigan, Report on Research Compliance
Molly Lang, *The Blue Sheet,* F-D-C Reports
Elizabeth Mendelsohn, UCSF Office of Research
Leah Mendelsohn, Johns Hopkins Bloomberg School of Public Health
Virginia Morrison, Health Care Mediations, Inc.
Janet Myers, UCSF Medicine
Edward Opton, Jr.
Sangeeta Panicker, American Psychological Association
Kevin Prohaska, Office for Human Research Protections
Mercedes Rubio, American Sociological Association
William Ruby, Gilead Sciences, Inc.
Sandra Sanford, George Mason University
Jeffrey Schomisch, Guide to Good Clinical Practice
Angela Sharpe, Consortium of Social Science Associations
Barbara Solt, Institute for the Advancement of Social Work Research
Anne Spaulding, Medical College of Georgia/
Georgia Correctional Health Care, Infectious Disease
Mary Sylla, Centerforce
Sara Tobin, Stanford University Center for Biomedical Ethics
Christie Visher, The Urban Institute
Cheryl Crawford Watson, National Institute of Justice
Donna Willmott, Legal Services for Prisoners with Children

Information Center, National Technical Information Service, and Excerpta Medica Database. Search terms used included *IRB composition, multisite study/studies, risk-benefit, informed consent, undue influence, vulnerable populations, payment, biomedical research, behavioral research, environment, clinical trials, medication development, FDA, data storage, record keeping, privacy, placebo-control trials, standard of care, follow-up care, follow-up monitoring, data monitoring, HIV/AIDS, tuberculosis, infectious diseases, substance abuse, mental health, women, females, juveniles, adolescents,* and *mental illness.* These search terms were cross-matched with the following subject terms: *inmate(s), prisoner(s), incarcerate(d), jail(s).* The preliminary search resulted in more than 14,000 articles. The search was then limited to the past 5 years, which resulted in a selection of 1,870 articles.

A random sampling of 20 percent of the 1,870 articles was selected as the final sample. Of these 374 studies, a total of 327 were studies that included human subjects. The remaining 47 included the following types of articles: review articles, commentaries, introductions to special editions, letters to the editor, position pieces, editorials, theory articles, news articles, legal reviews, opinion pieces, discussion pieces, and news type articles.

All of the articles were reviewed and coded using the standard criteria. The results follow.

Results

The results of the survey to assess the general characteristics of published research with prisoners are summarized in the following figures.

Funding Sources

Funding stemmed from a variety of sources, including the federal government, state agencies, universities, and the private sector (Figures A-1, A-2).

Mechanism of Approval

Most studies (66 percent) did not report the mechanism by which they were approved (Figure A-3). Fifteen percent indicated institutional review board approval; other entity review was 19 percent.

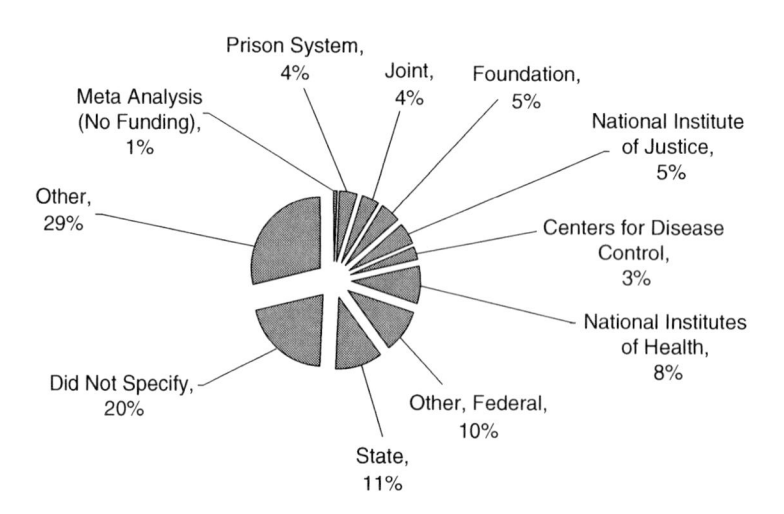

FIGURE A-1 Source of funding.

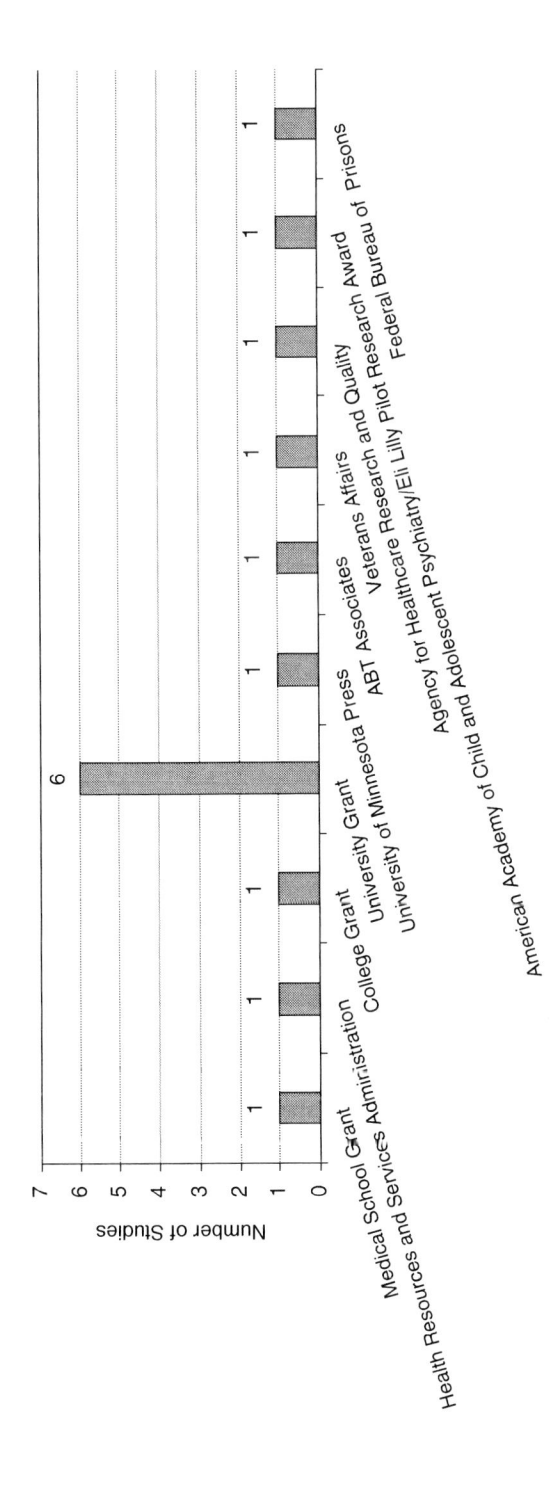

FIGURE A-2 Number of studies with other or other federal sources of funding.

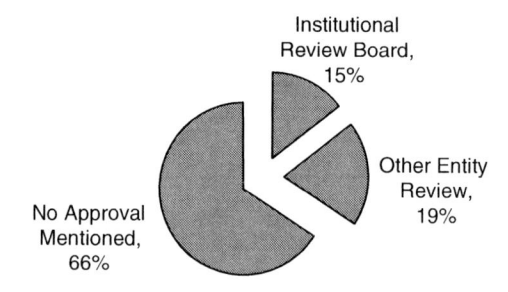

182 ETHICAL CONSIDERATIONS FOR RESEARCH INVOLVING PRISONERS

FIGURE A-3 Mechanism of approval.

Study Design

As shown in Figure A-4, epidemiological studies were the most common (39 percent). Other common study designs included correlational studies (27 percent) and those assessing behavioral outcomes (14 percent).

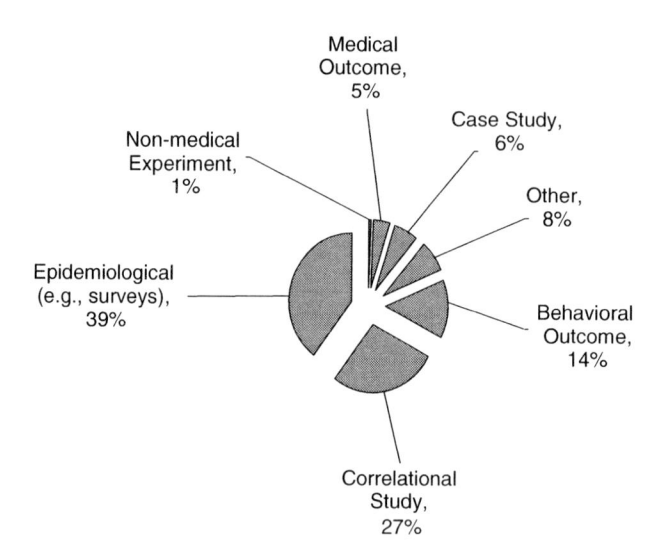

FIGURE A-4 Study design.

Type of Study

Most of the studies (41 percent) in the sample had a sociobehavioral focus, lacked a therapeutic purpose, and had minimal risk to participants (Figure A-5). Program evaluations (26 percent) and record reviews (21 percent) were also common.

APPENDIX A

Pie chart showing:
- Medical, Therapeutic, No Standard of Care, 1%
- Biomedical, Nontherapeutic, 1%
- Medical, Therapeutic, Standard of Care Exists, 2%
- Social/Behavioral, Nontherapeutic, Greater than Minimal Risk, 0%
- Other, 2%
- Social/Behavioral, Therapeutic, 6%
- Social/Behavioral, Nontherapeutic, Minimal Risk, 41%
- Administrative Records Review, 21%
- Department of Corrections Program Evaluation, 26%

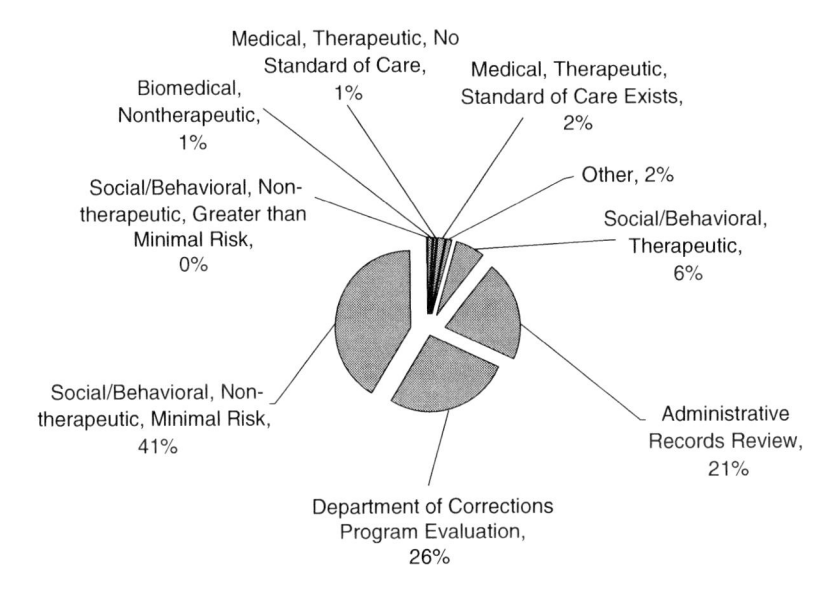

FIGURE A-5 Type of study. (Same as Figure 2-3).
NOTE: Greater than minimal risk included any biomedical (nontherapeutic) study; any medical therapeutic study (regardless of the existence of a standard of care); any social/behavioral therapeutic study; and any nontherapeutic study involving a manipulation that the research assistant judged to involve potentially serious physical or emotional stress (e.g., long sleep deprivation). Not greater than minimal risk included any study based on review of administrative records; any program evaluation study; any nontherapeutic social/behavioral study that either involved no manipulation (e.g., innocuous questionnaires/surveys) or involved a manipulation that the research assistant judged did not involve potentially serious physical or emotional stress (e.g., long sleep deprivation).

Studies were largely focused on health status (43 percent) and personality characteristics (19 percent) (Figure A-6).

Facilities/Locations

More than half of the studies (53 percent) were conducted in prisons or jails (Figure A-7). Another large proportion of the studies (37 percent) were conducted in alternate settings, such as treatment programs or postincarceration settings (Figures A-7, A-8).

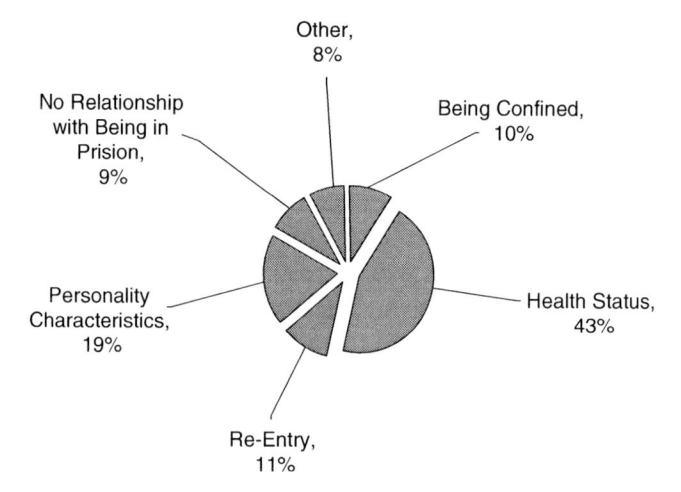

FIGURE A-6 Categories of research.

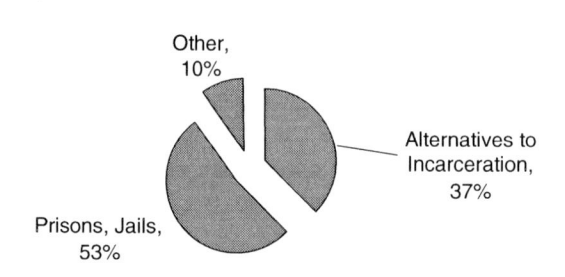

- Other, 8%
- Being Confined, 10%
- Health Status, 43%
- Re-Entry, 11%
- Personality Characteristics, 19%
- No Relationship with Being in Prision, 9%

FIGURE A-7 Facilities/location of studies.

- Other, 10%
- Alternatives to Incarceration, 37%
- Prisons, Jails, 53%

Number and Demographics of Research Participants

The number of participants in a published article ranged from 1 to 336,668. Most studies (272) included 1,000 or fewer participants (Figure A-9).

Gender More studies included male participants than female participants (Figure A-10).

Age Most studies included adult participants; few included participants younger than 18 years (Figure A-11).

APPENDIX A   185

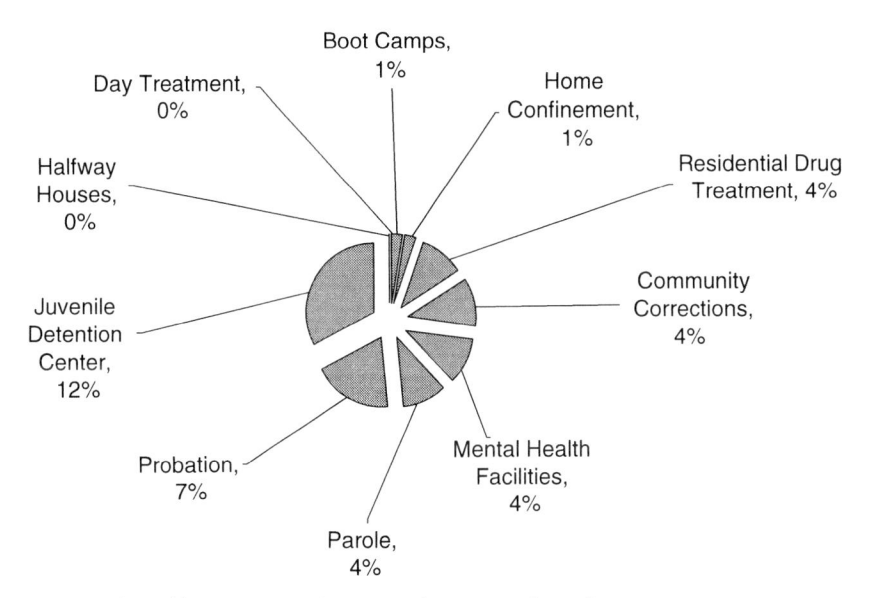

FIGURE A-8 Alternatives to incarceration research settings.
NOTE: This graph corresponds to the "Alternatives to Incarceration" slice in Figure A-7. Juvenile detention centers were included in this analysis because the committee decided to limit its focus to adults after this literature assessment was conducted.

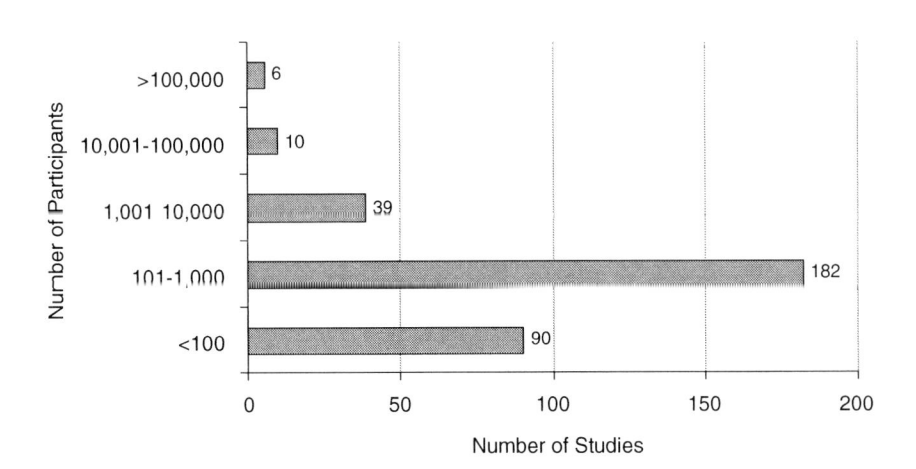

FIGURE A-9 Number of research participants.

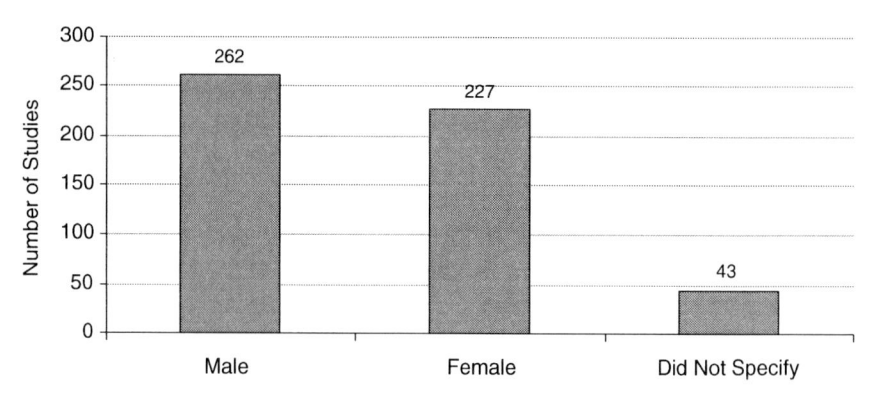

186   ETHICAL CONSIDERATIONS FOR RESEARCH INVOLVING PRISONERS

FIGURE A-10 Number of studies by gender of participants.

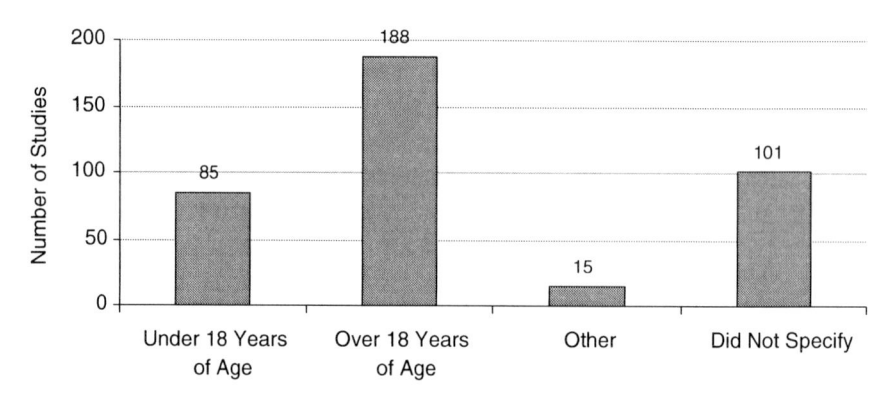

FIGURE A-11 Number of studies by age of participants.

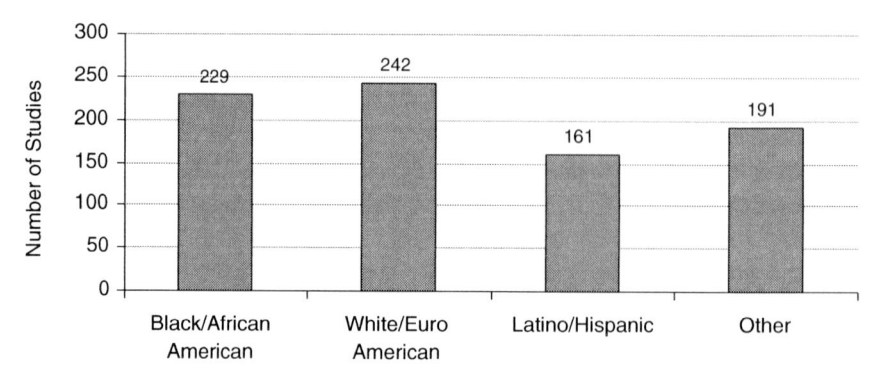

FIGURE A-12 Number of studies by race/ethnicity of research participants.

FIGURE A-13 Number of studies with participants of "other" race/ethnicity.

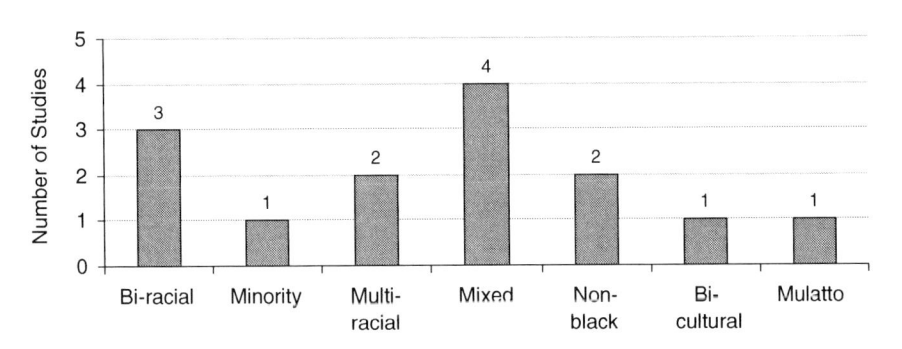

FIGURE A-14 Number of studies with nonwhite participants.

Race/Ethnicity Most studies included Caucasians, closely followed by African Americans, and Latinos/Hispanics (Figure A-12). Other racial and ethnic groups were represented to a lesser extent (Figures A-13, A-14).

SITE VISITS

The committee conducted two site visits to correctional facilities. On July 20, 2005, the committee visited San Quentin Prison in San Francisco and the California Medical Facility (CMF) at Vacaville, California. During their site visits, the committee had guided tours of both facilities and unstructured discussions with peer educators (i.e., inmates who are trained to be peer educators) about research experiences and needed protections when participating in research.

SURVEY OF STATE DEPARTMENTS OF CORRECTIONS

As part of its data collection activities, the committee collected information from state DOCs regarding research policies and practices. The committee conducted telephone interviews with six states and sent a survey to the remaining states and District of Columbia by e-mail.

Telephone Interviews

The committee collected information from DOCs in six states via telephone interviews: New York, California, Iowa, Texas, Florida, and Utah. The interviews covered the following:

- types of research that are conducted,
- number of studies that have been undertaken in recent years,
- requirements for informed consent,
- degree of risk to which research subjects are subjected,
- procedures for processing research proposals,
- credentials and qualifications of the people charged with the responsibility of approving research,
- problems or concerns that have arisen in connection with such research, and
- impact of laws and regulations on proposed or actual research projects.

Chapter 2 includes summary results of those telephone interviews.

E-Mail Survey

In the interest of reaching all 50 states and the District of Columbia, similar information to that which was collected by telephone interviews was requested from the DOCs of the remaining 44 states and Washington, D.C., in an e-mail survey. The purpose of this survey was to poll the states' DOCs about their research activities and practices. All but three (Delaware, Illinois, Wyoming) DOCs responded, bringing to 48 the total number of DOCs about which the committee had information (6 from telephone interviews, 42 from e-mail survey). Table A-1 presents the survey questions and a summary of DOC responses.

189

TABLE A-1 Summary of Results from Department of Corrections (DOC) Survey

Question	Yes	No	Other
For questions 1–8, is this type of research permitted in your DOC?			
1. *Purely DOC records review*, typically descriptive studies (e.g., demographics of prison population) or correlational studies (e.g., association of prisoner characteristics with type of index crime, number/type of disciplinary infractions) based on information routinely gathered by the DOC outside the framework of a specific research protocol	40	2	
2. *Evaluation studies of DOC programs* that evaluate the process or outcomes of an internal DOC program such as an educational program (e.g., impact of new classroom technique on GED test performance), or health or mental program (e.g., drug/substance abuse education; sex offender treatment)	40	2	
3. *Nontherapeutic social/behavioral studies* involving minimal risk such as administration of interviews and/or questionnaires to assess personality features and personal history for development of a risk assessment measure; reaction time studies (e.g., how quickly inmates respond to different visual stimuli presented on a computer screen)	30	10	1/case by case 1/yes–no[a]
4. *Nontherapeutic social/behavioral studies* involving greater than minimal risk (e.g., evaluate the effects of prolonged sleep deprivation)	4	34	1/not likely 2/case by case 1/yes–no[b]
5. *Evaluation of behavioral clinical interventions* developed and administered by outside agencies (e.g., university researchers implement and evaluate a group therapy treatment protocol for PTSD that is not part of DOC standard services).	20	19	2/case by case 1/yes–no[a]
6. *Medical research–therapeutic studies* (e.g., AIDS, hepatitis C, breast/prostate cancer, reproductive medicines/devices) in which study involvement permits inmates to have access to experimental treatments that would not be otherwise available	13	27	1/case by case 1/yes–no[a]

continued

TABLE A-1 Continued

Question	Yes	No	Other
7. *Medical research–therapeutic studies* of diseases for which there is an established standard of care (e.g., new asthma medications)	14	26	1/case by case 1/yes–no[a]
8. *Biomedical studies of a nontherapeutic nature*, including studies that involve exposure to a biological or chemical agent to assess the effects on and reactions of humans (e.g., effects of cosmetic or cleaning agents on skin)	3	38	1/not likely
9. If you answered "no" to any of the questions above, is it the case that some of these types of research are explicitly prohibited by your DOC policy or by legislation? Answer the following questions only if at least one of the types of research described above is permitted in your DOC. To ensure the safety of research subjects, in many research settings any study that involves human beings as research participants must be evaluated and approved by an institutional review board (IRB) before the study can commence. Please answer each of the questions below regarding IRB involvement in research at your organization.	31	8	3/NA
10. Does your DOC require IRB approval before research can commence?	29	10	3/NA
11a. Does your DOC have its own IRB within the organization?	13	26	3/NA
11b. If you answered *yes* to Question 11a, are there prisoner representatives on the DOC's IRB?	5	13	24/NA
12. Does your DOC have an adverse events reporting process or procedure?	18	20	4/NA

NOTE: DOC, Department of Corrections; IRB, institutional review board; NA, not applicable; GED, General Education Development (tests); PTSD, post-traumatic stress disorder.
[a]Vermont stated that the DOC is part of an umbrella Agency of Human Services (AHS). The AHS operates an IRB for review of all research, including DOC-related studies. No research involving minimal or greater risk to participants may proceed without IRB approval.
[b]Only with IRB approval.

B

The National Commission's Deliberations and Findings

NATIONAL RESEARCH ACT

The National Commission for the Protection of Human Subjects of Biomedical and Behavioral Research (NCPHSBBR) was created in 1973 by the National Research Act[1] and charged with submitting periodic reports to the President, Congress, and Secretary of the Department of Health, Education and Welfare (DHEW) about protecting humans involved in research. The commissioners were specifically charged to look into protections for certain classes of research subjects that included children, the "institutionally mentally infirm," and prisoners. Title II of the act, which applies to prisoners, is presented in Box B-1.

The commission was further required by Section 202(a)(3) to make recommendations to Congress for developing laws that could be implemented at other agencies that would protect persons involved in biomedical and behavioral research, including research on prisoners that may have been supported by those non-DHEW agencies.

In its charge to the commission concerning research with prisoners, Congress identified informed consent as the locus of ethical concern. In particular, Congress directed the commission to attend to three components of informed consent: (1) the nature of the consent; (2) the adequacy of the information given; and (3) the competence and freedom of the prisoners or their legal representatives to make a choice.[2]

---

[1] Pub. L. No. 93-348
[2] National Research Act, § 202(a)(2).

> **BOX B-1**
> **National Research Act Section 202(a)(2)**
>
> The Commission shall identify the requirements for informed consent to participation in biomedical and behavioral research by . . . prisoners . . . The Commission shall investigate and study biomedical and behavioral research conducted or supported under programs administered by the Secretary [DHEW] and involving prisoners...to determine the nature of the consent obtained from such persons or their legal representatives before such persons were involved in such research; the adequacy of the information given them respecting the nature and purpose of the research, procedures to be used, risks and discomforts, anticipated benefits from their research, and other matters necessary for informed consent; and the competence and the freedom of the persons to make a choice for or against involvement in such research. On the basis of such investigation and study the Commission shall make such recommendations to the Secretary as it determines appropriate to assure that biomedical and behavioral research conducted or supported under programs administered by him meets the requirements respecting informed consent identified by the Commission.

In carrying out this charge, the commission used elements of a principle-based ethical framework that would be more fully fleshed out in the Belmont Report (NCPHSBBR, 1976a), a response to its charge to identify the relevant ethical principles that relate to and support research with human subjects. This 20-page document discussed the line to be drawn between practice of biomedical and behavioral therapy and research in those areas. It identified three philosophical principles or general prescriptive judgments that were particularly relevant to research with human subjects: respect for persons, beneficence, and justice.

The first principle—respect for persons—"incorporates at least two ethical convictions: first, that individuals should be treated as autonomous agents, and second, that persons with diminished autonomy are entitled to protection" (NCPHSBBR, 1979a). The second principle—beneficence—demands that persons be "treated in an ethical manner not only by respecting their decisions and protecting them from harm, but also by making efforts to secure their well-being" (NCPHSBBR, 1979a). The concerns of the final principle—justice—are found in the answer to the question that the report poses: "Who ought to receive the benefits of research and bear its burdens?" (NCPHSBBR, 1979a). It is clear that the concerns raised by the report remain central to the analysis of this document.

NATIONAL COMMISSION METHODOLOGY

The national commission determined that research involving prisoners was so complex that a special section of regulations was needed to (1) provide severe restraints on the sorts of research that could be performed to protect the rights and interests of inmates, and (2) impose specific rules and procedures for institutional review boards reviewing protocols for correctional settings. The current inquiry, almost 30 years later, asks whether that special set of regulations is still sufficient and valid. The national commission noted that research in correctional settings presented problems largely relating to coercion and challenges to autonomous consent and refusal.

The national commission conducted a number of information-gathering activities as part of the development of its report on prisoners. Commission members made site visits to four prison facilities that conducted research with their inmate populations and two research facilities that were not penal institutions but that used prisoners as research subjects. During these visits, commission members and staff talked with inmates who did and did not participate in research projects, with prison administrators who had oversight responsibilities, and with directors of the research programs at the facilities.

When the National Commission visited the Jackson State Prison in Michigan on November 14, 1975, they met with a group of highly articulate prisoners. The leader of the group greeted them with the following opening statement: "Ladies and gentlemen: You are in a place where death at random is a way of life. We have noticed that the only place in this prison that people don't die is in the research unit. Just what is it that you think you are protecting us from?" (Dubler and Sidel, 1989).

In addition, commission members held hearings to allow for comment by those who would be most affected by any proposed protections. Groups represented at these hearings included members of the scientific community, advocates for the rights of prisoners, attorneys who provided legal services to prisoners, representatives from the pharmaceutical industry, and members of the general public. A National Minority Conference on Human Experimentations was also held to allow for groups representing minority concerns to receive a more in-depth hearing.

In addition to these activities, members of the commission staff authored papers, completed surveys, and wrote other reports that helped to inform the commission's deliberations. Papers were written by others as well. Topics for these papers were

- alternatives to the use of inmates as research subjects,
- a review of foreign practices on developing new pharmaceutical medications with prison subjects,

- a review of philosophical, sociological, and legal views of the use of inmates in research,
- behavioral perspectives on using inmate subjects, and
- a survey of research review procedures, principal investigators, and inmate subjects at five facilities.

The state of the art, as reported to the commissioners, was unsettled and unsettling. The pharmaceutical industry and various stakeholders, other than prisoners, were crafting the research agenda in correctional settings. Inmates often agreed to participate, with the hope of improving their living conditions or their chances for probation or parole.

Finally, members of the national commission held a series of public hearings that began in January 1976. During these hearings, commissioners discussed findings and identified and developed recommendations that were included in the final report, which was released in October 1976 (NCPHSBBR, 1976a).

NATIONAL COMMISSION DELIBERATIONS, FINDINGS, AND CONCLUSIONS

The national commission began its report by acknowledging some of the history of research with prisoners and noting that sensitivities to abuses in the United States and other countries had led to a generally growing concern about the propriety of research in prisons.

It then noted that there were two specific sets of concerns that were directly relevant to the report and recommendations: first, a set of general concerns about the "serious deficiencies in living conditions and health care that generally prevail in prisons" (NCPHSBBR, 1976b) and, second, a set of ethical concerns asking (1) do prisoners bear a fair share of the burdens and receive a fair share of the benefits of research? and (2) are prisoners, in the words of the Nuremberg Code (1949) "so situated as to be able to exercise free power of choice." That is, can prisoners give truly voluntary consent to participate in research?

These two dilemmas relate to two of the basic ethical principles: justice, which requires that persons and groups be treated fairly, and respect for persons, which requires that the autonomy of persons be promoted and protected. In discussing these issues, the commission noted that in its judgment the "appropriate expression of respect consists in protection from exploitation" (NCPHSBBR, 1976b). On the issue of justice, it stated that the concern is:

> To ensure the equitable distribution of the burdens of research no matter how large or small those burdens may be. The Commission is concerned

that the status of being a prisoner makes possible the perpetration of certain systemic injustices. For example, the availability of a population living in conditions of social and economic deprivation makes it possible for researchers to bring to these populations types of research that persons better situated would ordinarily refuse. It also establishes an enterprise whose fair administration can be readily corrupted by prisoner control or arbitrarily manipulated by prison authorities. And finally, it allows an inequitable distribution of burdens and benefits, in that those social classes from which prisoners often come are seldom full beneficiaries of improvements in medical care and other benefits accruing to society from the research enterprise. (NCPHSBBR, 1976b)

Chapter 2 of this report makes clear that today's correctional environments have the same characteristics that were of concern to the commission 30 years ago plus new, important features as well.

The commission completed its deliberations with five recommendations, which largely, although not entirely, became the guiding elements for 45 C.F.R. Part 46, Subpart C. They are listed in Box B-2.

The commission's deliberations came after the late 1960s and early 1970s saw a series of exposés documenting abuses in connection with nontherapeutic research in U.S. prisons (Mitford, 1973a,b; Rugaber, 1969). Many of those who were most vocal about the plight of prisoners, journalists and the staff of prisoner advocacy and civil liberties groups, saw research with prisoners largely under the twin headings of coercion and exploitation (Mitford, 1973a,b; NCPHSBBR, 1976;[3] Rugaber, 1969). For the most part, these groups pushed for restriction rather than reform of the prison research enterprise. Although the commission did not recommend a ban on all research with prisoners, its work and the aftermath have been described as tending toward that end: "The result of these regulations has been, as was their goal, the virtual elimination of biomedical research activity in prisons and jails" (Dubler and Sidel, 1989). According to one informed estimate, in the late 1990s only about 15 percent of institutions engaged in clinical research in the United States included prisoners in their research protocols (Hoffman, 2000[4]). In 1997, New York State had the

---

[3]See the summaries of presentations made to the commission (pp. 44–48) by Gabe Kaimowitz, a senior staff attorney for Michigan Legal Services; Matthew L. Myers, from the National Prison Project of the American Civil Liberties Foundation; Allan H. Lawson, executive director of the Prisoners' Rights Council of Pennsylvania; and the Rev. Americus Roy of the Prisoners Aid Association of Maryland, at a public hearing held on January 9, 1976.

[4]Hoffman was citing a 1998 estimate by Paula Knudson, executive coordinator of the University of Texas Health Science Center Committee for the Protection of Human Subjects. One factor to be considered may be state bans on biomedical research with prisoners; Hoffman cites a survey from the American Correctional Health Services Association finding that 22 states have such total bans.

> **BOX B-2**
> **National Commission Recommendations**
>
> 1. Recommended that studies of the possible causes, effects, and processes of incarceration and studies of prisons as institutional structures or of prisoners as incarcerated persons may be conducted or supported provided that (a) they present minimal or no risk and no more than mere inconvenience to the subjects, and (b) the requirements under Recommendation 4 are fulfilled.
> 2. Research on practices both innovative and accepted, which have the intent and reasonable probability of improving the health or well-being of the individual prisoner, may be conducted or supported provided the requirements under Recommendation 4 are fulfilled.
> 3. Discussed the need for a national ethical review body to determine that the research fulfills an important social and scientific need, that the involvement of the prisoners satisfies conditions of equity, and that a high degree of voluntariness is required. This recommendation led to requirements for certain sorts of secretarial review in the actual regulations but did not mirror the commission's list of mandatory characteristics of the prison, which included many requirements for conditions of confinement, such as adequate living space, existence of single occupancy cells, operable toilets, access to clean and working showers, existence of good-quality medical facilities in the prison that are adequately staffed and equipped and approved by an outside medical accrediting organization, among others. This requirement for the specifics of prison existence did not become part of the regulations.
> 4. This recommendation had two parts:
>   - The head of the responsible federal department or agency should determine that the competence of the investigators and the adequacy of the research facilities involved are sufficient for the conduct of any research project in which prisoners are to be involved.
>   - All research involving prisoners should be reviewed by at least one human subjects review committee.
> 5. A grandfathering provision that permitted research in existence to continue for at least 1 year.

largest estimated number of HIV-infected prisoners of any prison system (9,456), but only 8 (less than 0.001 percent) were enrolled in clinical trials (Lazzarini and Altice, 2000).

REFERENCES

Dubler N, Sidel V. 1989. On research on HIV infection and AIDS. *The Milbank Quarterly* 67(2):171–207.

Hoffman S. 2000. Beneficial and unusual punishment: An argument in support of prisoner participation in clinical trials. *Indiana Law Review* 33:475.

Lazzarini Z, Altice FL. 2000. A review of the legal and ethical issues for the conduct of HIV-related research in prisons. *AIDS and Public Policy Journal* 15(3/4):105–135.

Mitford J. 1973a. Experiments behind bars: Doctors, drug companies, and prisoners. *Atlantic Monthly* 23:64–73.

Mitford J. 1973b. *Kind and Usual Punishment: The Prison Business.* New York: Alfred A. Knopf.

NCPHSBBR (National Commission for the Protection of Human Subjects of Biomedical and Behavioral Research). 1976a. *The Belmont Report: Ethical Principles and Guidelines for the Protection of Human Subjects of Research.* Washington, DC: U.S. Department of Health, Education, and Welfare.

NCPHSBBR. 1976b. *Report and Recommendations: Research Involving Prisoners.* DHEW Publication No. (OS) 76-131. Washington, DC: U.S. Department of Health, Education, and Welfare.

Nuremburg Code. 1949. *Trials of War Criminals Before the Nuremburg Military Tribunals Under Control Council Law No. 10, Vol. 2.* Washington, DC: U.S. Government Printing Office.

Rugaber W. 1969, July 29. Prison drug and plasma projects leave fatal trail. *New York Times*, p. 20.

C

Report of the SACHRP Subcommittee and Human Subjects Protections

In 2003, the Secretary's Advisory Committee on Human Research Protections (SACHRP) asked its Subpart C Subcommittee to review the text and application of Subpart C primarily to determine whether the current Department of Health and Human Services (DHHS) interpretation and application of Subpart C's requirements should be modified.[1]

Among the topics the subcommittee addressed were

- the definition of the term *prisoner* under Subpart C,
- the application of research protections to those who become incarcerated after agreeing to participate in a nonprisoner study,
- issues with identifying a prisoner representative for prisoner research institutional review boards (IRBs) and particularly in multisite studies,
- conduct of expedited review in prisoner research,
- the definition of *minimal risk* under Subpart C (which is different from the Subpart A definition), and
- the requirement of secretarial review when prisoners in the control group are merely provided the standard of care.

These topics and the subcommittee's recommendations for further consideration by the Institute of Medicine (IOM) are discussed in more detail below.

---

[1] The full report of the subcommittee's findings is available at http://www.hhs.gov/ohrp/sachrp/mtgings/present/SubpartC.htm.

DEFINITION OF PRISONER

The subcommittee recommended that a modified Subpart A analysis apply when a subject who is enrolled in a study may not be fully within the definition of the term *prisoner* for the duration of the study. First, the subcommittee affirmed that the interpretation of *prisoner* should remain defined by the words of the regulation and not expanded to include other subjects whose liberty is restricted, such as those in community correctional facilities or on probation or parole. Although those subjects deserve heightened protection, the subcommittee recommended that the DHHS rely on Subpart A's protections for subjects "vulnerable to coercion or undue influence" without including those subjects as prisoners under Subpart C. Likewise, when a subject is incarcerated after becoming enrolled in a study, the concerns about coercion and undue influence are not as great; at the same time, it may be difficult to modify the research protocol to comply with Subpart C. Therefore, the subcommittee suggested that Subpart A's general requirement of heightened protection apply instead. The subcommittee recommended that an IRB should review a researcher's request to continue the research when a subject subsequently becomes incarcerated, taking into account the new conditions of incarceration but without fully engaging in a new Subpart C approval process.

PRISONER IRB REPRESENTATIVE

The subcommittee discussed a variety of problems with identifying a representative who would be skilled and knowledgeable enough to be effective but not so unlike the rest of the IRB as to be marginalized. The subcommittee recommended that the Office of Human Research Protections (OHRP) assist IRBs in searching for an appropriate prisoner representative, which might include family members of prisoners, former prisoners (especially people in recovery from substance addiction who have also had experience as prisoners), and service providers who assist in the correctional process. It was recommended that the OHRP should provide functional criteria that might help IRBs (and investigators, who are also responsible for the composition of an IRB that will properly evaluate ethical issues) identify persons who can be an effective voice for prisoners within the IRB. With respect to multisite studies, the subcommittee recommended that, although Subpart C only requires one prisoner representative on a central IRB for multisite research, the IRB must nevertheless consider the individual circumstances of each prison site, which can vary widely. In addition, with respect to expedited review, the subcommittee recommended that, if expedited review of a protocol is required, a prisoner representative should be one of the reviewers.

DEFINING MINIMAL RISK AND BENEFIT TO PARTICIPANT

The subcommittee considered two issues regarding the distinction between using as the ethical baseline other healthy prisoners as opposed to other healthy persons generally. First, the subcommittee affirmed that the different definition of minimal risk in the Subpart C regulations compared with Subpart A regulations was appropriate. The Subpart C regulations specify that the determination of minimal risk must be in comparison to the ordinary experience of a healthy person, which the subcommittee interpreted as referring to a healthy person outside the prison environment. The subcommittee cautioned that the greater situational risk in the prison setting should not influence the baseline for the IRB's decision; rather, the minimal risk should be compared with the risk to a healthy person in a safe environment. The OHRP should provide guidance, using examples, of how the minimal risk might be viewed in different protocols.

At the same time, the subcommittee viewed the current OHRP interpretation of when a protocol does not provide a benefit to the participant as overly restrictive. The OHRP's position is that using standard of care as a control arm does not provide any benefit to the participant and thus requires secretarial review and expert panel consideration. The subcommittee's view is that, because the participant receives the standard of care and does ultimately benefit from the results of the research, even if not immediately, such a control arm should not require heightened review. The subcommittee recommended that only when the control group is placebo only (and thus deviating from the standard of care) should the protocol be considered to include an arm not benefiting from the research.

The subcommittee also pointed out the problems with the jurisdiction of Subpart C. Because it has been adopted by so few agencies, it has limited application to federally funded research. In addition, it does not automatically apply to institutions that have signed a federal-wide assurance (FWA) unless they specifically request that it be part of their obligation. Because of these two enormous gaps in coverage, most research involving prisoners does not fall under the special protections of Subpart C.

RECOMMENDATIONS FOR FURTHER CONSIDERATION BY THE INSTITUTE OF MEDICINE

In addition to its recommendations on the issues discussed previously, the subcommittee noted with approval that the IOM had been charged with studying the human research protections for prisoners. The subcommittee recommended the IOM committee consider the need for a requirement that research only be conducted in prisons providing standard of care to the general population (and how best to get such services in place); the interpretation of the requirement that follow-up care be provided when the prisoner has been released from confinement; and the limited jurisdiction of Subpart C (i.e., to DHHS-supported research only).

OTHER FEDERAL HUMAN SUBJECTS PROTECTIONS

The full panoply of DHHS protections for prisoners in Subpart C presently only apply to research funded by DHHS, the Central Intelligence Agency, and the Social Security Administration. Some of the other 14 departments and agencies that have adopted the Common Rule accept the OHRP-approved FWA as assurance of compliance with ethical regulations regarding human research subjects. However, those departments and agencies have not adopted Subpart C, so the assurance only requires certification of compliance with the Common Rule (Subpart A).[2] Although institutions holding an FWA and engaging in research funded by one of the other departments or agencies may voluntarily extend their protections to include those under the other subparts (including Subpart C)—the OHRP estimates that this applies to approximately 60 percent of institutions holding an FWA—they are not required to do so.

Moreover, prisoner research that is funded by another department or agency (other than DHHS) falls outside of the protections of the OHRP oversight even if the institution has requested in its FWA that Subpart C apply because the OHRP does not monitor the institution's compliance with a voluntary assurance regarding Subpart C. Additionally, an organization that does not receive its funding from any of these sources generally does not hold an FWA and is not required to comply with the Common Rule or any of the subparts (see Table C-1).

At the same time, certain federal departments or agencies that have adopted a form of the Common Rule have also adopted their own additional rules protecting certain categories of human research subjects other than Subpart C. Of particular interest are the Department of Justice, because it includes the Bureau of Prisons, and the Food and Drug Administration, because its regulations govern a majority of biomedical research (regardless of whether the subjects of the study are prisoners).

---

[2]One exception is the Department of Education, which has adopted Subpart D but has not adopted Subparts B or C of the DHHS regulations.

TABLE C-1 Overview of Regulations Applicable to Research Involving Prisoners as Subjects, Independent of Funding Source

	Federal–Adult	Federal–Juvenile	State–Adult	State–Juvenile
Medical treatment–nontherapeutic/cosmetic	Not permitted	Not permitted	FDA Subpart A, state policy	FDA Subpart A, FDA Subpart D, state policy
Pharmaceutical/medical device–therapeutic (for specific inmate's condition)	DOJ Subpart A, FDA Subpart A, DHHS (Subpart C)	DOJ Subpart A, FDA Subpart A, DHHS (Subpart C), FDA Subpart D	FDA Subpart A, FDA Subpart D, state policy	FDA Subpart A, FDA Subpart D, state policy
Non-FDA regulated medical treatment–therapeutic	DOJ Subpart A, DHHS (Subpart C)	DOJ Subpart A, DHHS (Subpart C)	Varies by state	Varies by state
Nonmedical research	DOJ Subpart A, BOP research policy	DOJ Subpart A, BOP research policy	Varies by state	Varies by state

D

Code of Federal Regulations
Title 45: Public Welfare
Part 46: Protection of Human Subjects

This appendix contains the text of Part 46 Protection of Human Subjects of Title 45 Public Welfare of the Code of Federal Regulations (C.F.R.). Part 46 of the C.F.R.s were revised June 23, 2005, and made effective that day. Below is a table of contents listing the sections of Subparts A through D. Following are sections that cover each subpart in turn.

Subpart A:
Basic DHHS Policy for Protection of Human Research Subjects

Sec.	
46.101	To what does this policy apply?
46.102	Definitions
46.103	Assuring compliance with this policy—research conducted or supported by any federal department or agency
46.104–46.106	[Reserved]
46.107	IRB membership
46.108	IRB functions and operations
46.109	IRB review of research
46.110	Expedited review procedures for certain kinds of research involving no more than minimal risk and for minor changes in approved research
46.111	Criteria for IRB approval of research
46.112	Review by institution

46.113	Suspension or termination of IRB approval of research
46.114	Cooperative research
46.115	IRB records
46.116	General requirements for informed consent
46.117	Documentation of informed consent
46.118	Applications and proposals lacking definite plans for involvement of human subjects
46.119	Research undertaken without the intention of involving human subjects
46.120	Evaluation and disposition of applications and proposals for research to be conducted or supported by a federal department or agency
46.121	[Reserved]
46.122	Use of federal funds
46.123	Early termination of research support: evaluation of applications and proposals
46.124	Conditions

Subpart B:
Additional Protections for Pregnant Women, Human Fetuses, and Neonates Involved in Research

Sec.

46.201	To what do these regulations apply?
46.202	Definitions
46.203	Duties of IRBs in connection with research involving pregnant women, fetuses, and neonates
46.204	Research involving pregnant women or fetuses
46.205	Research involving neonates
46.206	Research involving, after delivery, the placenta, the dead fetus, or fetal material
46.207	Research not otherwise approvable which presents an opportunity to understand, prevent, or alleviate a serious problem affecting the health or welfare of pregnant women, fetuses, or neonates

Subpart C:
Additional Protections Pertaining to Biomedical and Behavioral Research Involving Prisoners as Subjects

Sec.

46.301	Applicability
46.302	Purpose

46.303	Definitions
46.304	Composition of IRBs where prisoners are involved
46.305	Additional duties of the IRBs where prisoners are involved
46.306	Permitted research involving prisoners

Subpart D:
Additional Protections for Children Involved as Subjects in Research

Sec.

46.401	To what do these regulations apply?
46.402	Definitions
46.403	IRB duties
46.404	Research not involving greater than minimal risk
46.405	Research involving greater than minimal risk but presenting the prospect of direct benefit to the individual subjects
46.406	Research involving greater than minimal risk and no prospect of direct benefit to individual subjects, but likely to yield generalizable knowledge about the subject's disorder or condition
46.407	Research not otherwise approvable which presents an opportunity to understand, prevent, or alleviate a serious problem affecting the health or welfare of children
46.408	Requirements for permission by parents or guardians and for assent by children
46.409	Wards

The authority for these federal regulations can be found in 5 U.S.C. 301 and 42 U.S.C. 289(a).

Note that the Department of Health and Human Services (DHHS) issued a notice of waiver regarding the requirements set forth in Part 46, relating to protection of human subjects, as they pertain to demonstration projects, approved under section 1115 of the Social Security Act, which test the use of cost-sharing, such as deductibles, copayment, and coinsurance, in the Medicaid program. For further information see 47 *Federal Register* 9208, Mar. 4, 1982.

As revised, Subpart A of the DHHS regulations incorporates the Federal Policy for the Protection of Human Subjects (56 FR 28003). Subpart D of the DHHS regulations has been amended at Section 46.401(b) to reference the revised Subpart A.

The Federal Policy for the Protection of Human Subjects is also codified at the following:

7 C.F.R. Part 1c	Department of Agriculture
10 C.F.R. Part 745	Department of Energy
14 C.F.R. Part 1230	National Aeronautics and Space Administration
15 C.F.R. Part 27	Department of Commerce
16 C.F.R. Part 1028	Consumer Product Safety Commission
22 C.F.R. Part 225	International Development Cooperation Agency, Agency for International Development
24 C.F.R. Part 60	Department of Housing and Urban Development
28 C.F.R. Part 46	Department of Justice
32 C.F.R. Part 219	Department of Defense
34 C.F.R. Part 97	Department of Education
38 C.F.R. Part 16	Department of Veterans Affairs
40 C.F.R. Part 26	Environmental Protection Agency
45 C.F.R. Part 690	National Science Foundation
49 C.F.R. Part 11	Department of Transportation

Subpart A: Basic DHHS Policy for Protection of Human Research Subjects
Authority: 5 U.S.C. 301; 42 U.S.C. 289(a); 42 U.S.C. 300v-1(b).
Source: 56 FR 28003, June 18, 1991; 70 FR 36325, June 23, 2005.

§46.101 To what does this policy apply?

(a) Except as provided in paragraph (b) of this section, this policy applies to all research involving human subjects conducted, supported, or otherwise subject to regulation by any federal department or agency which takes appropriate administrative action to make the policy applicable to such research. This includes research conducted by federal civilian employees or military personnel, except that each department or agency head may adopt such procedural modifications as may be appropriate from an administrative standpoint. It also includes research conducted, supported, or otherwise subject to regulation by the federal government outside the United States.

(1) Research that is conducted or supported by a federal department or agency, whether or not it is regulated as defined in §46.102(e), must comply with all sections of this policy.

(2) Research that is neither conducted nor supported by a federal department or agency but is subject to regulation as defined in §46.102(e) must be reviewed and approved, in compliance with §46.101, §46.102, and §46.107 through §46.117 of this policy, by an institutional review board (IRB) that operates in accordance with the pertinent requirements of this policy.

(b) Unless otherwise required by department or agency heads, research activities in which the only involvement of human subjects will be in one or more of the following categories are exempt from this policy:
(1) Research conducted in established or commonly accepted educational settings, involving normal educational practices, such as (i) research on regular and special education instructional strategies, or (ii) research on the effectiveness of or the comparison among instructional techniques, curricula, or classroom management methods.
(2) Research involving the use of educational tests (cognitive, diagnostic, aptitude, achievement), survey procedures, interview procedures or observation of public behavior, unless:
(i) information obtained is recorded in such a manner that human subjects can be identified, directly or through identifiers linked to the subjects; and (ii) any disclosure of the human subjects' responses outside the research could reasonably place the subjects at risk of criminal or civil liability or be damaging to the subjects' financial standing, employability, or reputation.
(3) Research involving the use of educational tests (cognitive, diagnostic, aptitude, achievement), survey procedures, interview procedures, or observation of public behavior that is not exempt under paragraph (b)(2) of this section, if:
(i) the human subjects are elected or appointed public officials or candidates for public office; or (ii) federal statute(s) require(s) without exception that the confidentiality of the personally identifiable information will be maintained throughout the research and thereafter.
(4) Research involving the collection or study of existing data, documents, records, pathological specimens, or diagnostic specimens, if these sources are publicly available or if the information is recorded by the investigator in such a manner that subjects cannot be identified, directly or through identifiers linked to the subjects.
(5) Research and demonstration projects which are conducted by or subject to the approval of department or agency heads, and which are designed to study, evaluate, or otherwise examine:
(i) Public benefit or service programs; (ii) procedures for obtaining benefits or services under those programs; (iii) possible changes in or alternatives to those programs or procedures; or (iv) possible changes in methods or levels of payment for benefits or services under those programs.
(6) Taste and food quality evaluation and consumer acceptance studies, (i)

if wholesome foods without additives are consumed or (ii) if a food is consumed that contains a food ingredient at or below the level and for a use found to be safe, or agricultural chemical or environmental contaminant at or below the level found to be safe, by the Food and Drug Administration or approved by the Environmental Protection Agency or the Food Safety and Inspection Service of the U.S. Department of Agriculture.

(c) Department or agency heads retain final judgment as to whether a particular activity is covered by this policy.

(d) Department or agency heads may require that specific research activities or classes of research activities conducted, supported, or otherwise subject to regulation by the department or agency but not otherwise covered by this policy, comply with some or all of the requirements of this policy.

(e) Compliance with this policy requires compliance with pertinent federal laws or regulations which provide additional protections for human subjects.

(f) This policy does not affect any state or local laws or regulations which may otherwise be applicable and which provide additional protections for human subjects.

(g) This policy does not affect any foreign laws or regulations which may otherwise be applicable and which provide additional protections to human subjects of research.

(h) When research covered by this policy takes place in foreign countries, procedures normally followed in the foreign countries to protect human subjects may differ from those set forth in this policy. [An example is a foreign institution which complies with guidelines consistent with the World Medical Assembly Declaration (Declaration of Helsinki amended 1989) issued either by sovereign states or by an organization whose function for the protection of human research subjects is internationally recognized.] In these circumstances, if a department or agency head determines that the procedures prescribed by the institution afford protections that are at least equivalent to those provided in this policy, the department or agency head may approve the substitution of the foreign procedures in lieu of the procedural requirements provided in this policy. Except when otherwise required by statute, Executive Order, or the department or agency head, notices of these actions as they occur will be published in the Federal Register or will be otherwise published as provided in department or agency procedures.

(i) Unless otherwise required by law, department or agency heads may waive the applicability of some or all of the provisions of this policy to specific research activities or classes or research activities otherwise covered by this policy. Except when otherwise required by statute or Executive Order, the department or agency head shall forward advance notices of these actions to the Office for Human Research Protections, Department of Health and Human Services (DHHS), or any successor office, and shall also publish them in the Federal Register or in such other manner as provided in department or agency procedures.[1]

§46.102 Definitions.

(a) *Department or agency head* means the head of any federal department or agency and any other officer or employee of any department or agency to whom authority has been delegated.

(b) *Institution* means any public or private entity or agency (including federal, state, and other agencies).

(c) *Legally authorized representative* means an individual or judicial or other body authorized under applicable law to consent on behalf of a prospective subject to the subject's participation in the procedure(s) involved in the research.

(d) *Research* means a systematic investigation, including research development, testing, and evaluation, designed to develop or contribute to generalizable knowledge. Activities which meet this definition constitute research for purposes of this policy, whether or not they are conducted or supported under a program which is considered research for other purposes. For example, some demonstration and service programs may include research activities.

---

[1] Institutions with DHHS-approved assurances on file will abide by provisions of Title 45 C.F.R. Part 46 Subparts A-D. Some of the other departments and agencies have incorporated all provisions of Title 45 C.F.R. Part 46 into their policies and procedures as well. However, the exemptions at 45 C.F.R. § 46.101(b) do not apply to research involving prisoners, Subpart C. The exemption at 45 C.F.R. § 46.101(b)(2), for research involving survey or interview procedures or observation of public behavior, does not apply to research with children, Subpart D, except for research involving observations of public behavior when the investigator(s) do not participate in the activities being observed.
[56 FR 38012, 28022, June 18, 1991; 56 FR 29756, June 28, 1991; 70 FR 36325, June 23, 2005]

(e) *Research subject to regulation* and similar terms are intended to encompass those research activities for which a federal department or agency has specific responsibility for regulating as a research activity, (for example, investigational new drug requirements administered by the Food and Drug Administration). It does not include research activities which are incidentally regulated by a federal department or agency solely as part of the department's or agency's broader responsibility to regulate certain types of activities whether research or nonresearch in nature (for example, wage and hour requirements administered by the Department of Labor).

(f) *Human subject* means a living individual about whom an investigator (whether professional or student) conducting research obtains:
(1) Data through intervention or interaction with the individual, or
(2) Identifiable private information.
Intervention includes both physical procedures by which data are gathered (for example, venipuncture) and manipulations of the subject or the subject's environment that are performed for research purposes. Interaction includes communication or interpersonal contact between investigator and subject.
Private information includes information about behavior that occurs in a context in which an individual can reasonably expect that no observation or recording is taking place, and information which has been provided for specific purposes by an individual and which the individual can reasonably expect will not be made public (for example, a medical record). Private information must be individually identifiable (i.e., the identity of the subject is or may readily be ascertained by the investigator or associated with the information) in order for obtaining the information to constitute research involving human subjects.

(g) *IRB* means an institutional review board established in accord with and for the purposes expressed in this policy.

(h) *IRB approval* means the determination of the IRB that the research has been reviewed and may be conducted at an institution within the constraints set forth by the IRB and by other institutional and federal requirements.

(i) *Minimal risk* means that the probability and magnitude of harm or discomfort anticipated in the research are not greater in and of themselves than those ordinarily encountered in daily life or during the performance of routine physical or psychological examinations or tests.

(j) *Certification* means the official notification by the institution to the supporting department or agency, in accordance with the requirements of

APPENDIX D

this policy, that a research project or activity involving human subjects has been reviewed and approved by an IRB in accordance with an approved assurance.

§46.103 Assuring compliance with this policy-research conducted or supported by any federal department or agency.

(a) Each institution engaged in research which is covered by this policy and which is conducted or supported by a federal department or agency shall provide written assurance satisfactory to the department or agency head that it will comply with the requirements set forth in this policy. In lieu of requiring submission of an assurance, individual department or agency heads shall accept the existence of a current assurance, appropriate for the research in question, on file with the Office for Human Research Protections, DHHS, or any successor office, and approved for federal-wide use by that office. When the existence of an DHHS-approved assurance is accepted in lieu of requiring submission of an assurance, reports (except certification) required by this policy to be made to department and agency heads shall also be made to the Office for Human Research Protections, DHHS, or any successor office.

(b) Departments and agencies will conduct or support research covered by this policy only if the institution has an assurance approved as provided in this section, and only if the institution has certified to the department or agency head that the research has been reviewed and approved by an IRB provided for in the assurance, and will be subject to continuing review by the IRB. Assurances applicable to federally supported or conducted research shall at a minimum include:
(1) A statement of principles governing the institution in the discharge of its responsibilities for protecting the rights and welfare of human subjects of research conducted at or sponsored by the institution, regardless of whether the research is subject to federal regulation. This may include an appropriate existing code, declaration, or statement of ethical principles, or a statement formulated by the institution itself. This requirement does not preempt provisions of this policy applicable to department-supported, agency-supported, or regulated research and need not be applicable to any research exempted or waived under §46.101 (b) or (i).
(2) Designation of one or more IRBs established in accordance with the requirements of this policy, and for which provisions are made for meeting space and sufficient staff to support the IRB's review and recordkeeping duties.
(3) A list of IRB members identified by name; earned degrees; representative capacity; indications of experience such as board certifications, licenses,

etc., sufficient to describe each member's chief anticipated contributions to IRB deliberations; and any employment or other relationship between each member and the institution; for example: full-time employee, part-time employee, member of governing panel or board, stockholder, paid or unpaid consultant. Changes in IRB membership shall be reported to the department or agency head, unless in accord with §46.103(a) of this policy, the existence of an DHHS-approved assurance is accepted. In this case, change in IRB membership shall be reported to the Office for Human Research Protections, DHHS, or any successor office.

(4) Written procedures which the IRB will follow (i) for conducting its initial and continuing review of research and for reporting its findings and actions to the investigator and the institution; (ii) for determining which projects require review more often than annually and which projects need verification from sources other than the investigators that no material changes have occurred since previous IRB review; and (iii) for ensuring prompt reporting to the IRB of proposed changes in a research activity, and for ensuring that such changes in approved research, during the period for which IRB approval has already been given, may not be initiated without IRB review and approval except when necessary to eliminate apparent immediate hazards to the subject.

(5) Written procedures for ensuring prompt reporting to the IRB, appropriate institutional officials, and the department or agency head of (i) any unanticipated problems involving risks to subjects or others or any serious or continuing noncompliance with this policy or the requirements or determinations of the IRB; and (ii) any suspension or termination of IRB approval.

(c) The assurance shall be executed by an individual authorized to act for the institution and to assume on behalf of the institution the obligations imposed by this policy and shall be filed in such form and manner as the department or agency head prescribes.

(d) The department or agency head will evaluate all assurances submitted in accordance with this policy through such officers and employees of the department or agency and such experts or consultants engaged for this purpose as the department or agency head determines to be appropriate. The department or agency head's evaluation will take into consideration the adequacy of the proposed IRB in light of the anticipated scope of the institution's research activities and the types of subject populations likely to be involved, the appropriateness of the proposed initial and continuing review procedures in light of the probable risks, and the size and complexity of the institution.

(e) On the basis of this evaluation, the department or agency head may approve or disapprove the assurance, or enter into negotiations to develop an approvable one. The department or agency head may limit the period during which any particular approved assurance or class of approved assurances shall remain effective or otherwise condition or restrict approval.

(f) Certification is required when the research is supported by a federal department or agency and not otherwise exempted or waived under §46.101 (b) or (i). An institution with an approved assurance shall certify that each application or proposal for research covered by the assurance and by §46.103 of this policy has been reviewed and approved by the IRB. Such certification must be submitted with the application or proposal or by such later date as may be prescribed by the department or agency to which the application or proposal is submitted. Under no condition shall research covered by §46.103 of the policy be supported prior to receipt of the certification that the research has been reviewed and approved by the IRB. Institutions without an approved assurance covering the research shall certify within 30 days after receipt of a request for such a certification from the department or agency, that the application or proposal has been approved by the IRB. If the certification is not submitted within these time limits, the application or proposal may be returned to the institution.

(Approved by the Office of Management and Budget under control number 0990-0260.)

[56 FR 38012, 28022, June 18, 1991; 56 FR 29756, June 28, 1991; 70 FR 36325, June 23, 2005]

§§46.104–46.106 [Reserved]

§46.107 IRB membership.

(a) Each IRB shall have at least five members, with varying backgrounds to promote complete and adequate review of research activities commonly conducted by the institution. The IRB shall be sufficiently qualified through the experience and expertise of its members, and the diversity of the members, including consideration of race, gender, and cultural backgrounds and sensitivity to such issues as community attitudes, to promote respect for its advice and counsel in safeguarding the rights and welfare of human subjects. In addition to possessing the professional competence necessary to review specific research activities, the IRB shall be able to ascertain the acceptability of proposed research in terms of institutional commitments and regulations, applicable law, and standards of professional conduct and practice. The IRB shall therefore include persons knowledgeable in these areas. If an IRB regularly reviews research that involves a vulnerable category of subjects, such as children, prisoners, pregnant women, or handicapped or mentally disabled persons, consideration shall be given to the inclusion of one or more individuals who are knowledgeable about and experienced in working with these subjects.

(b) Every nondiscriminatory effort will be made to ensure that no IRB consists entirely of men or entirely of women, including the institution's consideration of qualified persons of both sexes, so long as no selection is made to the IRB on the basis of gender. No IRB may consist entirely of members of one profession.

(c) Each IRB shall include at least one member whose primary concerns are in scientific areas and at least one member whose primary concerns are in nonscientific areas.

(d) Each IRB shall include at least one member who is not otherwise affiliated with the institution and who is not part of the immediate family of a person who is affiliated with the institution.

(e) No IRB may have a member participate in the IRB's initial or continuing review of any project in which the member has a conflicting interest, except to provide information requested by the IRB.

(f) An IRB may, in its discretion, invite individuals with competence in special areas to assist in the review of issues which require expertise beyond or in addition to that available on the IRB. These individuals may not vote with the IRB.

§46.108 IRB functions and operations.

In order to fulfill the requirements of this policy each IRB shall:

(a) Follow written procedures in the same detail as described in §46.103(b)(4) and to the extent required by §46.103(b)(5).

(b) Except when an expedited review procedure is used (see §46.110), review proposed research at convened meetings at which a majority of the members of the IRB are present, including at least one member whose primary concerns are in nonscientific areas. In order for the research to be approved, it shall receive the approval of a majority of those members present at the meeting.

APPENDIX D

§46.109 IRB review of research.

(a) An IRB shall review and have authority to approve, require modifications in (to secure approval), or disapprove all research activities covered by this policy.

(b) An IRB shall require that information given to subjects as part of informed consent is in accordance with §46.116. The IRB may require that information, in addition to that specifically mentioned in §46.116, be given to the subjects when in the IRB's judgment the information would meaningfully add to the protection of the rights and welfare of subjects.

(c) An IRB shall require documentation of informed consent or may waive documentation in accordance with §46.117.

(d) An IRB shall notify investigators and the institution in writing of its decision to approve or disapprove the proposed research activity, or of modifications required to secure IRB approval of the research activity. If the IRB decides to disapprove a research activity, it shall include in its written notification a statement of the reasons for its decision and give the investigator an opportunity to respond in person or in writing.

(e) An IRB shall conduct continuing review of research covered by this policy at intervals appropriate to the degree of risk, but not less than once per year, and shall have authority to observe or have a third party observe the consent process and the research.

(Approved by the Office of Management and Budget under control number 0990-0260.)

§46.110 Expedited review procedures for certain kinds of research involving no more than minimal risk, and for minor changes in approved research.

(a) The Secretary, DHHS, has established, and published as a Notice in the *Federal Register*, a list of categories of research that may be reviewed by the IRB through an expedited review procedure. The list will be amended, as appropriate, after consultation with other departments and agencies, through periodic republication by the Secretary, DHHS, in the *Federal Register*. A copy of the list is available from the Office for Human Research Protections, DHHS, or any successor office.

(b) An IRB may use the expedited review procedure to review either or both of the following:
(1) some or all of the research appearing on the list and found by the reviewer(s) to involve no more than minimal risk,
(2) minor changes in previously approved research during the period (of one year or less) for which approval is authorized.
Under an expedited review procedure, the review may be carried out by the IRB chairperson or by one or more experienced reviewers designated by the chairperson from among members of the IRB. In reviewing the research, the reviewers may exercise all of the authorities of the IRB except that the reviewers may not disapprove the research. A research activity may be disapproved only after review in accordance with the nonexpedited procedure set forth in §46.108(b).

(c) Each IRB which uses an expedited review procedure shall adopt a method for keeping all members advised of research proposals which have been approved under the procedure.

(d) The department or agency head may restrict, suspend, terminate, or choose not to authorize an institution's or IRB's use of the expedited review procedure.

§46.111 Criteria for IRB approval of research.

(a) In order to approve research covered by this policy the IRB shall determine that all of the following requirements are satisfied:
(1) Risks to subjects are minimized: (i) By using procedures which are consistent with sound research design and which do not unnecessarily expose subjects to risk, and (ii) whenever appropriate, by using procedures already being performed on the subjects for diagnostic or treatment purposes.
(2) Risks to subjects are reasonable in relation to anticipated benefits, if any, to subjects, and the importance of the knowledge that may reasonably be expected to result. In evaluating risks and benefits, the IRB should consider only those risks and benefits that may result from the research (as distinguished from risks and benefits of therapies subjects would receive even if not participating in the research). The IRB should not consider possible long-range effects of applying knowledge gained in the research (for example, the possible effects of the research on public policy) as among those research risks that fall within the purview of its responsibility.
(3) Selection of subjects is equitable. In making this assessment the IRB should take into account the purposes of the research and the setting in which the research will be conducted and should be particularly cognizant

of the special problems of research involving vulnerable populations, such as children, prisoners, pregnant women, mentally disabled persons, or economically or educationally disadvantaged persons.
(4) Informed consent will be sought from each prospective subject or the subject's legally authorized representative, in accordance with, and to the extent required by §46.116.
(5) Informed consent will be appropriately documented, in accordance with, and to the extent required by §46.117.
(6) When appropriate, the research plan makes adequate provision for monitoring the data collected to ensure the safety of subjects.
(7) When appropriate, there are adequate provisions to protect the privacy of subjects and to maintain the confidentiality of data.

(b) When some or all of the subjects are likely to be vulnerable to coercion or undue influence, such as children, prisoners, pregnant women, mentally disabled persons, or economically or educationally disadvantaged persons, additional safeguards have been included in the study to protect the rights and welfare of these subjects.

§46.112 Review by institution.

Research covered by this policy that has been approved by an IRB may be subject to further appropriate review and approval or disapproval by officials of the institution. However, those officials may not approve the research if it has not been approved by an IRB.

§46.113 Suspension or termination of IRB approval of research.

An IRB shall have authority to suspend or terminate approval of research that is not being conducted in accordance with the IRB's requirements or that has been associated with unexpected serious harm to subjects. Any suspension or termination of approval shall include a statement of the reasons for the IRB's action and shall be reported promptly to the investigator, appropriate institutional officials, and the department or agency head.

(Approved by the Office of Management and Budget under control number 0990-0260.)

§46.114 Cooperative research.

Cooperative research projects are those projects covered by this policy which involve more than one institution. In the conduct of cooperative research projects, each institution is responsible for safeguarding the rights and welfare of human subjects and for complying with this policy. With the approval of the department or agency head, an institution participating in a cooperative project may enter into a joint review arrangement, rely upon the review of another qualified IRB, or make similar arrangements for avoiding duplication of effort.

§46.115 IRB records.

(a) An institution, or when appropriate an IRB, shall prepare and maintain adequate documentation of IRB activities, including the following:
(1) Copies of all research proposals reviewed, scientific evaluations, if any, that accompany the proposals, approved sample consent documents, progress reports submitted by investigators, and reports of injuries to subjects.
(2) Minutes of IRB meetings which shall be in sufficient detail to show attendance at the meetings; actions taken by the IRB; the vote on these actions including the number of members voting for, against, and abstaining; the basis for requiring changes in or disapproving research; and a written summary of the discussion of controverted issues and their resolution.
(3) Records of continuing review activities.
(4) Copies of all correspondence between the IRB and the investigators.
(5) A list of IRB members in the same detail as described in §46.103(b)(3).
(6) Written procedures for the IRB in the same detail as described in §46.103(b)(4) and §46.103(b)(5).
(7) Statements of significant new findings provided to subjects, as required by §46.116(b)(5).

(b) The records required by this policy shall be retained for at least 3 years, and records relating to research which is conducted shall be retained for at least 3 years after completion of the research. All records shall be accessible for inspection and copying by authorized representatives of the department or agency at reasonable times and in a reasonable manner.

(Approved by the Office of Management and Budget under control number 0990-0260.)

§46.116 General requirements for informed consent.

Except as provided elsewhere in this policy, no investigator may involve a human being as a subject in research covered by this policy unless the investigator has obtained the legally effective informed consent of the sub-

APPENDIX D

ject or the subject's legally authorized representative. An investigator shall seek such consent only under circumstances that provide the prospective subject or the representative sufficient opportunity to consider whether or not to participate and that minimize the possibility of coercion or undue influence. The information that is given to the subject or the representative shall be in language understandable to the subject or the representative. No informed consent, whether oral or written, may include any exculpatory language through which the subject or the representative is made to waive or appear to waive any of the subject's legal rights, or releases or appears to release the investigator, the sponsor, the institution or its agents from liability for negligence.

(a) Basic elements of informed consent. Except as provided in paragraph (c) or (d) of this section, in seeking informed consent the following information shall be provided to each subject:
(1) A statement that the study involves research, an explanation of the purposes of the research and the expected duration of the subject's participation, a description of the procedures to be followed, and identification of any procedures which are experimental;
(2) A description of any reasonably foreseeable risks or discomforts to the subject;
(3) A description of any benefits to the subject or to others which may reasonably be expected from the research;
(4) A disclosure of appropriate alternative procedures or courses of treatment, if any, that might be advantageous to the subject;
(5) A statement describing the extent, if any, to which confidentiality of records identifying the subject will be maintained;
(6) For research involving more than minimal risk, an explanation as to whether any compensation and an explanation as to whether any medical treatments are available if injury occurs and, if so, what they consist of, or where further information may be obtained;
(7) An explanation of whom to contact for answers to pertinent questions about the research and research subjects' rights, and whom to contact in the event of a research-related injury to the subject; and
(8) A statement that participation is voluntary, refusal to participate will involve no penalty or loss of benefits to which the subject is otherwise entitled, and the subject may discontinue participation at any time without penalty or loss of benefits to which the subject is otherwise entitled.

(b) Additional elements of informed consent. When appropriate, one or more of the following elements of information shall also be provided to each subject:

(1) A statement that the particular treatment or procedure may involve risks to the subject (or to the embryo or fetus, if the subject is or may become pregnant) which are currently unforeseeable;
(2) Anticipated circumstances under which the subject's participation may be terminated by the investigator without regard to the subject's consent;
(3) Any additional costs to the subject that may result from participation in the research;
(4) The consequences of a subject's decision to withdraw from the research and procedures for orderly termination of participation by the subject;
(5) A statement that significant new findings developed during the course of the research which may relate to the subject's willingness to continue participation will be provided to the subject; and
(6) The approximate number of subjects involved in the study.

(c) An IRB may approve a consent procedure which does not include, or which alters, some or all of the elements of informed consent set forth above, or waive the requirement to obtain informed consent provided the IRB finds and documents that:
(1) The research or demonstration project is to be conducted by or subject to the approval of state or local government officials and is designed to study, evaluate, or otherwise examine: (i) public benefit or service programs; (ii) procedures for obtaining benefits or services under those programs; (iii) possible changes in or alternatives to those programs or procedures; or (iv) possible changes in methods or levels of payment for benefits or services under those programs; and
(2) The research could not practicably be carried out without the waiver or alteration.

(d) An IRB may approve a consent procedure which does not include, or which alters, some or all of the elements of informed consent set forth in this section, or waive the requirements to obtain informed consent provided the IRB finds and documents that:
(1) The research involves no more than minimal risk to the subjects;
(2) The waiver or alteration will not adversely affect the rights and welfare of the subjects;
(3) The research could not practicably be carried out without the waiver or alteration; and
(4) Whenever appropriate, the subjects will be provided with additional pertinent information after participation.

(e) The informed consent requirements in this policy are not intended to preempt any applicable federal, state, or local laws which require additional information to be disclosed in order for informed consent to be legally effective.

(f) Nothing in this policy is intended to limit the authority of a physician to provide emergency medical care, to the extent the physician is permitted to do so under applicable federal, state, or local law.

(Approved by the Office of Management and Budget under control number 0990-0260.)

§46.117 Documentation of informed consent.

(a) Except as provided in paragraph (c) of this section, informed consent shall be documented by the use of a written consent form approved by the IRB and signed by the subject or the subject's legally authorized representative. A copy shall be given to the person signing the form.

(b) Except as provided in paragraph (c) of this section, the consent form may be either of the following:
(1) A written consent document that embodies the elements of informed consent required by §46.116. This form may be read to the subject or the subject's legally authorized representative, but in any event, the investigator shall give either the subject or the representative adequate opportunity to read it before it is signed; or
(2) A short form written consent document stating that the elements of informed consent required by §46.116 have been presented orally to the subject or the subject's legally authorized representative. When this method is used, there shall be a witness to the oral presentation. Also, the IRB shall approve a written summary of what is to be said to the subject or the representative. Only the short form itself is to be signed by the subject or the representative. However, the witness shall sign both the short form and a copy of the summary, and the person actually obtaining consent shall sign a copy of the summary. A copy of the summary shall be given to the subject or the representative, in addition to a copy of the short form.

(c) An IRB may waive the requirement for the investigator to obtain a signed consent form for some or all subjects if it finds either:
(1) That the only record linking the subject and the research would be the consent document and the principal risk would be potential harm resulting from a breach of confidentiality. Each subject will be asked whether the subject wants documentation linking the subject with the research, and the subject's wishes will govern; or
(2) That the research presents no more than minimal risk of harm to sub-

jects and involves no procedures for which written consent is normally required outside of the research context.

In cases in which the documentation requirement is waived, the IRB may require the investigator to provide subjects with a written statement regarding the research.

(Approved by the Office of Management and Budget under control number 0990-0260.)

§46.118 Applications and proposals lacking definite plans for involvement of human subjects.

Certain types of applications for grants, cooperative agreements, or contracts are submitted to departments or agencies with the knowledge that subjects may be involved within the period of support, but definite plans would not normally be set forth in the application or proposal. These include activities such as institutional type grants when selection of specific projects is the institution's responsibility; research training grants in which the activities involving subjects remain to be selected; and projects in which human subjects' involvement will depend upon completion of instruments, prior animal studies, or purification of compounds. These applications need not be reviewed by an IRB before an award may be made. However, except for research exempted or waived under §46.101 (b) or (i), no human subjects may be involved in any project supported by these awards until the project has been reviewed and approved by the IRB, as provided in this policy, and certification submitted, by the institution, to the department or agency.

§46.119 Research undertaken without the intention of involving human subjects.

In the event research is undertaken without the intention of involving human subjects, but it is later proposed to involve human subjects in the research, the research shall first be reviewed and approved by an IRB, as provided in this policy, a certification submitted, by the institution, to the department or agency, and final approval given to the proposed change by the department or agency.

§46.120 Evaluation and disposition of applications and proposals for research to be conducted or supported by a federal department or agency.

(a) The department or agency head will evaluate all applications and proposals involving human subjects submitted to the department or agency

APPENDIX D 225

through such officers and employees of the department or agency and such experts and consultants as the department or agency head determines to be appropriate. This evaluation will take into consideration the risks to the subjects, the adequacy of protection against these risks, the potential benefits of the research to the subjects and others, and the importance of the knowledge gained or to be gained.

(b) On the basis of this evaluation, the department or agency head may approve or disapprove the application or proposal, or enter into negotiations to develop an approvable one.

§46.121 [Reserved]

§46.122 Use of federal funds.

Federal funds administered by a department or agency may not be expended for research involving human subjects unless the requirements of this policy have been satisfied.

§46.123 Early termination of research support: evaluation of applications and proposals.

(a) The department or agency head may require that department or agency support for any project be terminated or suspended in the manner prescribed in applicable program requirements, when the department or agency head finds an institution has materially failed to comply with the terms of this policy.

(b) In making decisions about supporting or approving applications or proposals covered by this policy the department or agency head may take into account, in addition to all other eligibility requirements and program criteria, factors such as whether the applicant has been subject to a termination or suspension under paragraph (a) of this section and whether the applicant or the person or persons who would direct or has/have directed the scientific and technical aspects of an activity has/have, in the judgment of the department or agency head, materially failed to discharge responsibility for the protection of the rights and welfare of human subjects (whether or not the research was subject to federal regulation).

§46.124 Conditions.

With respect to any research project or any class of research projects the department or agency head may impose additional conditions prior to or at the time of approval when in the judgment of the department or agency head additional conditions are necessary for the protection of human subjects.

Subpart B: Additional Protections for Pregnant Women, Human Fetuses, and Neonates Involved in Research
Source: 66 FR 56778, Nov. 13, 2001, unless otherwise noted.

§46.201 To what do these regulations apply?

(a) Except as provided in paragraph (b) of this section, this subpart applies to all research involving pregnant women, human fetuses, neonates of uncertain viability, or nonviable neonates conducted or supported by the Department of Health and Human Services (DHHS). This includes all research conducted in DHHS facilities by any person and all research conducted in any facility by DHHS employees.

(b) The exemptions at §46.101(b)(1) through (6) are applicable to this subpart.

(c) The provisions of §46.101(c) through (i) are applicable to this subpart. Reference to state or local laws in this subpart and in §46.101(f) is intended to include the laws of federally recognized American Indian and Alaska native tribal governments.

(d) The requirements of this subpart are in addition to those imposed under the other subparts of this part.

§46.202 Definitions.

The definitions in §46.102 shall be applicable to this subpart as well. In addition, as used in this subpart:

(a) Dead fetus means a fetus that exhibits neither heartbeat, spontaneous respiratory activity, spontaneous movement of voluntary muscles, nor pulsation of the umbilical cord.

(b) Delivery means complete separation of the fetus from the woman by expulsion or extraction or any other means.

(c) Fetus means the product of conception from implantation until delivery.

(d) Neonate means a newborn.

(e) Nonviable neonate means a neonate after delivery that, although living, is not viable.

(f) Pregnancy encompasses the period of time from implantation until delivery. A woman shall be assumed to be pregnant if she exhibits any of the pertinent presumptive signs of pregnancy, such as missed menses, until the results of a pregnancy test are negative or until delivery.

(g) Secretary means the Secretary of Health and Human Services and any other officer or employee of the Department of Health and Human Services to whom authority has been delegated.

(h) Viable, as it pertains to the neonate, means being able, after delivery, to survive (given the benefit of available medical therapy) to the point of independently maintaining heartbeat and respiration. The Secretary may from time to time, taking into account medical advances, publish in the *Federal Register* guidelines to assist in determining whether a neonate is viable for purposes of this subpart. If a neonate is viable then it may be included in research only to the extent permitted and in accordance with the requirements of subparts A and D of this part.

§46.203 Duties of IRBs in connection with research involving pregnant women, fetuses, and neonates.

In addition to other responsibilities assigned to IRBs under this part, each IRB shall review research covered by this subpart and approve only research which satisfies the conditions of all applicable sections of this subpart and the other subparts of this part.

§46.204 Research involving pregnant women or fetuses.

Pregnant women or fetuses may be involved in research if all of the following conditions are met:

(a) Where scientifically appropriate, preclinical studies, including studies on pregnant animals, and clinical studies, including studies on nonpregnant women, have been conducted and provide data for assessing potential risks to pregnant women and fetuses;

(b) The risk to the fetus is caused solely by interventions or procedures that hold out the prospect of direct benefit for the woman or the fetus; or, if there is no such prospect of benefit, the risk to the fetus is not greater than minimal and the purpose of the research is the development of important biomedical knowledge which cannot be obtained by any other means;

(c) Any risk is the least possible for achieving the objectives of the research;
(d) If the research holds out the prospect of direct benefit to the pregnant woman, the prospect of a direct benefit both to the pregnant woman and the fetus, or no prospect of benefit for the woman nor the fetus when risk to the fetus is not greater than minimal and the purpose of the research is the development of important biomedical knowledge that cannot be obtained by any other means, her consent is obtained in accord with the informed consent provisions of Subpart A of this part;

(e) If the research holds out the prospect of direct benefit solely to the fetus then the consent of the pregnant woman and the father is obtained in accord with the informed consent provisions of Subpart A of this part, except that the father's consent need not be obtained if he is unable to consent because of unavailability, incompetence, or temporary incapacity or the pregnancy resulted from rape or incest;

(f) Each individual providing consent under paragraph (d) or (e) of this section is fully informed regarding the reasonably foreseeable impact of the research on the fetus or neonate;

(g) For children as defined in §46.402(a) who are pregnant, assent and permission are obtained in accord with the provisions of Subpart D of this part;

(h) No inducements, monetary or otherwise, will be offered to terminate a pregnancy;

(i) Individuals engaged in the research will have no part in any decisions as to the timing, method, or procedures used to terminate a pregnancy; and

(j) Individuals engaged in the research will have no part in determining the viability of a neonate.

§46.205 Research involving neonates.

(a) Neonates of uncertain viability and nonviable neonates may be involved in research if all of the following conditions are met:
(1) Where scientifically appropriate, preclinical and clinical studies have been conducted and provide data for assessing potential risks to neonates.
(2) Each individual providing consent under paragraph (b)(2) or (c)(5) of

this section is fully informed regarding the reasonably foreseeable impact of the research on the neonate.
(3) Individuals engaged in the research will have no part in determining the viability of a neonate.
(4) The requirements of paragraph (b) or (c) of this section have been met as applicable.

(b) Neonates of uncertain viability. Until it has been ascertained whether or not a neonate is viable, a neonate may not be involved in research covered by this subpart unless the following additional conditions have been met:
(1) The IRB determines that (i) The research holds out the prospect of enhancing the probability of survival of the neonate to the point of viability, and any risk is the least possible for achieving that objective, or (ii) The purpose of the research is the development of important biomedical knowledge which cannot be obtained by other means and there will be no added risk to the neonate resulting from the research; and
(2) The legally effective informed consent of either parent of the neonate or, if neither parent is able to consent because of unavailability, incompetence, or temporary incapacity, the legally effective informed consent of either parent's legally authorized representative is obtained in accord with Subpart A of this part, except that the consent of the father or his legally authorized representative need not be obtained if the pregnancy resulted from rape or incest.

(c) Nonviable neonates. After delivery nonviable neonate may not be involved in research covered by this subpart unless all of the following additional conditions are met:
(1) Vital functions of the neonate will not be artificially maintained;
(2) The research will not terminate the heartbeat or respiration of the neonate;
(3) There will be no added risk to the neonate resulting from the research;
(4) The purpose of the research is the development of important biomedical knowledge that cannot be obtained by other means; and
(5) The legally effective informed consent of both parents of the neonate is obtained in accord with Subpart A of this part, except that the waiver and alteration provisions of §46.116(c) and (d) do not apply. However, if either parent is unable to consent because of unavailability, incompetence, or temporary incapacity, the informed consent of one parent of a nonviable neonate will suffice to meet the requirements of this paragraph (c)(5), except that the consent of the father need not be obtained if the pregnancy resulted from rape or incest. The consent of a legally authorized representative of either or both of the parents of a nonviable neonate will not suffice to meet the requirements of this paragraph (c)(5).

(d) Viable neonates. A neonate, after delivery, that has been determined to be viable may be included in research only to the extent permitted by and in accord with the requirements of subparts A and D of this part.

§46.206 Research involving, after delivery, the placenta, the dead fetus or fetal material.

(a) Research involving, after delivery, the placenta; the dead fetus; macerated fetal material; or cells, tissue, or organs excised from a dead fetus, shall be conducted only in accord with any applicable federal, state, or local laws and regulations regarding such activities.

(b) If information associated with material described in paragraph (a) of this section is recorded for research purposes in a manner that living individuals can be identified, directly or through identifiers linked to those individuals, those individuals are research subjects and all pertinent subparts of this part are applicable.

§46.207 Research not otherwise approvable which presents an opportunity to understand, prevent, or alleviate a serious problem affecting the health or welfare of pregnant women, fetuses, or neonates.

The Secretary will conduct or fund research that the IRB does not believe meets the requirements of §46.204 or §46.205 only if:

(a) The IRB finds that the research presents a reasonable opportunity to further the understanding, prevention, or alleviation of a serious problem affecting the health or welfare of pregnant women, fetuses or neonates; and

(b) The Secretary, after consultation with a panel of experts in pertinent disciplines (for example: science, medicine, ethics, law) and following opportunity for public review and comment, including a public meeting announced in the Federal Register, has determined either:
(1) That the research in fact satisfies the conditions of §46.204, as applicable; or
(2) The following: (i) The research presents a reasonable opportunity to further the understanding, prevention, or alleviation of a serious problem affecting the health or welfare of pregnant women, fetuses or neonates; (ii) The research will be conducted in accord with sound ethical principles; and (iii) Informed consent will be obtained in accord with the informed consent provisions of Subpart A and other applicable subparts of this part.

Subpart C: Additional Protections Pertaining to Biomedical and Behavioral Research Involving Prisoners as Subjects
Source: 43 FR 53655, Nov. 16, 1978, unless otherwise noted

§46.301 Applicability.

(a) The regulations in this subpart are applicable to all biomedical and behavioral research conducted or supported by the Department of Health and Human Services involving prisoners as subjects.

(b) Nothing in this subpart shall be construed as indicating that compliance with the procedures set forth herein will authorize research involving prisoners as subjects, to the extent such research is limited or barred by applicable state or local law.

(c) The requirements of this subpart are in addition to those imposed under the other subparts of this part.

§46.302 Purpose.

Inasmuch as prisoners may be under constraints because of their incarceration which could affect their ability to make a truly voluntary and uncoerced decision whether or not to participate as subjects in research, it is the purpose of this subpart to provide additional safeguards for the protection of prisoners involved in activities to which this subpart is applicable.

§46.303 Definitions.

As used in this subpart:

(a) *Secretary* means the Secretary of Health and Human Services and any other officer or employee of the Department of Health and Human Services to whom authority has been delegated.

(b) *DHHS* means the Department of Health and Human Services.

(c) *Prisoner* means any individual involuntarily confined or detained in a penal institution. The term is intended to encompass individuals sentenced to such an institution under a criminal or civil statute, individuals detained in other facilities by virtue of statutes or commitment procedures which provide alternatives to criminal prosecution or incarceration in a penal institution, and individuals detained pending arraignment, trial, or sentencing.

(d) *Minimal risk* is the probability and magnitude of physical or psychological harm that is normally encountered in the daily lives, or in the routine medical, dental, or psychological examination of healthy persons.

§46.304 Composition of institutional review boards where prisoners are involved.

In addition to satisfying the requirements in §46.107 of this part, an institutional review board, carrying out responsibilities under this part with respect to research covered by this subpart, shall also meet the following specific requirements:

(a) A majority of the board (exclusive of prisoner members) shall have no association with the prison(s) involved, apart from their membership on the board.

(b) At least one member of the board shall be a prisoner, or a prisoner representative with appropriate background and experience to serve in that capacity, except that where a particular research project is reviewed by more than one board only one board need satisfy this requirement.
[43 FR 53655, Nov. 16, 1978, as amended at 46 FR 8366, Jan. 26, 1981]

§46.305 Additional duties of the institutional review boards where prisoners are involved.

(a) In addition to all other responsibilities prescribed for institutional review boards under this part, the board shall review research covered by this subpart and approve such research only if it finds that:
(1) The research under review represents one of the categories of research permissible under §46.306(a)(2);
(2) Any possible advantages accruing to the prisoner through his or her participation in the research, when compared to the general living conditions, medical care, quality of food, amenities and opportunity for earnings in the prison, are not of such a magnitude that his or her ability to weigh the risks of the research against the value of such advantages in the limited choice environment of the prison is impaired;
(3) The risks involved in the research are commensurate with risks that would be accepted by nonprisoner volunteers;
(4) Procedures for the selection of subjects within the prison are fair to all prisoners and immune from arbitrary intervention by prison authorities or prisoners. Unless the principal investigator provides to the board justification in writing for following some other procedures, control subjects must

be selected randomly from the group of available prisoners who meet the characteristics needed for that particular research project;

(5) The information is presented in language which is understandable to the subject population;

(6) Adequate assurance exists that parole boards will not take into account a prisoner's participation in the research in making decisions regarding parole, and each prisoner is clearly informed in advance that participation in the research will have no effect on his or her parole; and

(7) Where the board finds there may be a need for follow-up examination or care of participants after the end of their participation, adequate provision has been made for such examination or care, taking into account the varying lengths of individual prisoners' sentences, and for informing participants of this fact.

(b) The board shall carry out such other duties as may be assigned by the Secretary.

(c) The institution shall certify to the Secretary, in such form and manner as the Secretary may require, that the duties of the board under this section have been fulfilled.

§46.306 Permitted research involving prisoners.

(a) Biomedical or behavioral research conducted or supported by DHHS may involve prisoners as subjects only if:

(1) The institution responsible for the conduct of the research has certified to the Secretary that the institutional review board has approved the research under §46.305 of this subpart; and

(2) In the judgment of the Secretary the proposed research involves solely the following: (i) Study of the possible causes, effects, and processes of incarceration, and of criminal behavior, provided that the study presents no more than minimal risk and no more than inconvenience to the subjects; (ii) Study of prisons as institutional structures or of prisoners as incarcerated persons, provided that the study presents no more than minimal risk and no more than inconvenience to the subjects; (iii) Research on conditions particularly affecting prisoners as a class (for example, vaccine trials and other research on hepatitis which is much more prevalent in prisons than elsewhere; and research on social and psychological problems such as alcoholism, drug addiction, and sexual assaults) provided that the study may proceed only after the Secretary has consulted with appropriate experts including experts in penology, medicine, and ethics, and published notice, in the *Federal Register*, of his intent to approve such research; or (iv)

Research on practices, both innovative and accepted, which have the intent and reasonable probability of improving the health or well-being of the subject. In cases in which those studies require the assignment of prisoners in a manner consistent with protocols approved by the IRB to control groups which may not benefit from the research, the study may proceed only after the Secretary has consulted with appropriate experts, including experts in penology, medicine, and ethics, and published notice, in the *Federal Register*, of the intent to approve such research.

(b) Except as provided in paragraph (a) of this section, biomedical or behavioral research conducted or supported by DHHS shall not involve prisoners as subjects.

Subpart D: Additional Protections for Children Involved as Subjects in Research
Source: 48 FR 9818, March 8, 1983, unless otherwise noted

§46.401 To what do these regulations apply?

(a) This subpart applies to all research involving children as subjects, conducted or supported by the Department of Health and Human Services.
(1) This includes research conducted by department employees, except that each head of an operating division of the department may adopt such nonsubstantive, procedural modifications as may be appropriate from an administrative standpoint.
(2) It also includes research conducted or supported by the Department of Health and Human Services outside the United States, but in appropriate circumstances, the Secretary may, under paragraph (i) of §46.101 of Subpart A, waive the applicability of some or all of the requirements of these regulations for research of this type.

(b) Exemptions at §46.101(b)(1) and (b)(3) through (b)(6) are applicable to this subpart. The exemption at §46.101(b)(2) regarding educational tests is also applicable to this subpart. However, the exemption at §46.101(b)(2) for research involving survey or interview procedures or observations of public behavior does not apply to research covered by this subpart, except for research involving observation of public behavior when the investigator(s) do not participate in the activities being observed.

(c) The exceptions, additions, and provisions for waiver as they appear in paragraphs (c) through (i) of §46.101 of Subpart A are applicable to this subpart.

[48 FR 9818, Mar.8, 1983; 56 FR 28032, June 18, 1991; 56 FR 29757, June 28, 1991.]

§46.402 Definitions.

The definitions in §46.102 of Subpart A shall be applicable to this subpart as well. In addition, as used in this subpart:

(a) *Children* are persons who have not attained the legal age for consent to treatments or procedures involved in the research, under the applicable law of the jurisdiction in which the research will be conducted.

(b) *Assent* means a child's affirmative agreement to participate in research. Mere failure to object should not, absent affirmative agreement, be construed as assent.

(c) *Permission* means the agreement of parent(s) or guardian to the participation of their child or ward in research.

(d) *Parent* means a child's biological or adoptive parent.

(e) *Guardian* means an individual who is authorized under applicable state or local law to consent on behalf of a child to general medical care.

§46.403 IRB duties.

In addition to other responsibilities assigned to IRBs under this part, each IRB shall review research covered by this subpart and approve only research which satisfies the conditions of all applicable sections of this subpart.

§46.404 Research not involving greater than minimal risk.

DHHS will conduct or fund research in which the IRB finds that no greater than minimal risk to children is presented, only if the IRB finds that adequate provisions are made for soliciting the assent of the children and the permission of their parents or guardians, as set forth in §46.408.

§46.405 Research involving greater than minimal risk but presenting the prospect of direct benefit to the individual subjects.

DHHS will conduct or fund research in which the IRB finds that more than minimal risk to children is presented by an intervention or procedure that holds out the prospect of direct benefit for the individual subject, or by a monitoring procedure that is likely to contribute to the subject's well-being, only if the IRB finds that:

(a) The risk is justified by the anticipated benefit to the subjects;

(b) The relation of the anticipated benefit to the risk is at least as favorable to the subjects as that presented by available alternative approaches; and

(c) Adequate provisions are made for soliciting the assent of the children and permission of their parents or guardians, as set forth in §46.408.

§46.406 Research involving greater than minimal risk and no prospect of direct benefit to individual subjects, but likely to yield generalizable knowledge about the subject's disorder or condition.

DHHS will conduct or fund research in which the IRB finds that more than minimal risk to children is presented by an intervention or procedure that does not hold out the prospect of direct benefit for the individual subject, or by a monitoring procedure which is not likely to contribute to the well-being of the subject, only if the IRB finds that:

(a) The risk represents a minor increase over minimal risk;

(b) The intervention or procedure presents experiences to subjects that are reasonably commensurate with those inherent in their actual or expected medical, dental, psychological, social, or educational situations;

(c) The intervention or procedure is likely to yield generalizable knowledge about the subjects' disorder or condition which is of vital importance for the understanding or amelioration of the subjects' disorder or condition; and

(d) Adequate provisions are made for soliciting assent of the children and permission of their parents or guardians, as set forth in §46.408.

§46.407 Research not otherwise approvable which presents an opportunity to understand, prevent, or alleviate a serious problem affecting the health or welfare of children.

DHHS will conduct or fund research that the IRB does not believe meets the requirements of §46.404, §46.405, or §46.406 only if:

(a) The IRB finds that the research presents a reasonable opportunity to further the understanding, prevention, or alleviation of a serious problem affecting the health or welfare of children; and

(b) The Secretary, after consultation with a panel of experts in pertinent disciplines (for example: science, medicine, education, ethics, law) and following opportunity for public review and comment, has determined either: (1) That the research in fact satisfies the conditions of §46.404, §46.405, or §46.406, as applicable, or (2) the following: (i) The research presents a reasonable opportunity to further the understanding, prevention, or alleviation of a serious problem affecting the health or welfare of children; (ii) The research will be conducted in accordance with sound ethical principles; (iii) Adequate provisions are made for soliciting the assent of children and the permission of their parents or guardians, as set forth in §46.408.

§46.408 Requirements for permission by parents or guardians and for assent by children.

(a) In addition to the determinations required under other applicable sections of this subpart, the IRB shall determine that adequate provisions are made for soliciting the assent of the children, when in the judgment of the IRB the children are capable of providing assent. In determining whether children are capable of assenting, the IRB shall take into account the ages, maturity, and psychological state of the children involved. This judgment may be made for all children to be involved in research under a particular protocol, or for each child, as the IRB deems appropriate. If the IRB determines that the capability of some or all of the children is so limited that they cannot reasonably be consulted or that the intervention or procedure involved in the research holds out a prospect of direct benefit that is important to the health or well-being of the children and is available only in the context of the research, the assent of the children is not a necessary condition for proceeding with the research. Even where the IRB determines that the subjects are capable of assenting, the IRB may still waive the assent requirement under circumstances in which consent may be waived in accord with §46.116 of Subpart A.

(b) In addition to the determinations required under other applicable sections of this subpart, the IRB shall determine, in accordance with and to the extent that consent is required by §46.116 of Subpart A, that adequate provisions are made for soliciting the permission of each child's parents or guardian. Where parental permission is to be obtained, the IRB may find that the permission of one parent is sufficient for research to be conducted under §46.404 or §46.405. Where research is covered by §46.406 and §46.407 and permission is to be obtained from parents, both parents must give their permission unless one parent is deceased, unknown, incompetent, or not reasonably available, or when only one parent has legal responsibility for the care and custody of the child.

(c) In addition to the provisions for waiver contained in §46.116 of Subpart A, if the IRB determines that a research protocol is designed for conditions or for a subject population for which parental or guardian permission is not a reasonable requirement to protect the subjects (for example, neglected or abused children), it may waive the consent requirements in Subpart A of this part and paragraph (b) of this section, provided an appropriate mechanism for protecting the children who will participate as subjects in the research is substituted, and provided further that the waiver is not inconsistent with federal, state, or local law. The choice of an appropriate mechanism would depend upon the nature and purpose of the activities described in the protocol, the risk and anticipated benefit to the research subjects, and their age, maturity, status, and condition.

(d) Permission by parents or guardians shall be documented in accordance with and to the extent required by §46.117 of Subpart A.

(e) When the IRB determines that assent is required, it shall also determine whether and how assent must be documented.

§46.409 Wards.

(a) Children who are wards of the state or any other agency, institution, or entity can be included in research approved under §46.406 or §46.407 only if such research is:
(1) Related to their status as wards; or
(2) Conducted in schools, camps, hospitals, institutions, or similar settings in which the majority of children involved as subjects are not wards.

(b) If the research is approved under paragraph (a) of this section, the IRB shall require appointment of an advocate for each child who is a ward, in addition to any other individual acting on behalf of the child as guardian or in loco parentis. One individual may serve as advocate for more than one child. The advocate shall be an individual who has the background and experience to act in, and agrees to act in, the best interests of the child for the duration of the child's participation in the research and who is not associated in any way (except in the role as advocate or member of the IRB) with the research, the investigator(s), or the guardian organization.

E

Committee, Expert Advisor, Liaison Panel, and Staff Biographies

COMMITTEE

Lawrence O. Gostin, JD, LLD *(Chair)* is an internationally recognized scholar in law and public health. He has been awarded degrees from the Georgetown University School of Law and The Johns Hopkins University School of Public Policy. He is an elected member of the Institute of Medicine (IOM) of the National Academies and an elected fellow of the Hastings Center. At the National Academy of Sciences (NAS), he currently serves on the Board on Health Promotion and Disease Prevention, is a member of the Committee to Enhance the Effectiveness of the Centers for Disease Control and Prevention (CDC) Quarantine Station Expansion Plan for U.S. Points of Entry, and recently served as chair of the Committee on Genomics and the Public's Health in the 21st Century. Professor Gostin is the health law and ethics editor of the *Journal of the American Medical Association* and serves on the editorial boards of many other scholarly journals. His recent books include *The AIDS Pandemic: Complacency, Injustice, and Unfulfilled Expectations* (2004), *The Human Rights of Persons with Intellectual Disabilities: Different But Equal* (2003, with S. S. Herr, H. H. Koh, eds.), *Public Health Law and Ethics: A Reader* (2002), and *Public Health Law: Power, Duty, Restraint* (2000). Professor Gostin is the John Carroll Research Professor of Law at the Georgetown University Law School. He also directs the Centers for Disease Control and Prevention's Collaborating Center Promoting Health Through Law.

Hortensia Amaro, PhD, is a distinguished professor of health sciences at the Bouve College of Health Sciences at Northeastern University (NEU) and director of the Institute on Urban Health Research at NEU. She received her doctoral degree from the University of California, Los Angeles in 1982 and was awarded an honorary doctoral degree in humane letters by Simmons College in 1994. Over the last 20 years, Dr. Amaro's work has focused on improving the connections between public health research and public health practice. Her research has focused on epidemiological and community-based studies of alcohol and drug use among adolescents and adults, on the effectiveness of HIV/AIDS prevention programs, and on substance abuse and mental health treatment issues for women. In 1996, Dr. Amaro was appointed to the Board of the Boston Public Health Commission by Mayor Thomas Menino. She currently serves as vice-chair of the board. She has recently served as an appointed member of the National Advisory Council of the National Institute on Drug Abuse. Dr. Amaro has also served on several committees at the National Research Council related to social and behavioral research; substance abuse, mental health, and AIDS; and legal and ethical issues for women in clinical studies.

Patricia Blair, PhD, JD, is vice-president and university counsel at the University of Texas Health Center in Tyler, Texas and adjunct associate professor in the School of Nursing. She is also university compliance office and university ethics officer. Her research has focused on nursing ethics, law and policy; legal and ethical issues related to correctional health care; and the provision of health-care services in prison settings. Dr. Blair is a member of the board of directors of the American Association of Nurse Attorneys. She received her MSN from the University of Texas Medical Branch at Galveston, her JD from Texas Southern University, her LLM in Health Law and Policy from the University of Houston Law School, and her PhD from the University of Texas Medical Branch in Clinical Sciences Health Services Research with a focus on health disparities research.

Steve Cambra, Jr., is co-owner of Cambra, Larson & Associates, a criminal justice consulting firm that advises prison facilities on compliance with federal and state regulations. He has spent 35 years working in the corrections industry. Mr. Cambra began as a corrections officer in 1970 at the California Men's Colony and was gradually promoted through management and administrative ranks. He served as warden of Pelican Bay State Prison for almost 3 years before being promoted to chief deputy director for field operations with the California Department of Corrections. Mr. Cambra also served as director of the California Department of Corrections. In this position, he was responsible for approximately 122,000 parolees and 160,000 inmates in a system that included 33 prisons, 38 conservation camps, 16 community correctional facilities, 35 work furlough and prisoner mother community-based programs, and more than 100 parole offices statewide. He currently advises the California Youth Authority. Mr. Cambra earned a BA in social science at Stanislaus State College.

G. David Curry, PhD, is an ex-prisoner. He is a professor in the Department of Criminology and Criminal Justice at the University of Missouri, St. Louis. He is currently conducting outcome evaluations of a number of St. Louis programs designed to reduce youth violence. Dr. Curry is coauthor of *Confronting Gangs: Crime and Community* (2002) and author of *Sunshine Patriots: Punishment and the Vietnam Offender* (1985) as well as book chapters and research articles. He is a member of the American Society of Criminology, American Association for the Advancement of Science, and Academy of Criminal Justice Sciences. He has received the Boys and Girls Club of America Advocacy Award (2001) and his university's Chancellor's Award for Excellence in Service (2004). Dr. Curry received his PhD in sociology from the University of Chicago. He also completed postdoctoral studies there with a specialization in evaluation research methods. Dr. Curry served as chair of a university institutional review board (IRB) committee (2 years) and as a prisoner representative on an IRB (6 years).

Cynthia A. Gómez, PhD, is the founding director of Health Equity Initiatives at San Francisco State University where she leads efforts to enhance and integrate campus research, curricula, community service, and training programs that address health disparities and/or promote health equity in the United States. She previously served as codirector of the Center for AIDS Prevention Studies (CAPS) at the University of California at San Francisco where she was also an associate professor in the Department of Medicine and leading scientist in HIV prevention research since 1991. She received her master's degree in psychology from Harvard and her PhD in Clinical Psychology from Boston University. Prior to her work with CAPS, Dr. Gómez spent 12 years working in community health settings, including five as director of a child and family mental health center in Boston. Dr. Gómez is considered a pioneer in the areas of cultural determinants in sexual behaviors among Latinos, in the role of power dynamics in sexual risk among women, and in the development of HIV prevention interventions, including interventions for people living with HIV. Dr Gómez is a nationally renowned speaker and an expert in the field of HIV prevention and sexual health. She has served on several national committees including the Center for Disease Control's HIV and STD Advisory Council, the National Institute on Drug Abuse's (NIDA) National Hispanic Science Network, and the Substance Abuse and Mental Health Services Administration's (SAMHSA) Advisory Committee on Women's Services.

She is a member and past chair of the board of directors of the Guttmacher Institute. She serves on several other boards of directors including the National AIDS Fund, Public Responsibility in Medicine & Research, and the Pacific Institute for Women's Health. Dr Gómez was also an appointed member to the Presidential Advisory Council on HIV/AIDS under both WJ Clinton and GW Bush administrations.

Bradford H. Gray, PhD, is a principal research associate at the Urban Institute and editor of *The Milbank Quarterly,* a journal of population health and health policy. He was formerly a study director at the IOM, a faculty member at Yale University, and director of the health policy division at the New York Academy of Medicine. He earlier served on the staff of the National Commission for the Protection of Human Subjects of Biomedical and Behavioral Research and was a consultant on IRBs to the President's Commission for the Study of Ethical Problems in Medicine and Research. He has published extensively on matters pertaining to the ethics of human experimentation, for-profit and nonprofit health care, and the changing conditions of medical professionalism. His books include *Human Subjects in Medical Experimentation: The Conduct and Regulation of Clinical Research (1975)* and *The Profit Motive and Patient Care: The Changing Accountability of Doctors and Hospitals* (1991). Dr. Gray holds bachelor's and master's degrees from Oklahoma State University and a PhD in sociology from Yale University. He is a fellow of The Hastings Center, AcademyHealth, and the New York Academy of Medicine. Dr. Gray is a member of the IOM.

Michael S. Hamden, JD, is executive director of North Carolina Prisoner Legal Services, Inc., a public service, nonprofit organization for prisoners and others detained in the criminal justice system in North Carolina. He also serves as a prisoner representative for the Research Triangle Institute's IRBs. Mr. Hamden is a member of the North Carolina Bar Association, where he currently serves as chair of the Section on Constitutional Rights and Responsibilities. He is also a member of the North Carolina Academy of Trial Lawyers and served as chair of the North Carolina Legal Services Planning Council. Mr. Hamden is a member of the American Bar Association, serving as cochair on the Corrections and Sentencing Committee and as liaison to the American Correctional Association (ACA). In the ACA, Mr. Hamden is a member of the Standards Committee and the Commission on Accreditation for Corrections, both as commissioner and as a member of the Executive Committee. He has written extensively on the provision of legal services to prison populations, most recently coediting *The Law and Policy of Sentencing and Corrections* (7th ed., 2005) with law professor

Lynn S. Branham. Hamden earned a JD at the University of Tennessee College of Law and a bachelor of music degree at Berklee College of Music.

Jeffrey L. Metzner, MD, is clinical professor in the Departments of Psychiatry and Pediatrics at the University of Colorado School of Medicine and associate director of the Forensic Psychiatry Fellowship Program. He is a member of the American Psychiatric Association and immediate past chair of its Council on Psychiatry and the Law. He also holds memberships with the American Academy of Psychiatry and Law, American Academy of Forensic Sciences, American College of Legal Medicine, and American Correctional Association. Dr. Metzner has written extensively on the psychiatric care of prison populations. He received his MD from the University of Maryland Medical School.

Jonathan Moreno, PhD, is the Emily Davie and Joseph S. Kornfield Professor of Biomedical Ethics and director of the Center for Biomedical Ethics at the University of Virginia. Dr. Moreno is an elected member of the IOM, a bioethics consultant for the Howard Hughes Medical Institute, a senior fellow at the Center for American Progress, a faculty affiliate of the Kennedy Institute of Ethics at Georgetown University, and a fellow of the Hastings Center. He was a member of the National Human Research Protection Advisory Committee and during 1994–1995 was senior policy and research analyst for the President's Advisory Committee on Human Radiation Experiments. He is currently a member of the Health Sciences Policy Board of the IOM and served as cochair for the Committee on Guidelines for Human Embryonic Stem Cell Research. Among his books are *Is There an Ethicist in the House: On the Cutting Edge of Bioethics* (2005) and *Undue Risk: Secret State Experiments on Humans* (2001).

Larry Palmer, LLB, is the endowed chair in urban health policy at the University of Louisville, Kentucky, with appointments in the Department of Family and Community Medicine, Institute for Bioethics, Health Policy and Law, and School of Public Health and Information Sciences. Before joining the University of Louisville, he was a professor at Cornell University Law School in Ithaca, New York. Professor Palmer is the author of *Law, Medicine, and Social Justice* (1989), *Endings and Beginnings: Law, Medicine and Society in Assisted Life and Death* (2000), and numerous articles dealing with law, medicine, and health policy. Professor Palmer is also the executive producer and author of the study guide of the prize-winning educational video *Susceptible to Kindness: Miss Evers' Boys and the Tuskegee Syphilis Study*. He is a member of the board of directors of the Hastings Center in Garrison, New York. Previously, Professor Palmer served as a director of the National Patient Safety Foundation (1997–2002) and a trustee of the Phillips Exeter Academy (1990–2000). He was a member of the Committee on Establishing a National Cord Blood Stem Cell Bank Program with the IOM.

Norman Poythress, PhD, is professor in the Department of Mental Health Law and Policy at the Florida Mental Health Institute at the University of South Florida. He received his PhD in clinical psychology from the University of Texas, Austin in 1977. Dr. Poythress has previously worked at the Center for Forensic Psychiatry in Ann Arbor, Michigan, and the Taylor Hardin Secure Medical Facility in Tuscaloosa, Alabama. He is a past president of the American Psychology-Law Society (Division 41 of the American Psychological Association) and was the recipient in 1990 of the American Academy of Forensic Psychology's Award for Distinguished Contributions to Forensic Psychology. Dr. Poythress was a consultant to the MacArthur Foundation Research Network on Mental Health and the Law from 1989 to 1996. He is coauthor of *Psychological Evaluations for the Courts: A Handbook for Mental Health Professionals and Lawyers,* and his current research interests include forensic evaluation, psychopathy, and risk assessment. He is a member of the American Psychological Association and the International Association for Forensic Mental Health Services.

William J. Rold, JD, CC HP-A, is a practicing civil rights attorney in New York City. A substantial part of his practice involves representing prisoners in lawsuits concerning health care and other rights. He also publishes, lectures, and consults with correctional health-care officials throughout the United States and abroad. He was a staff attorney for the Prisoners' Rights Project in New York for 10 years. Mr. Rold represents the American Bar Association on the board of directors of the National Commission on Correctional Health Care and has served on the IRB of the New York City Department of Health for research involving prisoner subjects. Mr. Rold earned his juris doctor in 1977 from Georgetown University Law Center and holds his advanced certification as a correctional health-care professional. He serves on the editorial board of the *Journal of Prison Health.* He was honored with the Bernard P. Harrison Award of Merit for his service to correctional health care by the National Commission on Correctional Health Care in St. Louis in 2000. Mr. Rold was recently appointed a vice-chair of the Corrections Committee of the American Bar Association.

Janette Y. Taylor, PhD, is associate professor in the College of Nursing at the University of Iowa. She is a certified women's health-care nurse practitioner with specialization in obstetrics, gynecological, and neonatal nursing. Dr. Taylor's research has focused on race/ethnicity as variables in nursing research, African American women's experience of domestic violence, the health of women prisoners, reconnecting incarcerated women with their children, and using narrative art therapy with incarcerated abused women. She completed her PhD at the University of Washington.

Wendy Visscher, PhD, is director of RTI International's Office of Research Protection and Ethics. RTI is an independent, nonprofit organization that conducts research and development projects for government and commercial clients worldwide. Dr. Visscher oversees the operation of RTI's three IRBs and chairs one of these committees. The IRBs review, approve, and monitor all human subjects research conducted by RTI, including both biomedical and sociobehavioral research. Dr. Visscher maintains RTI's federal-wide assurance with the U.S. Department of Health and Human Services' (DHHS) Office for Human Research Protections. She has expertise in DHHS and Food and Drug Administration human subjects protection regulations, the Health Insurance Portability and Accountability Act and other privacy laws, and international guidelines and state laws that relate to research. She provides guidance and training for researchers and legal and regulatory staff on human subjects and privacy issues and earned her certified IRB professional (CIP) rating in 2002. Dr. Visscher is also an experienced researcher and holds a master's of public health and a PhD in epidemiology from the University of Minnesota.

Barry Zack, MPH, is executive director of Centerforce, a nongovernment organization working with prisoners, their families, and persons recently released from jails and prisons in Northern and Central California. He is also an associate clinical professor at the University of California, San Francisco, in the Department of Community Health Systems at the School of Nursing. He has been a direct service provider and community researcher working with incarcerated populations since 1986. Mr. Zack has published research and presented at professional conferences on behavioral intervention strategies to prevent HIV, hepatitis, and sexually transmitted diseases and reduce risk behavior among prisoners; he has consulted with many department of corrections on effective behavioral interventions in the correctional setting. He is on the editorial board of *Infectious Diseases in Corrections Report (formerly HEPP Report)* and the *Journal of Correctional Health Care*. Mr. Zack was an external consultant for the CDC's Prevention and Control of Infections with Hepatitis Viruses in Correctional Settings program as well as the Surgeon General's "Call to Action on Corrections and Community Health."

EXPERT ADVISER

Nancy Neveloff Dubler, LLB, is the director of the Division of Bioethics, Department of Epidemiology and Population Health, Montefiore Medical Center and Professor of Epidemiology and Population Health at the Albert Einstein College of Medicine. She received her BA from Barnard College and her LLB from the Harvard Law School. Ms. Dubler directs the Bioethics Consultation Service at Montefiore Medical Center (founded in 1978) as a support for analysis of difficult clinical cases presenting ethical issues in the health-care setting; this service uses mediation as its process. She lectures extensively and is the author of numerous articles and books on termination of care, home care and long-term care, geriatrics, prison and jail health care, and AIDS. She is codirector of the Certificate Program in Bioethics and the Medical Humanities, conducted jointly by Montefiore Medical Center/Albert Einstein College of Medicine with Cardozo Law School of Yeshiva University. Her most recent books are: *Ethics On Call: Taking Charge of Life-and Death Choices in Today's Health Care System*, with David Nimmons, Vintage Press, (1993); *Bioethics Mediation: A Guide to Shaping Shared Solutions*, coauthor, Carol Liebman, United Hospital Fund, (2004); *The Ethics and Regulation of Research with Human Subjects*, Carl Coleman, Jerry Menikoff, Jesse Goldner, and Nancy Dubler, LexisNexis, (2005). She consults often with federal agencies, national working groups, and bioethics centers.

LIAISON PANEL:
FORMER PRISONERS AND PRISONER ADVOCATES

Edward Anthony was an inmate in Philadelphia's Holmesburg Prison in the 1960s. During that time he took part in a series on medical experiments that included patch tests, diet studies, and psychotropic drug experiments for the U.S. Army. Since becoming fully aware of how he and other former prisoners were used and misused as experimental material in the book *Acres of Skin*, Mr. Edwards has become an activist on the subject of ethical research and has spoken at numerous colleges, including Brown, Pennsylvania State, and Holy Family Universities. Mr. Edwards is currently working on a book with Allen Hornblum of Temple University concerning his life as a human guinea pig.

Jack Beck has been the director of the Prison Visiting Project at the Correctional Association (CA) of New York since October 2004. The CA has statutory authority to inspect prisons in New York State and to report findings to the legislature and public. In addition, the project has issued major reports on prison health care, disciplinary segregation, and treatment of inmates with mental illness. Before his association with CA, Mr. Beck was a senior supervising attorney at the Prisoners' Right Project of the Legal Aid Society, where he worked for 23 years. He specialized in medical care issues, with particular focus on HIV/AIDS and hepatitis C. Mr. Beck is also a member of several statewide coalitions concerned with medical and mental health care in prisons that have been advocating for legislation to improve care of inmates. Mr. Beck has been a member of the New York Academy of Medicine IRB as the prisoner representative for 6 years. From 2003 to 2005, he was a member of the DHHS Secretary's Advisory Committee on Human Research Protections, Subcommittee on Subpart C: Prisoners Research.

Debra Breuklander is a nurse consultant at MECCA, a residential inpatient substance abuse treatment program in Des Moines, Iowa. She previously worked as therapeutic community mentor and staff assistant while incarcerated at the Iowa Correctional Institution for Women. Ms. Breuklander has presented on child abuse prevention, reentry programs, and family transition in prison populations. She is currently vice-president of the Iowa Correctional Institution for Women Therapeutic Community Advisory Board and a member of the Friends of Iowa Women Prisoners.

James Dahl is a clinical psychologist and sociologist focused on research development, field implementation of evidence-based treatment, and collaborative community projects. He is currently directing research development for the largest substance abuse treatment organization in the United States, Phoenix House, managing a portfolio of competitive research grants in applied research related to therapeutic community and related treatment strategies for substance abuse. Dr. Dahl formerly served as director of Research Development, Research Foundation of City University of New York, driving a strategic research development program in biomedical and other bio-based technology, photonics, and aquaculture for the 20-campus system, which supports $250 million in research annually. He also served as vice-president of Washington based University Research Corporation for more than six years, specializing in federally sponsored research to application of evidence-based programs through training and site development. Dr. Dahl has held positions as a university professor at the State University of New York at Stony Brook (School of Medicine/Psychiatry and School of Social Work) and Hofstra University. He was a senior grants officer for a private foundation and a consultant for Washington-based WESTAT and Macro International, delivering technical assistance to state drug treatment programs for SAMHSA's Center for Substance Abuse Treatment as well as Atlanta University, Crime and Justice Institute, and Howard University, Center for Drug Abuse Research. He also served for six years as vice-president of the University Research Corporation in Bethesda, Maryland, conducting federal research and practice dissemination projects for the National Institute of Justice (NIJ), Office of Juvenile Justice and Delinquency Prevention, and Department of Education. He is currently a review panelist for SAMHSA, U.S. Department of Justice (DOJ), and National Institute of Drug Abuse Clinical Trials Network Concept Wave Reviews. Dr. Dahl is a current member of the American Psychological Association, American Psychological Society, and the New York Academy of Sciences. He is board certified in cognitive-behavioral therapy and hypnotherapy.

Allen Hornblum has spent many years in government and has an extensive background working in the criminal justice system. He has served as chief of staff of the Philadelphia Sheriff's Office and on the boards of the Pennsylvania Crime Commission, the Pennsylvania Commission of Crime and Delinquency, and the Philadelphia Prison System Board of Trustees. Mr. Hornblum's book *Acres of Skin* is the leading work on the subject of America's use of prison inmates as test subjects for medical experiments. He has recently completed a documentary on the Holmesburg experiments. Mr. Hornblum has also lectured on the subject at an array of institutions of higher learning, including Brown and Columbia universities, the National Institutes of Health (NIH), and the British Medical Association. Mr. Hornblum has also written *Philadelphia City Hall* (2003), a photographic history of Philadelphia's City Hall and *Confessions of a Second Story Man: Junior Kripplebauer and the K&A Gang*, which is scheduled for release in May 2005. He is currently working on two books, one of which will document the life of a former inmate test subject and his lasting resentment toward the medical establishment.

Daniel Murphy is currently a professor in the Department of Political Science and Justice Studies at Appalachian State University. He is also author of "Aspirin Ain't Gonna Help the Kind of Pain I'm In: Health Care Delivery in the Federal Bureau of Prisons," which appears in *Convict Criminology*. Dr. Murphy's research is based on his personal experience, having been imprisoned in the federal Bureau of Prisons (BOP) for 5 years. He is also an active member of the Convict Criminologists group. Dr. Murphy is cochair of the Federal Citizens United for the Rehabilitation of Errants' (FedCURE) Legislative Action Committee. He also serves as a member of FedCURE's Board of Directors.

Barry Nakell, Esq., is a former professor of law and an attorney who has been an advocate for the rights of prisoners over the last 30 years. Mr. Nakell represented the prisoner class in the seminal case, *Bounds v. Smith*, which established that prisoners have a right of access to the courts. After his victory in that case, in 1978 Mr. Nakell was the moving force in the creation of North Carolina Prisoner Legal Services, Inc., and has continuously served as a member of its board of directors.

Osvaldo Rivera is a 50-year-old Latino, born and raised in Puerto Rico. He has worked in the field of human services for approximately 10 years. Mr. Rivera was a member of the Consumer Advisory Board for the Massachusetts Department of Public Health. He currently serves on the Ryan White Planning Council. For the last five years, Mr. Rivera's work consisted of providing reintegration services to offenders and ex-offenders. He is affiliated with Span Inc., which specializes in providing reintegration services in the greater Boston, Massachusetts, area. Mr. Rivera's main focus is HIV/AIDS-positive men and those who are at high risk for acquiring and transmitting HIV/AIDS, hepatitis, and other sexually transmitted infections. After a long battle with addiction and many years spent in and out of prisons, Mr. Rivera made the commitment to work with people like himself. He went to school to further his education and became a certified addiction specialist and a licensed alcohol and drug counselor. He earned respect and a good reputation within his community as a positive role model and leader. Mr. Rivera's desire is to continue his positive work in order to empower and strengthen others in need.

Jeffrey Ian Ross is an associate professor in the Division of Criminology, Criminal Justice, and Social Policy and a research fellow at the Center for Comparative and International Law at the University of Baltimore. He has conducted research, written, and lectured on national security, political violence, political crime, policing, and corrections for more than 15 years. His work has appeared in many academic journals and books as well as popular magazines. He is the author of *Making News of Police Violence* (Praeger, 2000), coauthor (with Stephen C. Richards) of *Behind Bars: Surviving Prison* (Macmillan, 2002), editor of *Controlling State Crime* (2nd ed., Transaction Books, 2000), *Violence in Canada: Sociopolitical Perspectives* (Oxford University Press, 1995), *Cutting the Edge: Current Perspectives in Radical/Critical Criminology and Criminal Justice* (Praeger, 1998), *Varieties of State Crime and Its Control* (Criminal Justice Press, 1999), and coeditor, with Stephen C. Richards, of *Convict Criminology* (Wadsworth, 2002). In 1986 Ross was the lead expert witness for the Senate of Canada's Special Committee on Terrorism and Public Safety. He received his PhD in political science from the University of Colorado and was a social science analyst with the NIJ, a division of the DOJ, before coming to the University of Baltimore.

Jean Scott is the Deputy Regional Director of the New York City and Correctional Treatment Programs at Phoenix Houses of New York, the largest substance abuse treatment organization in the United States. Ms. Scott first joined Phoenix House in 1970; subsequently served as Manager of Purchasing and Corporate Relations; Senior Director/Assistant to the Associate Director of Phelan Place; Regional and Facility Director at the Hart Island complex; and Assistant Director of the Far Rockaway facility. From 1983 to 2000 she served as Vice-President, Director of Adult Programs and in 2000, she was promoted to Deputy Regional Director, New York City and Correctional Treatment Programs for Phoenix Houses of New York, where she oversees budgets in excess of $10 million for residential programs. She was also responsible for development, coordination, and implementation of a joint initiative with the New York State Department of Corrections, providing drug treatment for incarcerated offenders. She has served on the OASAS Credentialing Board; the Argus Community, Inc., ACT I, Private Sector Advisory Board; and the Board of Trustees at St. Francis College. In 1993, she received the 9th Fannie Lou Hamer award and in 1996 the 7th Annual Founders award from the Black Agency Executives. Ms. Scott is a credentialed alcohol and substance abuse counselor (CASAC), a certified addictions specialist (CAS) and a certified criminal justice addictions specialist (CCJAS); and she currently sits on the OASAS Appeals Board.

STAFF

Andrew Pope, PhD, is director of the board on Health Sciences Policy in the IOM. With a PhD in physiology and biochemistry, his primary interests are in science policy, biomedical ethics, and the environmental and occupational influences on human health. During his tenure at the National Academies and since 1989 at the IOM, Dr. Pope has directed numerous studies on topics that range from injury control, disability prevention, and biologic markers to the protection of human subjects of research, NIH priority-setting processes, organ procurement and transplantation policy, and the role of science and technology in countering terrorism. Dr. Pope is the recipient of the NAS President's Special Achievement Award and the IOM's Cecil Award.

Adrienne Stith Butler, PhD, is a senior program officer in the Board on Health Sciences Policy of the IOM. She is currently study director for the IOM Committee on Understanding Premature Birth and Assuring Healthy Outcomes. Previously, Dr. Stith Butler served as study director for the IOM report, *Preparing for the Psychological Consequences of Terrorism: A Public Health Strategy* conducted within the Board on Neuroscience and Behavioral Health. She has also served as a staff officer for IOM reports, *In the Nation's Compelling Interest: Ensuring Diversity in the Health-Care Workforce* and *Unequal Treatment: Confronting Racial and Ethnic Disparities in Health Care*, conducted within the Board on Health Sciences Policy. Before working at the IOM, Dr. Stith Butler served as the James Marshall Public Policy Scholar, a fellowship cosponsored by the Society for the Psychological Study of Social Issues and the American Psychological Association (APA). In this position, based at the APA in Washington, D.C., she engaged in policy analysis and monitored legislative issues related to ethnic disparities in health care and health research, racial profiling, and mental health counseling provisions in the reauthorization of the Elementary and Secondary Education Act. Dr. Stith Butler, a clinical psychologist, received her doctorate in 1997 from the University of Vermont. She completed postdoctoral fellowships in adolescent medicine and pediatric psychology at the University of Rochester Medical Center in Rochester, New York.

Susan McCutchen is a research associate for this study. She has been on staff at the National Academies for nearly 25 years, assisting committees focused on a wide variety of subjects, including studies for the Agency for International Development, technology transfer, aeronautics and space research, various kinds of natural disasters, HIV and needle exchange, human factors and engineering, the polygraph, poison control centers, education and testing issues (e.g., "No Child Left Behind"), ethics in research, and social security (i.e., representative payees, disability determinations). She has a BA in French from Miami University in Ohio and an MA in French with a minor in English from Kent State University.

Eileen Santa, MA, is a research associate working with the premature birth and the prisoner research ethics committees. She earned her master's degree in clinical psychology from the University of Massachusetts, where she is currently a doctoral candidate. Her research focuses on the cultural factors that contribute to healthy outcomes for Latina mothers and children.

Vilija Teel works as the senior project assistant for this study, providing administrative support for the project. Mrs. Teel plans and coordinates logistical arrangements for committee meetings, including coordinating travel and lodging for committee members, overseeing the attendee registration process during open sessions, and providing support throughout the committee meeting. She also provides support for the project's financial management, including processing payment requests and ensuring timely reimbursement of travel and incidental expenses. Mrs. Teel earned a BA in English/Linguistics from Vilnius University and has taken additional course work in finance and management areas. She is proficient in all of the major office-environment software programs. In addition to English, she has a good grasp of many other languages.

Jason Farley is currently working as an intern for this study. Mr. Farley is completing a PhD in the School of Nursing at The Johns Hopkins University. He holds a bachelor's degree in nursing from the University of Alabama, a master's degree in public health from the University of Alabama, Birmingham, and a master's degree in nursing from The Johns Hopkins University School of Nursing. He is certified as an adult nurse practitioner with a clinical practice both in infectious disease and emergency medicine. His doctoral study was recently funded by a National Research Service Award by the National Institute of Health. His research will investigate the molecular epidemiology of methicillin-resistant *Staphylococcus aureus* in the Baltimore City jail system.

Index

A

Abuses. *See also* Substance abuse
    intervening to curtail, 14
ACA. *See* American Correctional Association
Accountability, 7, 159–160
Acquired immunodeficiency syndrome (AIDS), 1–2, 22, 24, 29, 43, 54, 119
Acres of Skin: Human Experiments at Holmesburg Prison, 54, 121
Addictions. *See* Substance abuse
Adoption of DHHS Human Subjects Protection Regulations, 74–84
    the Common Rule, 76–78
    Report of the SACHRP Subcommittee, 81–84
    Subpart C: Prisoners as Research Subjects, 79–81
Adverse events (AE)
    in reviewing prisoner research, 151
Agency head, defined, 211
Ages
    of inmates, 40–42
    of research participants, 184, 186
AIDS. *See* Acquired immunodeficiency syndrome
Alternatives to comprehensive regulation, 99–100
Alternatives to incarceration, 23–24, 33
    research settings, 185
    that may be available to offenders, 104
Amendment review, of prisoner research, 151
American Correctional Association (ACA), 133
American Journal of Public Health, 37
American Psychiatric Association, 44
Animal Welfare Act, 64
Antiviral therapies, 43
Anxiety disorders, 45
Applicability, in Subpart C, 231
Applications lacking definite plans for involvement of human subjects, in Subpart A, 224
Assault. *See* Sexual assaults
Assent, defined, 235

B

Ballard v. Woodard, 58
Belmont Report, 10, 192
Beyond Consent: Seeking Justice in Research, 117, 132
Biologics, registry of clinical research on, 7
Biomedical research, 8–9, 67
    distrust regarding, x
    guidance on, 125–127
    interventions, 9

253

BJS. *See* Bureau of Justice Statistics
Black prisoners, 38–39
BOP. *See* Bureau of Prisons
BRRB. *See* Bureau Research Review Board
Bureau of Justice Statistics (BJS), 31, 33, 37–38, 44, 47–48, 89n, 105, 123
Bureau of Prisons (BOP), 6, 74, 85, 89–93, 99, 176, 202
Bureau Research Review Board (BRRB), 92–93

C

California, 40, 42–43, 59
California Department of Corrections and Rehabilitation (CDCR), 51
California Medical Facility (CMF), 187
California prison system medical care system in receivership, 29–30, 51
Care. *See* Health-care services; Standards of care
CDC. *See* Centers for Disease Control and Prevention
CDCR. *See* California Department of Corrections and Rehabilitation
Centers for Disease Control and Prevention (CDC), 63, 66–67, 73
Central Intelligence Agency (CIA), 74, 79, 158
Certification, defined, 212–213
Cervical cancer, 37
Children, 3n
 defined, 235
 excluded from study, 26n
 requirements in Subpart D for assent by, 237–238
 of women under correctional supervision, 38
Chronic diseases of inmates, 29, 44
CIA. *See* Central Intelligence Agency
Clinical Investigations Using Human Subjects, 74
CMF. *See* California Medical Facility
Code of Federal Regulations Title 45: Public Welfare; Part 46: Protection of Human Subjects, xi, 2, 23, 27, 76, 88, 205–238
 Subpart A: Basic DHHS Policy for Protection of Human Research Subjects, 23, 208–226
 Subpart B: Additional Protections for Pregnant Women, Human Fetuses, and Neonates Involved in Research, 226–230
 Subpart C: Additional Protections Pertaining to Biomedical and Behavioral Research Involving Prisoners as Subjects, 23, 231–234
 Subpart D: Additional Protections for Children Involved as Subjects in Research, 234–238
Coleman v. Wilson, 30
Collaborative research approach, 10–11, 16, 27, 127–130
Commission of Correction v. Myers, 58
Commissioned papers, 59, 176
Committee on Ethical Considerations (for Revisions to the DHHS Regulations) for Protection of Prisoners Involved in Research, ix, 22
 individuals and organizations that addressed, 177
 presentations before, 44
 task and approach, 24–26
Common Rule, 2, 6, 24, 74, 76–78, 202. *See also* Code of Federal Regulations Title 45; Subpart A: Basic DHHS Policy for Protection of Human Research Subjects
 informed consent, 77–78
 institutional assurances, 78
 IRBs, 77
Communicable diseases of inmates, 1–2, 24, 29, 42–44, 53
 hepatitis, 42–43
 HIV/AIDS, 43
 of inmates, 42–44
 tuberculosis, 43–44
Communication skill levels, 38
Community service, 103
Community settings, 4–6, 105–109
Compliance with policies, assuring, in all research conducted or supported by any federal department or agency, 213–215
Conditions, in Subpart A, 9, 225–226
Confidentiality
 in DOJ regulations, 91
 of health information, 56
 protecting, 25

INDEX 255

Congress, 14–15, 42, 115, 159
  scope of spending power, 96–99
Connecticut, 43
Consent. *See* Informed consent
Consumer Product Safety Commission, 208
Continuing review, of prisoner research, 151
Continuity of care, 111
Cooperative research, in Subpart A, 219–220
Correctional population. *See* Prisoner population
Correctional settings, 4–6, 101–112
  current regulations pertinent to places of prisoner research, 102–103
  delineation of settings, 109–110
  encompassing more than prisons and jails, 103–105
  ethical foundations of current research regulations, 101–102
  overcrowding of, 1–2
  when liberty status changes, 110–111
  when proposed regulations should apply, 109–110
  when proposed regulations should not apply, 110
Criminal justice system
  agencies and facilities in California, 106–107
  harm inflicted on those it punishes, 11–12
  restrictions imposed by, 4–6, 30, 105–109
Criteria for IRB approval of research, in Subpart A, 218–219
Cruzan v. Missouri Department of Health, 57
Current regulations pertinent to places of prisoner research, 102–103
Current research environment, 59–67
Current status of prisoner research, 59

D

Data sources and methods, 175–190. *See also* Public database
  data retrieval needing improving, 64–66
  literature survey to assess general characteristics of research with prisoners, 178–187

  open sessions and workshops, 175–178
  site visits, 187–188
  survey of state Departments of Corrections, 188–190
Decision making, autonomous, 15
Declaration of Helsinki, 210
Definitions, 82–84, 211–213, 226–227, 231–232, 235. *See also* individual terms and acronyms
  of minimal risk and benefit to participants, 83–84, 201
  of prisoner, 1, 21n, 27, 33, 65, 82–83, 105–109, 200, 231
  of prisoner research, 138–151
Demographics
  ability of prisoners to provide ethically adequate informed consent, 56
  barriers to privacy and right to consent or refuse care, 56–58
  descriptions of prisons, jails, and other correctional settings, 30–31
  and the ethical conduct of research, 55–58
  and health issues, 30–59
  implications for the ethical conduct of research on the prisoner population, 55–58
  prisoner population, 31–58
Department head, defined, 211
Department of Agriculture, 64, 208
Department of Commerce, 208
Department of Corrections (DOC), 111, 128, 142, 164. *See also* State Departments of Corrections survey
Department of Defense, 86n, 208
Department of Education, 84n, 208
Department of Energy, 208
Department of Health, Education, and Welfare (DHEW), 191
Department of Health and Human Services (DHHS), ix, xl, 1, 3, 4–10, 13–14, 22, 65–66, 105–109, 123–127, 138–139, 157–159, 199–202, 226, 234–237
  agencies of, 86–88
  defined, 231
  regulations of, 59, 73–100
  and Subpart A, 2
Department of Housing and Urban Development, 208

Department of Justice (DOJ), 6–7, 47, 65–66, 74, 93, 202, 208
  confidentiality, 91
  informed consent, 91–92
  regulations, 89–93
  review of research protocols, 92–93
  statistics and trends, 31
Department of Labor, 212
Department of Transportation, 208
Department of Veterans Affairs, 63, 208
Depression, major, 45
DHEW. *See* Department of Health, Education, and Welfare
DHHS. *See* Department of Health and Human Services
Diabetes, 29
Disadvantaged populations, 1–2. *See also* individual populations
Dislocation of inmates, from local to distant jurisdictions, 49
District of Columbia, 38
DOC. *See* Department of Corrections
Documentation of informed consent, in Subpart A, 223–224
DOJ. *See* Department of Justice
Downsizing Prisons, 34
Drug rehabilitation programs, 37
Drugs
  registry of clinical research on, 7
  war on, 23, 29, 33

E

E-mail survey, of state Departments of Corrections (DOCs), 188
Early termination. *See* Termination of research support—evaluation of applications and proposals
Education As Crime Prevention: Providing Education to Prisoners, 39
Educational attainment
  for correctional populations and the general population, 40
  and reading skills of prisoners, 38–40
Educational programs, participation in since most recent incarceration or sentence for state and federal prison inmates, local jail inmates, and probationers, 41
Electronic monitoring programs, 24, 33, 103

Environmental Protection Agency, 208
Estelle v. Gamble, 30, 50, 57
Ethical considerations, for revisions to DHHS regulations for protection of prisoners involved in research, 5
Ethical foundations, of current research regulations, 101–102
Ethical framework for research involving prisoners, x, 7, 26, 113–135
  1976 Commission's ethical framework, 114–116
  historical context, 114
  justice, 115–116, 127–135
  versus research involving nonprisoners, 25
  respect for persons, 115–127
  updated, 116–135
Ethical research, 11, 15
  prerequisites of, 1–2
European Convention for the Prevention of Torture and Inhuman or Degrading Treatment or Punishment, 153
Evaluation and disposition of applications and proposals for research to be conducted or supported by a federal department or agency, in Subpart A, 224–225
Expedited review procedures for certain kinds of research involving no more than minimal risk and for minor changes in approved research, in Subpart A, 217–218

F

Facilities/locations, of research with prisoners, 60–61, 183–184
FBOP. *See* Federal Bureau of Prisons
FDA. *See* Food and Drug Administration
Federal Bureau of Prisons (FBOP), 52
Federal funds, use of in Subpart A, 225
Federal human subjects protections, 6–7, 84–95
  in the Report of the SACHRP Subcommittee, 202
Federal-level review, 14
Federal Register, 80, 85, 88, 167–168, 210–211, 217, 233–234
Federal regulatory landscape, 73–100
  adoption of DHHS Human Subjects Protection Regulations, 74–84

INDEX   257

alternatives to comprehensive regulation,
    99–100
analysis, 94–100
DOJ regulations, 89–93
existing authority for broader regulation,
    95–96
FDA regulations, 86–88
guaranteeing the DHHS broader
    authority, 96–99
other DHHS agencies, 86–88
other federal human subjects
    protections, 84–93
Subpart D, 85–86
Federal Security Agency, 96
Federal-wide assurance (FWA), 78, 84–85,
    138, 142, 201–202
Florida, 59
Food and Drug Administration (FDA), 8,
    73, 85, 95, 125, 144, 170, 202,
    212
    regulations, 86–88, 99
For-profit prisons, 34, 49
Former prisoners/prisoner advocates liaison
    group, 176
Funding sources, 180–181
    in the published literature of prisoner
        studies, 63
FWA. *See* Federal-wide assurance

G

GAO. *See* General Accounting Office
GED. *See* General Equivalency Development
    test
Gender of research participants, 184
    numbers of studies by, 186
*Gender-Responsive Strategies for Women
    Offenders,* 36
General Accounting Office (GAO), 36
General Equivalency Development (GED)
    test, 39
Georgia, 43
Gonzales v. Oregon, 97n, 99
Guardians
    defined, 235
    requirements in Subpart D for
        permission by, 237–238
Guidelines for human subjects research,
    establishing uniform, 6–7, 94–95

H

Halfway houses, 24
Health-care services. *See also* Standards of
    care
    access to adequate, 2, 11, 133–134
    potentially inadequate, 1–2, 22–23, 29
Health Insurance Portability and
    Accountability Act (HIPAA), 150
Health status of inmates, 1, 12, 42–48
    chronic diseases, 44
    communicable diseases, 42–44
    gender factor in, 36
    injury, violence, rape, and suicide, 47–48
    mental illness, 44–47
    substance abuse, 47
*Health Status of Soon-to-Be-Released
    Inmates, The,* 42
Helvering v. Davis, 96
Hepatitis, 1–2, 22, 24, 29, 42–43, 128
High school completion, 39
HIPAA. *See* Health Insurance Portability
    and Accountability Act
Hispanic prisoners, 38–39
History, of research with prisoners, 3, 54–
    55
HIV. *See* Human immunodeficiency virus
Holmesburg Prison, 54–55
HRPPP. *See* Human Research Participant
    Protection Program
HRW. *See* Human Rights Watch
Human immunodeficiency virus (HIV), 1–2,
    24, 29, 43, 114, 128, 144–145, 196
    coinfections involving, 44
    gender factor in, 36
Human research participant protection
    programs (HRPPPs), 8, 10–11, 16,
    94n, 130, 133–134, 142, 149
    creating a national resource for, 14
Human Rights Watch (HRW), 34, 46, 49
Human subjects
    defined, 212
    protections for, 199–203

I

Incarcerated population
    dislocation of, from local to distant
        jurisdictions, 49
    growing enormously, 31–33

quality of health care provided, 50–54
services for, 49–54
Incarceration
increased use of isolation in punishment of inmates, 49–50
purpose of, 11
varieties of, 21
Incentives, 67, 228
Informed consent, 21, 122
ability of prisoners to provide ethically adequate, 56
in the Common Rule, 77–78
in DOJ regulations, 91–92
providing integrity to process of, 15
voluntary, 2, 15, 147–149
Initial review, of prisoner research, 150–151
Injury during incarceration. *See also* Sexual assaults
reasons for, 47–48
Institute of Medicine (IOM), ix, xi, 1, 3, 22, 176, 199
Institution, defined, 211
Institutional assurances, in the Common Rule, 78
Institutional review boards (IRBs), xi, 2, 12–13, 30, 60, 103, 110–111, 123–124, 139–158, 161–170, 209, 212–227
approval by, 12, 212
in the Common Rule, 77
composition of where prisoners are involved, in Subpart C, 232
considerations for independent ethical review, modifying, 13, 156–157
defined, 212
duties, in Subpart D, 235
functions and operations, in Subpart A, 216
membership, in Subpart A, 215–216
postapproval monitoring in oversight of research with prisoners, 156–157
records, in Subpart A, 220
review of research, 3, 217
International Development Cooperation Agency, Agency for International Development, 208
IOM. *See* Institute of Medicine
IRBs. *See* Institutional review boards
Isolation, in punishment of inmates, increased use of, 49–50

J

Jackson State Prison, 121, 193
Jacobson, Michael, 33
Jacobson v. Massachusetts, 58
Jail inmates, numbers of, 32
Joint Commission on Accreditation of Healthcare Organizations (JCAHO), 133
JPI. *See* Justice Policy Institute
Justice, 27, 127–135
collaborative responsibility, 127–130
welfare of the prisoner population, 130–135
Justice Policy Institute (JPI), 31–32, 34
Juveniles, 26n, 108, 185

L

Legally authorized representative, defined, 211
Liberty status, changes in, 110–111
Likelihood of injury, based on time in prison, 48
Literature review of published prisoner studies, 61–64
facilities/locations, 183–184
funding sources, 63, 180–181
general characteristics of research with prisoners, 178–187
locus of research activity, 61–62
mechanisms of research approval, 63–64, 180–182
numbers and demographics of research participants, 184–187
results, 180–187
study content/design, 62–63
study design, 182
type of study, 62, 182–183
Local research review board (LRRB), 92–93

M

Maryland, 43
Mechanisms of research approval
in the published literature of prisoner studies, 63–64
of research with prisoners, 180–182
Mental institutions, closing of large, 29

Mentally ill inmates, 1–2, 24, 44–47
  excluded from study, 26n
  gender factor in, 36
  receiving mental health services while incarcerated, 30, 46
  vulnerabilities of in prison, 12
Michigan, 121, 193
Military personnel, 3n
  excluded from study, 26n
Minimal risk, defined, 25, 124, 212, 232
Minorities. *See* Race/ethnicity of research participants; individual minorities

N

National Aeronautics and Space Administration, 208
National Bioethics Advisory Commission (NBAC), 75, 117
National Center on Institutions and Alternatives, 38
National Commission for the Protection of Human Subjects of Biomedical and Behavioral Research (National Commission) (NCPHSBBR), ix, xi, 22, 29, 66, 79, 101–102, 113, 191–197
  deliberations, findings, and conclusions, 194–196
  methodology, 193–194
National Commission on Correctional Health Care (NCCHC), 42, 44, 50–51, 133
National Institute of Corrections (NIC), 36
National Institute of Justice (NIJ), 63
National Institute on Drug Abuse, 60
National Institutes of Health (NIH), 63, 66–67, 73–76
National Minority Conference on Human Experimentations, 193
National oversight, of research with prisoners, 157–160
National Research Act, 115n, 117–118, 191–192
  Section 202(a)(2), 192
National Science Foundation, 208
Nazi experiments, 114
NBAC. *See* National Bioethics Advisory Commission
NCCHC. *See* National Commission on Correctional Health Care

Neonate
  defined, 226
  nonviable, defined, 227
New Freedom Commission on Mental Health (NFCMH), 45
New Jersey, 37
New York, 59, 114, 195
New York City
  Department of Health and Mental Hygiene, 53
  Departments of Correction and Probation, 34
New York Times, 42, 51–52
NFCMH. *See* New Freedom Commission on Mental Health
NIC. *See* National Institute of Corrections
NIH. *See* National Institutes of Health
NIJ. *See* National Institute of Justice
Nonviable neonate, defined, 227
Nonwhite participants, numbers of studies with, 187
Nuremburg Code, 114, 194

O

Office for Human Research Protections (OHRP), xi, 1, 3, 6, 8–9, 13–15, 22, 24, 73, 77, 83, 103, 123, 125, 156–159, 175–176, 200–201, 211, 217
  enhancing capacity of, 13–14, 157–159
  prisoner certifications, 81–82
Office of Management and Budget, 217, 219–220, 223–224
Office of Research and Evaluation (ORE), 92–93
OHRP. *See* Office for Human Research Protections
Ombudsman, 155
Open sessions and workshops, 175–178
Open Society Institute (OSI), 34, 39
ORE. *See* Office of Research and Evaluation
OSI. *See* Open Society Institute
Out of Sight: Super Maximum Security Confinement in the United States, 49
Oversight of research with prisoners, 151–160
  IRB postapproval monitoring, 156–157
  national oversight, 157–160
  Prison Research Subject Advocates, 153–156

P

Parents
  defined, 235
  requirements in Subpart D for permission by, 237–238
Parole, 30–31
Pell Grants, 40
Pennsylvania, 54–55
Permission, defined, 235
Permitted research involving prisoners, in Subpart C, 233–234
Phases of human research, 131, 160
  Phase 3 testing, 9, 125
PHR. *See* Physicians for Human Rights
PHS. *See* Public Health Service
Physicians for Human Rights (PHR), 56
Policies and procedures, for application review and study, 60–61
Policy makers, informing, 11–12, 134–135
PREA. *See* Prison Rape Elimination Act
Pregnancy
  defined, 227
  high risk, 37
Prejudicial information, 155
Prison Health Services, Inc., 30, 52–53
Prison Rape Elimination Act (PREA), 48, 98–99
Prison research subject advocate (PRSA), 12–13, 118, 137, 147, 154–156, 164–168
  oversight of research with prisoners, 153–156
Prisoner IRB representatives, in the Report of the SACHRP Subcommittee, 83, 200
Prisoner Liaison Panel, xi, 50, 65, 120
Prisoner population, 31–58. *See also* Today's prisoners—changing demographics, health issues, and the current research environment
  ages of inmates, 29, 40–42
  causes of growth in, 23–24, 33–35
  defined, 1, 21n, 27, 33, 65, 82–83, 105–109, 200, 231
  echoes of Tuskegee and Retin-A, 22, 54–55
  educational level and reading skills of prisoners, 38–40
  enormous growth in, 23, 29, 31–33
  findings on changing demographics and health issues, 58–59
  by gender, 36
  health status of, 42–48
  history of research with, 3, 54–55
  implications of demographics for the ethical conduct of research, 55–58
  injury, violence, rape, and suicide of, 47–48
  under jurisdiction of state or federal correctional authorities by gender, 35
  more women entering, 35–38
  numbers of, 32
  obtaining input from, 10–11, 129–130
  racial and ethnic disparities, 38
  reentering society, 11–12, 134–135
  restrictions on liberty and autonomy, 1–2, 27
  subclasses of, 12
  vulnerabilities of, 12, 21
  welfare of, 130–135
  where incarcerated and how provided with services, 49–54
  who is in prisons and jails, 35–42
Prisoner studies, published, literature review of, 61–64
Prisons, jails, and other correctional settings
  descriptions of, 30–31
  everyday life in, 11
  for-profit, 34, 49
Privacy
  absolute, difficulty guaranteeing, 16, 21–22
  barriers to, and the ethical conduct of research, 1–2, 56–58
  protection of, 2, 15–16, 25, 149–150
Probation, 30–31, 103
Problems
  investigating reports of possible, 14, 21–22
  unexpected, in reviewing prisoner research, 151
Prohibited categories and types of research involving prisoners, 170
Proposals lacking definite plans for involvement of human subjects, in Subpart A, 224
Proposed regulations, 109–110. *See also* Recommendations
Protectionism, role of, 118–127
Protocols. *See* Research, protocols
PRSA. *See* Prison research subject advocate
Public database, of all research involving prisoners, 7, 65–66

INDEX

Public health implications, of inadequate health care for prisoners, 53–54
Public Health Service Act, 95
Public Health Service (PHS), 55, 74
Public meeting participants, 178–179
Published prisoner studies, literature review of, 61–64
"Punishing decade," 32
Purpose, in Subpart C, 231

Q

Quality assurance (QA), 140
Quality improvement (QI), 140–141, 151, 155
Quality of health care provided, 50–54
  public health implications of inadequate health care for prisoners, 53–54

R

RA. *See* Research assistant
Race/ethnicity of research participants, 1, 38–39, 45, 187. *See also* individual racial and ethnic groups
  disparities among, 23, 38
  numbers of studies by, 186
  vulnerabilities of in prison, 12
Rape. *See* Sexual assaults
Reading skill levels, 38
Rearrest rates, 34
Recidivism
  high rates of, 23, 34
  reducing, 11–12, 39, 134–135
Recommendations, 3–16, 196
  data retrieval needing improving, 64–66
  enhancing systematic oversight of research involving prisoners, xi, 1, 4, 12–16, 159
  ensuring universal, consistent ethical protection, xi, 1, 4, 6–7
  expanding definition of prisoner, xi, 1, 4–6, 105–109
  shifting from a category-based to a risk-benefit approach to research review, xi, 1, 4, 8–10
  updating the ethical framework to include collaborative responsibility, xi, 1, 4, 10–12

Recommendations for further consideration by the IOM, in the Report of the SACHRP Subcommittee, 84, 201–202
Registry of clinical research on drugs and biololgics, 7
Registry of research involving prisoners, need for a national, 7, 14, 158
Regulation, existing authority for broader, 95–96
Regulations for the protection of human subjects, 24
  applicable even to research not federally funded by any agency, 90
  applicable to research involving human subjects, 75
  applicable to research involving prisoners as subjects, independent of funding source, 203
  compliance with, 14
  DOJ, 89–93
  Subpart A, 208–209
  Subpart B, 226
  Subpart D, 234–235
Reiger, Darrel A., 44
Report and Recommendations: Research Involving Prisoners, 2, 66, 79, 113
Report of the SACHRP Subcommittee and Human Subjects Protections, 27, 81–84, 94, 199–203
  defining minimal risk and benefit to participants, 83–84, 201
  definition of prisoner, 82–83, 200
  prisoner IRB representatives, 83, 200
  recommendations for further consideration by the IOM, 84, 201–202
Requirements, for permission by parents or guardians and for assent by children, in Subpart D, 237–238
Research
  abuses in, 3
  categories of, 184
  involving, after delivery, the placenta, the dead fetus, or fetal material, in Subpart B, 230
  involving greater than minimal risk and no prospect of direct benefit to individual subjects, but likely to yield generalizable knowledge about the subject's disorder or condition, in Subpart D, 236

involving greater than minimal risk but presenting the prospect of direct benefit to the individual subjects, in Subpart D, 235–236
involving neonates, in Subpart B, 228–230
involving pregnant women or fetuses, in Subpart B, 227–228
not involving greater than minimal risk, in Subpart D, 235
not otherwise approvable which presents an opportunity to understand, prevent
  or alleviate a serious problem affecting the health or welfare of children, in Subpart D, 236–237
  or alleviate a serious problem affecting the health or welfare of pregnant women, fetuses, or neonates, in Subpart B, 230
protocols for, 10–11, 13, 22, 26, 92–93, 129–130, 156–157
safeguards for particular kinds of, 160–170
Research assistant (RA), 62n
Research involving prisoners, 184–187
age, 140–142, 184, 186
best practices gained from high-quality, 12, 135
defined, 211
echoes of Tuskegee and Retin-A, 22, 54–55
establishing uniform guidelines for, 6–7, 94–95
ethical framework for, 113–135
gender, 184
government support needed for, 11–12, 134–135
history of, 3, 54–55
monitoring, 12–13, 154–156
numbers of, 185
oversight of, 151–160
priorities for, 25
protecting privacy, 15–16, 149–150
race/ethnicity, 187
settings delineated, 109–110
subject to regulation, defined, 212
undertaken without the intention of involving human subjects, in Subpart A, 224

Respect for persons, 15, 27, 117–127, 192
expanded view of, 117–118
guidance on biomedical research, 125–127
role of protectionism, 118–127
Responsible Research: A Systems Approach to Protecting Research Participants, 129
Results
from Department of Corrections survey, 189–190
policies and procedures for application review and study, 60–61
of research with prisoners, 180–187
from the surveys with key DOC personnel, 60–61
types of research permitted and research personnel, 60
Retin-A, echoes of among the prisoner population, 22, 54–55
Reviewing prisoner research, 138–151
adverse events or unexpected problems, 151
amendment review, 151
continuing review, 151
how reviews are conducted, 143–150
initial review, 150–151
by institution, in Subpart A, 219
research protocols, in DOJ regulations, 92–93
what is reviewed, 139–141
when reviews are done, 150–151
who reviews, 141–142
Rhode Island, 53n
Right to consent or refuse care, and the ethical conduct of research, 56–58
Risk
minimal, defined, 25, 124, 212
threshold of, 26
Risk-benefit framework, applying to research review, 8–10, 122–127
Rumsfeld v. Forum for Academic and Institutional Rights, 97n

S

SACHRP. *See* Secretary's Advisory Committee on Human Research Protections
Safeguards for particular kinds of research, 160–170

INDEX 263

SAMHSA. *See* Substance Abuse and Mental Health Services Administration
Sample situations, 163–170
San Quentin Prison, 187
Sanctions, for non-compliance, imposing, 14
Schloendorff v. Society of New York Hospitals, 57
Search terms, 179
Secretary of DHHS, 9
 defined, 227, 231
Secretary's Advisory Committee on Human Research Protections (SACHRP), 24, 80–82, 199. *See also* Report of the SACHRP Subcommittee
Sentencing laws. *See also* The Sentencing Project (TSP)
 harsher, 23, 29
 mandatory minimums, 34
 three-strike laws, 34
Sexual assaults, repeated, in incarcerated populations, 9, 37, 48
Sexual offenders, 109
Sexually transmitted diseases (STDs), 42, 128
Single female heads of household, 37
Site visits, 187–188
Social Security Administration (SSA), 74, 79, 158
South Dakota v. Dole, 96–97
Special study design, and PRSA monitoring safeguards, 162–163
SSA. *See* Social Security Administration
Stakeholders, 170–174
 obtaining input from, 10–11, 129–130
 responsibilities of, 17–19, 170–174
Standards of care, ensuring adequate, 11, 133–134
State Departments of Corrections (DOCs) survey, 59, 140, 175, 188–190
 e-mail survey, 59, 188
 telephone interviews, 59, 188
STDs. *See* Sexually transmitted diseases
Study content/design of research with prisoners, 182
 in the published literature, 62–63
Subjects, of reviews, 139–141
Subpart A: Basic DHHS Policy for Protection of Human Research Subjects, 2, 208–226
 applications and proposals lacking definite plans for involvement of human subjects, 224
 assuring compliance with this policy— research conducted or supported by any federal department or agency, 213–215
 conditions, 225–226
 cooperative research, 219–220
 criteria for IRB approval of research, 218–219
 documentation of informed consent, 223–224
 early termination of research support— evaluation of applications and proposals, 225
 evaluation and disposition of applications and proposals for research to be conducted or supported by a federal department or agency, 224–225
 expedited review procedures for certain kinds of research involving no more than minimal risk and for minor changes in approved research, 217–218
 general requirements for informed consent, 220–223
 IRB functions and operations, 216
 IRB membership, 215–216
 IRB records, 220
 IRB review of research, 217
 research undertaken without the intention of involving human subjects, 224
 review by institution, 219
 suspension or termination of IRB approval of research, 219
 use of federal funds, 225
 to what this policy applies, 208–209
Subpart A definitions, 211–213
 agency head, 211
 certification, 212–213
 department head, 211
 human subject, 212
 institution, 211
 IRB, 212
 IRB approval, 212
 legally authorized representative, 211
 minimal risk, 212
 research, 211
 research subject to regulation, 212

Subpart B: Additional Protections for Pregnant Women, Human Fetuses, and Neonates Involved in Research, 226–230
  duties of IRBs in connection with research involving pregnant women, fetuses, and neonates, 227
  research involving, after delivery, the placenta, the dead fetus, or fetal material, 230
  research involving neonates, 228–230
  research involving pregnant women or fetuses, 227–228
  research not otherwise approvable which presents an opportunity to understand, prevent, or alleviate a serious problem affecting the health or welfare of pregnant women, fetuses, or neonates, 230
  to what these regulations apply, 226
Subpart B definitions, 226–227
  dead fetus, 226
  delivery, 226
  fetus, 226
  neonate, 226
  nonviable neonate, 227
  pregnancy, 227
  Secretary of DHHS, 227
  viable, 227
Subpart C: Additional Protections Pertaining to Biomedical and Behavioral Research Involving Prisoners as Subjects, xi, 2–6, 66, 79–81, 231–234
  additional duties of the IRBs where prisoners are involved, 232–233
  additional requirements for IRBs, 80–81
  applicability, 231
  composition of IRBs where prisoners are involved, 232
  key definitions within Subpart C, 79–80
  OHRP certification, 81
  permitted research involving prisoners, 233–234
  purpose, 231
  rewriting, 24
Subpart C definitions, 231–232
  DHHS, 231
  minimal risk, 232
  prisoners, 231
  Secretary of DHHS, 231
Subpart D: Additional Protections for Children Involved as Subjects in Research, 8–9, 85–86, 234–238
  framework, 87
  IRB duties, 235
  requirements for permission by parents or guardians and for assent by children, 237–238
  research involving greater than minimal risk and no prospect of direct benefit to individual subjects, but likely to yield generalizable knowledge about the subject's disorder or condition, 236
  research involving greater than minimal risk but presenting the prospect of direct benefit to the individual subjects, 235–236
  research not involving greater than minimal risk, 235
  research not otherwise approvable which presents an opportunity to understand, prevent, or alleviate a serious problem affecting the health or welfare of children, 236–237
  wards, 238
  to what these regulations apply, 234–235
Subpart D definitions, 235
  assent, 235
  children, 235
  guardian, 235
  parent, 235
  permission, 235
Substance Abuse and Mental Health Services Administration (SAMHSA), 73
Substance abuse of inmates, 37, 47
Surveys with key DOC personnel, results from, 60–61
Suspension or termination of IRB approval of research, in Subpart A, 219
Systems of oversight, safeguards, and protections, 137–174
  applying safeguards for particular kinds of research, 160–170
  defining and reviewing prisoner research, 138–151
  impact of committee recommendations on stakeholder responsibilities, 170–174

other prohibited categories and types of research involving prisoners, 170
sample situations, 163–170

T

TB. *See* Tuberculosis
Telephone interviews, of state Departments of Corrections (DOCs), 188
Termination of research support—evaluation of applications and proposals, early, in Subpart A, 225
Texas, 43, 52, 59
The Sentencing Project (TSP), 34, 40
Therapeutic research, 116
Thompson v. City of Los Angeles, 58
Three-strike laws, 34, 40, 42
Timing, 22–24
 of reviews, 150–151
Today's prisoners—changing demographics, health issues, and the current research environment, 29–71
 changing demographics and health issues, 30–59
 current research environment, 59–67
 current status of prisoner research, 59
 data retrieval needing improving, 64–66
 published literature—a review of selected prisoner studies, 61–64
 results from the surveys with key DOC personnel, 60–61
 summary of findings on current research environment, 66–67
Transparency, 7, 26, 64, 159–160
TSP. *See* The Sentencing Project
Tuberculosis (TB), 1–2, 24, 43–44
Tuskegee, echoes of among the prisoner population, 22, 54–55
Types of research with prisoners, 182–183
 permitted, and research personnel, 60
 in the published literature, 62

U

U.S. Constitution
 Eighth Amendment, 23, 50, 57
 role in guaranteeing the DHHS broader authority, 96

U.S. Patriot Act, 3n, 26n
U.S. Supreme Court, 30, 50, 56–57, 97

V

Viable, defined, 227
Violent Crime Control and Law Enforcement Act, 40
Viral diseases, 42–43
 antiviral therapies, 43
Virginia, 43
Voluntariness, in the prison setting, 25–26
Voluntary informed consent, 2, 15, 147–149

W

Wards, in Subpart D, 238
Washington State, 49
Washington v. Harper, 58
Weekend reporting programs, 33
Welfare of the prisoner population, 130–135
White prisoners, 39, 45
White v. Napoleon, 57–58
Women
 increasingly entering the correctional system, 1–2, 23, 35–38
 single female heads of household, 37–38
 vulnerabilities of in prison, 12, 36–38
Women Offenders: Programming Needs and Promising Approaches, 37
Work-release programs, 24, 33
World Medical Assembly Declaration, 210

Y

Young people, vulnerabilities of in prison, 12

Z

Zaire v. Dalsheim, 58